40.00/30.00

D1593209

Electrical

Contracting

2nd Edition

Michael Sammaritano

The Estimating Room Inc.

Library of Congress Cataloging-in-Publication Data

Michael Sammaritano
Electrical Contracting

Library of Congress Catalog Card No
2005933554

ISBN 0-9771541-0-6

List Price $79.50 USA Dollars

Printed in the United States of America

10 9 8 7 6 5 4 3 2

Visit our website at www.theestimatingroom.com

Book Tour

The World of Electrical Contracting

The Essentials of Contracting

Markets Defined

Sales

Estimating

Contracting the Job

Contract Administration

Doing the Job

Collecting Your Money

General Administration

Quick Start

Chapter 28 – Quick Start caters to those on the go. In it, you will find guidelines that will speed up whatever task you want to tackle or delegate in electrical contracting today.

INTRODUCTION

Taking control of modern technology, especially fast-moving programs, is the key to greater success in today's business world. As electrical contractors, we must revert to the fundamentals of contracting for in their simplicity lies control.

Typically, we attain our master licenses, buy a computer, and start pushing buttons without challenging the output. We just accept it and disregard our proficiency as masters of our trade.

This practice generates either too much unprofitable work or no work. In both cases, most of us lack the skills to convert our expertise into useful factor for our estimating and cost control programs.

Then there is the business of contracting, which deals not only with the general contractor, the owner, the architect, and the engineer, but also the building department, vendors, and with manufacturers. Most importantly, however, it concerns our staff and the workforce in the field.

When things get hectic, it's because we have not grasped the fundamentals of electrical contracting in their simplest form.

This book conveys those fundamentals, radically simplified.

Use them well,

Michael Sammaritano

A Word about the Author

Michael Sammaritano is the author of several books, among them:

Electrical Contracting – (The Estimating Room Inc 2005)
Smart Contracting – For the Construction Industry (CPI 2003)
Making it! Journeyman to Project Manager (CPI 2003)
Successful Electrical Contracting Methods (CPI 1995)
The Productive Electrician (CPI 1996)
The Essentials of Estimating and Selling the Job (CPI 1996)
The Office Administrator for the Electrical Contractor (CPI 1996)

In 1961, Michael attained his Master Electrician License in New York City; subsequently, in 1981 he was certified Electrical Contractor by the State of Florida.

As an electrical contractor, and at times as a general contractor, he has personally contracted and managed construction jobs ranging from wiring a doorbell to installing high-voltage transmission lines and switching stations in rugged terrains, airport expansions, and the like projects. Thanks to his natural gifts as an organizer, he has looked at contracting always in a different light than would a dedicated contractor.

TABLE OF CONTENTS

For Quick Start See Chapter 28

THE WORLD OF ELECTRICAL CONTRACTING

Chapter 1

THE BUSINESS OF
ELECTRICAL CONTRACTING

WHAT IS BUSINESS?

Business is that with which a person is principally and seriously concerned.

WHAT IS ELECTRICAL CONTRACTING?

Contracting is a tradesperson's business. Through contracting, a contractor sells his service in an attempt to make a profit. To an electrician, the phrase, 'sells his service in an attempt to make a profit' translates into a concise objective—service work.

If we are successful at service work, most likely it motivates us into contracting. One way to succeed in contracting is to keep on doing service work and carry over our successful methods into contracting.

This method serves well those who resist the temptation of seeking overnight success. Unfortunately, the beginner tends to abandon service work and invest much of his resources into selling electrical equipment rather than labor.

At heart, perhaps, we all feel at home with merchandising. As children, we sold cookies and candies in school and around the neighborhood. Selling expensive and sophisticated equipment, as adults, makes the game complex and risky, especially when we mix it with contracting.

A merchant is a person whose business is buying and selling goods (finished products) for profit. He is not involved in the production of the goods he sells. In addition to adequate financing, a merchant needs to market his products and protect his investment. His profits are dependent on his ability to collect his money—plus interest when delays in payment occur.

An electrical contractor, on the other hand, is a tradesperson whose business is selling his services for profit: he is involved in the production of the contracts he sells. He has the skills to install, alter, and repair a building's electrical wiring inside and out. His profit is in direct proportion to his ability to complete a job in the least number of labor hours.

The contrast between these two fields of contracting and merchandising makes it almost impossible for anyone to make a profit in both and still produce competitive bids. You will discover that in most bids the profit from one is often used up to offset the other.

A case in point is the contractor who cuts down the special-equipment quote to win a bid—no less, adding a markup and sales taxes to it. This contractor hopes that once he gets the job he'll be able to buy the equipment cheaper. Should he fail, his next plan of action is to make up the difference in labor savings—a feat that many attempt and most fail.

As we carry out the work, we must recognize opportunities that increase or protect profit. We do so by keeping a watchful eye out for changes in the scope of work that will affect cost and productivity. While some contractors are capable of achieving the latter by intuition, we must rely on facts.

As opposed to merchants, electrical contractors need limited financial resources to conduct business. We can negotiate contracts to leave the bulk of the financing in the hands of the owner or the general contractor—who are merchants at heart. In doing so, we reinforce the basic rule of electrical contracting:

> Minimize your financial investment in every job you take, thus maximizing the number of jobs you can do at lower risk and higher profit with the most cash flow.

We make most of our profit on labor-intensive jobs, not on buying and selling equipment.

Our expertise in controlling labor means we can earn a greater return per dollar invested in productive labor than in merchandising equipment. The more jobs we spread our investment over, the lower the risk.

That is, the more jobs we contract, the more productive labor hours we sell—and the more profit we stand to make. This is what we are in business for.

Never apologize for making profit.

PITFALLS OF CONTRACTING

Among the wealth of opportunities electrical contracting offers, there are pitfalls.

When starting out in service work, the most important thing is to get small jobs, buy and install the basic materials, pay the bills, and go on to the next job. Because we are good at what we do and pay close attention to our affairs, this simple business formula works well. We produce profits repeatedly, enabling us to provide a home, a new car, and more for our families and ourselves.

Some contractors will depart from service work prematurely and venture into the world of electrical contracting, where large projects are bid and won and larger profits are just around the corner. If you are not prepared for such a transition, your overconfidence can take you into unknown territory and possibly over a precipice.

In contracting, the rules are different from service work. Down payments, C.O.D. charges, and prompt payments are not the norm. One-sided contracts favoring the owner or the general contractor are customary. Business transactions with suppliers and surety companies that bear our personal guarantee and make our family and our family's heirs liable are also customary.

For the uninitiated, entering contracting can be as complex as entering the world of high finance. For an electrical contractor, the most dangerous trap is to get caught up in buying and selling equipment such as lighting fixtures and switching-gear packages, emergency generators, electronics systems and the like while neglecting job performance.

Another trap involves the supplier, whose business is buying and selling equipment. If the sale is direct, i.e. between the supplier and the owner, you are clear of liability. However, if the sale is made through you, via the so-called 'job account,' then be alert, because (contrary to what they tell you) you are responsible for any balance due at any time.

The supplier's concern is to protect his investment, even if it means putting you out of business and your family out of the very home you just bought. In making the sale, the supplier puts in motion a series of legal maneuvers to which you must pay attention. Whenever possible, avoid these kinds of closed circuit transactions. You should limit your liability for acquisitions on behalf of the customer.

Consider the case where we asked the customer to buy his or her own lighting fixtures. By doing this, we limited our financial liability and reduced our cash outlays almost to zero—not to mention the absence of paperwork. We only needed to buy pipe and wire. Doing the job can then be fun and making profit easy.

Regardless of the size of the job, we should never change that formula without compensation.

In support of that principle, it is worth noting that for some time, public agencies, utility companies, and large corporations—and not the electrical contractor—have acquired these pieces of equipment and other specials during the planning stage of the job. This practice of critical schedules and tight budgets for greater cost effectiveness is on the rise in small projects as well. For example, national chain storeowners make these purchases long before they let the job out for bid.

This principle is sound and it is here to stay because it favors the owner, the general contractor, the subcontractor, and the supplier. Here's how:

- The owner pays the supplier directly.

- The owner saves money and owns what he bought clear of liens.

- The contractor frees up his resources for other projects.

- Progress schedules are better kept.

What about the contractor's profit on the equipment? Ask yourself instead, "what about the profit on the last job I bid and lost?"

Theoretically, we cannot lose money on what we didn't do. In those situations, we can claim the loss-anticipated profits only.

Assuming we do the work, who is to say that anticipated profits won't turn into losses. If anticipated profits are what we are seeking, then just look around, for every business opportunity offers plenty.

However, if real profit is what we want, then let us turn the odds in our favor. Chances are we will make better profits on installation than on buying and selling special equipment.

In short, our financial exposure with respect to the acquisition of special equipment is—and should be—that of a contractor and not an owner. Unless our investment is protected and we are compensated, we should look for opportunities to exclude from our contracts the furnishing of special equipment (See Chapter 16 - Negotiations).

On the subject of compensation, most contractors that fail in business rarely fail because they misinterpret the National Electrical Code or make bad splices. They fail because they take the wrong job with the wrong general contractor; moreover, they lack the skills to deal with the inevitable change order and back charge, the filing of claims for loss of productivity and job delays, and, most of all, how to collect the ten percent retainer or reduce it to five percent when due.

The contractor who cannot resist the temptation of megabuck profits in large projects is often lured into risky projects just like a high roller being lured to the crap tables. Neither heeds warnings.

MERITS OF CONTRACTING

Despite its pitfalls, electrical contracting offers great opportunities for the entrepreneurial mind. Remember that every structure needs electrical servicing and every new project needs an array of electrical equipment wired and installed. From smart home and office electronics systems to very high voltage transmission lines that carry our nation's electrical power, the opportunities are plentiful.

SECTION II

THE ESSENTIALS OF CONTRACTING

Chapter 2 Market Yourself and Your Company

Market Yourself

Market Your Company

Marketing Results

Chapter 2

MARKET YOURSELF AND YOUR COMPANY

MARKET YOURSELF

Historically, illegal and unqualified contractors have often enticed prospective customers with low prices, which affect the legitimate electrical contractor. Shady contractors with slick presentations quite often take jobs away from qualified contractors.

As electrical contractors, we must recognize and deal with that trend as well as other competitive elements. We must implement a plan that allows us to market ourselves not only to prospective customers, but also to the industry, to our employees and associates.

Those who underestimate the value of such a marketing strategy usually leave behind a trail of misleading impressions that foster negative repercussions affecting everything else they do.

First Impressions

When we promote ourselves, either in person or through advertising, it is essential that we leave behind a favorable impression. In their minds, people will record forever the visual impact we first created along with our spoken words.

First impression is the product of our presentation and, once set, it's inerasable—no matter how hard we try to change it. Every subsequent contact with that person will always bring back that first impression. Therefore, unless we first present ourselves as businesspersons, even when performing service work, we cannot upgrade our image from that of a service person to that of a businessperson in the customer's mind. Regardless of the rank we choose—service or businessperson—we should never make careless or un-businesslike presentations.

Unprofessional presentations create long-lasting damage to our image that lead prospective customers either to look elsewhere for a better contractor or to treat us like any other shady contractor unworthy of their business—unless they can profit greatly from the venture. When this is the case, our lowest price is suddenly not low enough, no matter how hard we try to make the sale.

Although favorable impressions are not signed contracts, they do serve as door openers to better opportunities. We should treat them no differently than telephone calls generated by solicitations. What each opportunity generates is entirely up to us and to our ability to sell and close contracts.

Once we take on a job, our level of performance will complement our other qualities. This byproduct will determine the kind of relationship we will establish with each customer. If he calls back or refers us to others, then we can pat ourselves on the back for a job well done.

First Meetings

In making sales presentations, 'Who are you?' is the first question that crosses the prospective customer's mind. If you fail to answer that question and fail to answer promptly all other questions, you can find yourself in an uncomfortable and counter-productive meeting.

In a planned marketing approach, your promotional material has to lead up to your personal presentation. This approach will familiarize the prospective customer with your company and you and pave the way for productive sell-calls. Finally, when we meet the prospective customer, there will be no question of who you are. 'The job'—and not 'you'—will be the focal point of the meeting.

However, when you have to make 'cold calls' in person, one sure way to avoid embarrassment and win the confidence of a prospective customer is to be ready to answer all questions and to overcome the 'Who are we?' question within the first few seconds of the meeting.

This kind of presentation requires discipline and adherence to basic guidelines:

Personal Appearance

Most people observe others from their feet up. Good clean shoes, neatly groomed hair, and complementary attire will do the job.

Show yourself to be ready to do business by carrying a briefcase or a well-organized notebook.

General Attitude

- Be positive and enthusiastic about the topics under discussion. Show your expertise and genuine interest in the project.

- Pay close attention to what your prospective customer is saying.

- Express your opinions freely.

- Do not use the prospective customer's telephone for any other purposes than your presentation. When you have to, be very discreet.

- Don't clam up—converse with your prospective customer.

- Humor, when out of place, can be costly. Jokes and other trivial conversation are for water-cooler breaks.

- Do not hide your traits; they are your assets. Promote them appropriately.

- Do not throw ice cubes on a warming-up relationship. In other words, do not use phrases such as "Yes, Sir" or "Yes, Ma'am." There is nothing wrong with addressing customers by their names. When someone is warming up to you, it is because he is beginning to trust you and wants you to do the work. A too-formal conversation can distance the prospective customer irretrievably. Seize the moment and share his enthusiasm in the most cordial and friendly way. If he warms up to you, respond in the same way. The prospective customer, before he signs a contract, wants and needs to feel comfortable with you and your company.

- Do not make constant reference to the National Electrical Code. Use your mechanic's expert opinion. Remember, the N.E.C. requirements are minimum standards. Most projects are built above it.

- Do not criticize the design criteria of the job until you have learned the reasons behind it. If you feel you have to question the criteria, be tactful.

- No snow jobs: You are better off saying nothing than faking a compliment.

- Telling someone you are licensed adds little value to your presentation. The customer expects it. On the other hand, telling someone your work exceeds industry standards adds considerable value to your presentation.

MARKET YOUR COMPANY

Before we start on the subject of marketing our company, we need to address a misconception that applies across many industries. The primary intent behind marketing a company (not to be confused with marketing a company's product or service) is to present the company at its best to prospective customers.

Misleading promotional campaigns are the main cause for many consumer losses, with costly backlash for the promoting company itself; for example, a growing company working at creating demand for its services makes unjustified changes midstream to its marketing plans.

Many executives consider natural growth too slow. They begin to doubt sound marketing approaches, disregarding their company's ability to produce and, at the drop of a hat, embark on a new and more aggressive campaign, thus generating more sales than the company can handle. Such a misdirected campaign adversely affects the customer and the company as well, especially when orders are mishandled.

We need not be seasoned marketers to spot the problems facing these companies: they are not set up to handle overnight growth; for that matter, very few companies are. The additional workload can easily put them out of business.

We must lay out marketing plans thoughtfully, and then implement them carefully while we patiently nurture their results to produce long-term growth.

Promoting ourselves for a job for which we are undercapitalized or which we are not equipped to handle will burden our company's natural growth. We achieve growth by letting our business grow at its own pace and on its own merits. This means undertaking only profitable jobs that we can handle with ease. Consistent profit making gives us confidence in our marketing plan, which in turn nurtures good organization—an essential element for natural business growth.

Forced business growth, besides being a gamble, will lead to disorganized plans with daily tasks run on an emergency basis and new personnel training reduced to close to zero. If we put ourselves in this position, we will soon find ourselves with neither the resources nor the organization to complete the work.

To prevent such a situation, no matter how hard it is to turn down a customer or what seems to be a profitable job, once we have saturated our workload capacity, turn it down. We cannot take on additional work just on gut feeling. To make correct decisions, we must have facts and a good plan to expand our work capability (See Chapter 21- Controlling the Job).

Some may think this rule applies only to manufacturers or larger contractors, but nothing could be further from the truth—it applies more to the beginner than it does to established companies.

As electrical contractors, we must keep up to date on our financial status and production capabilities on a daily basis (See chapter 24 - Business Administration). This knowledge will give us the confidence to make wise decisions. With it, we can take calculated risks and undertake additional work, or we can build the courage to turn down jobs regardless of their anticipated profits.

However, we can turn this predicament into a marketing tool. Explaining to the customer why you are turning down his work will only strengthen your business ties. Everyone wants a winner. You will be planting a good seed for the future, thus creating greater demand for your company. This customer will not only call on you early for his next project, but he will also influence others to call on you as well by talking about your integrity and the way you operate.

Good, effective marketing plans grow at their own pace. After all, the seeds you plant in our business are the seeds for your personal future as well. Because so much rides on them, when we sense a delay or decline in sales, we tend to doubt the very plan we have implemented. However, these are the moments in life when we have to believe in ourselves and be patient and persistent.

This is not to suggest that marketing plans are written in stone. If we feel, we have given our marketing plan a reasonable chance to succeed, don't stand idly by—make adjustments as you go along. Nevertheless, do it prudently, because neither you nor anyone else can predict where, when, or how many seeds will germinate. Go ahead, make your changes, but don't stray too far from good marketing fundamentals.

The Marketing Plan

Most electrical contractors can implement marketing plans that are more effective at no additional cost, or even cut down their advertising budget. In most cases, they are already paying for some form of advertising, for example, company stationery, truck lettering, specialty items, yellow pages and the like, which can be reworked to meet their objectives better.

A common alternative to a comprehensive marketing plan is a random plan. As the title implies, it is a combination of traditional marketing elements—most often, those copied from others—and the adoption of randomly selected bits and pieces of advertising and specialty items.

Thanks to our compulsion to invest in advertising on one hand and cut expenses on the other, we sometimes create more costly and ineffective marketing plans then we might admit, squandering good promotional dollars.

Next time you are lettering a truck, make sure the overall layout sends the message you want. Then do the same with your stationery and so on (see details later on in this chapter).

In comparing cost versus effectiveness you will find that, in most cases, the least expensive marketing elements are the most effective. A well-written reference letter, for example, or the implementation of standard procedures aimed at enhancing the overall performance of the company is the most common among these items.

Starting out in business, most of us pay little or no attention to image setting and visual impact. Quite often, this will be the last thing on your mind. However, for the would-be contractor, starting up is the best time to follow your visions and plan where you want your company to be five, ten, or twenty years down the road.

For those committed to going the distance, the implementation of a marketing plan is a serious matter and as such, it should not be left in the hands of others. Copywriters and commercial artists can create only from what we show and tell them. If we want our experience and our wisdom reflected in their work, we have to provide them with specific guidelines and our visions as well.

Following is a list of the major marketing elements pertaining to electrical contracting. The commentary notes are designed to acquaint you with the accepted guidelines. Study these notes in detail, for they will give you the basics for defining an effective marketing plan.

Visual Impact

Logo

A logo is the catalyst of the company. Regardless of its size, the logo tells the world who you are and what you do—at a glance. Seen over time, it creates name recognition.

While the logo should be unique, it does not have to be complex. The best design for a logo has simple colors and layout. You should be able to reduce, enlarge, and photocopy it in black and white without losing its impact.

If the logo contains tiny details and too many shades of color, those details will be distorted when it is reduced or enlarged. Think in terms of faxing and e-mailing your logo. If it is not within those guidelines, it will not be much to look at when it comes out at the other end. The most effective logos are graphic in nature.

Truck Lettering

The best and most inexpensive mobile advertising is the space on the outside panels of your truck. You should use all sides, including the top when necessary. You rarely see the rear or the front panel used for advertising, and never the top.

Using the top panel of a service truck is effective advertising when serving business and residential communities with two-story buildings or higher. When you park between other vehicles, the top panel has a greater audience than the side panels. The people on the ground level are usually in a hurry, while the people up above, attracted by the novelty, have the time to write down your name and phone number. If you decide to use the top panel of your trucks, then share the space between the ladders and the sign. Move or stack the ladders to the opposite side of the sign.

The rear panel of your truck has the most exposure to those who follow on the road. Too many companies waste this valuable space trying to cut costs.

The general guidelines for truck lettering are as important as the location of the lettering on the truck.

Do not clutter the lettering with too much text. Every word you use, in its proper place and size, has to say something of value (No ego trips here).

The size of each line should be consistent. The name of the company should be full size, the telephone number 75% of that, a slogan 30%, and the rest of the text, if any, should be proportionally smaller.

License Numbers and The Like

Although they are required and reassuring to the public of your legitimacy, license numbers don't carry much advertising weight, no matter how large you letter them. Treat them as normal text—30% or less of the company's name.

Telephone Numbers

Whenever possible, avoid the use of multiple telephone numbers. This type of listing tends to clutter your truck lettering and takes the reader's attention from your message.

If the intent is convenience, then adopt an 800 number. The toll-free call also serves to overcome people's reluctance to call out-of-town contractors. It is a good business rule to pay for business calls generated by your advertising. In business, you always pay for leads one way or another.

Color and Font Typefaces

Don't use too many colors; use a maximum of three. The same applies to font and typeface styles for your letters.

Company Logo

A well-displayed logo on your truck or sign pulls more than printed business cards and letterheads put together. The truck or sign is exposed to larger audiences for greater periods than a business card or letterhead, which are seen only by those you solicit or write.

This is a comparison between outdoor signs and general stationery, and not a recommendation to remove the logo from your stationery. We show this comparison to encourage you to place the logo on your trucks and signs, something neglected by many contractors.

The logo delivers a visual impact for all your marketing tools.

Next time you want to cut your truck lettering costs, shop for better prices rather than omitting the logo. Most likely, other less effective items you can omit will bring the cost down and improve the overall message you are trying to convey.

Paint or Vinyl Lettering

For all your signage needs, use cut-to-specifications vinyl letters instead of hand-painted lettering whenever possible. The vinyl lettering lasts longer, resists the effects of weather better, and does not discolor as fast as painted letters do. The overall look is superior.

Many vinyl-lettering suppliers will cut letters and logos to your specifications. With a little guidance, you can install them yourself and save enough on labor to afford lettering for all five sides of the truck plus a logo.

Job Site Signs

The same rules that apply to trucks apply to sign lettering, with few exceptions:

- Unlike trucks, job site signs are fixed and passing traffic must get their message at a glance, thus limiting the amount of text. Your logo and company name should be the most prominent elements. Job site signs, when proportioned in line size, font, and color, pull a good share of the advertising load. Because they are placed at a job that you are working on, they act as a testimonial to your success and are therefore very effective. Placing one sign at each job site will give you strong credentials.

- Avoid popular layout signs where "Another Job By" or "Electrical Work By" lines are larger than the company name. If your sign is next to a construction site, it is obvious that you are doing the job. To add any other line will obscure your name and logo.

- Keep the lettering proportions the same as that of

the truck: Name and logo 100%, telephone number 75%, all other lines 30% or smaller. Check that every word says something of value. Don't clutter the sign with unnecessary words or lines. Use contrasting colors.

Uniforms

Uniforms are a necessity for service-oriented companies. Their color scheme and lettering should be in harmony with the rest of the company attire.

Identification tags

Use identification tags for each of your servicepersons instead of imprinting their names on the uniform. Identification tags project confidence and add prestige to your company. They tell the customer that you care and have taken the time to check and identify your employees, especially with a photo.

Identification tags make it easy for employees to exchange uniforms and they are a requirement in most security-sensitive areas. In your marketing reference letter, the mention of your company using uniforms and identification tags for your technicians often makes the difference between losing and getting a job or a maintenance contract.

Hard Hats

Hard hats are good safety devices. OSHA requires them on all jobs. From a marketing point of view, they are also very effective. The next time you see a cover page featuring a contractor at work, note the two main elements of visual impact. The hard hat and the company's name and logo enhance both the publication's feature story and the contractor. Visualize the same photos without hard hats and you will understand the power of visual impact.

Indisputably, hard hats make a statement about your company. Those who think it is inconvenient or unimportant should consider safety as well as marketing advantages first. The use of hard hats makes good business sense—for a relatively low cost, it creates a safer work environment, lower insurance premiums, and greater company visibility.

Communication

Stationery

A letter is the physical messenger of your thoughts. Its appearance dictates the impression you will create on the reader.

Many volumes have been written on business letter writing, text formats, and layout—including crafted letters for any business occasion. You may follow their guidelines, for they are excellent learning tools.

There are certain conventions used in letter writing that are well established, yet flexible enough to allow you to communicate exactly what you want to the reader. If you consider the appearance of the letter, format, length, and envelope, the reader will be drawn to it. Once the reader gives your letter his attention, your message is sure to get through.

The Envelope

The appearance of the envelope adds to the overall reception of your letter. With the exception of the two-letter abbreviation for the state, the address on the envelope should be the same as it appears on the letter.

The Letterhead

The letterhead usually consists of the logo, full business name and address, license number, phone and fax number.

THE ESSENTIALS OF CONTRACTING

This information should be uncluttered and readable. The design should be simple enough for the reader to find the information he needs without being distracted from reading the rest of the letter.

The fax number and email are an additional mailing address and as such, they belong with your address, possibly on the same line and right after the zip code. Contrary to conventional practices, they don't belong next to the telephone number. The telephone number should be by itself, clutter free.

Business stationeries are usually white or some other conservative color. The standard letter size is 8.5 by 11 inches.

The letterhead is always used as the first sheet of a letter. If the typed letter is more than one page, a plain sheet of paper matching the letterhead color can be used for all subsequent pages.

The length of any letter also affects its reception. Customers who receive a lot of correspondence are not going to react favorably to lengthy three-page letters that could have been written in one.

Come right to the point in your letters: they should be concise and limited to one page whenever possible.

Reference Letter

A reference letter is your passport to better accounts and better jobs. A reference letter is your company's Data Sheet (see below) with a Reference Sheet listing completed and active jobs with their respective customers' names and phone numbers. If you wish, you may list the projects' dollar values. Of the two sheets, the data sheet is the most important to your prospective customer.

Chapter 2 Market Yourself and Your Company   43

Company Data Sheet

Write the company's Data Sheet on a letterhead. It should start with a short welcome paragraph including the following:

- Your electrical license number, the issuing municipality or agency, and the territory it covers

- The FEIN (Federal Employer Identification Number)

- The license name and number of each municipal, county or state license(s) required to operate in your territory

- The Workman's Compensation and Employer Liability carrier, including the policy number

- Your commercial General Liability carrier, including coverage and policy number

- Your insurance agent, including contact name and phone number

- Any association with electrical contracting councils or boards and the like, including years of membership

- Operation - A short statement of company operating territories, including remote shops or branches where applicable

- Management - A short statement of your managerial philosophy and why your business method is beneficial to your prospective customer

- Banking - The bank you deal with, including contact person and telephone number

- References - Use this final statement to direct the

reader to the next page, the Company Reference Sheet. You could write,
"The following is a partial list of customers . . ." or any similar statement that makes the reader aware that there is more to your presentation.

Company Reference Sheet

- On this sheet, you may list your completed projects by category—residential, commercial, and industrial—or by territory, or both. The combinations are endless, but don't overdo it.

  Stay within one page. If you have presented your company well in the Data Sheet, then the Reference Sheet becomes secondary and you don't need to elaborate much.

- Insert a P.S. note at the end of the Reference Sheet stating, "For further information please call Mr. John Doe at (123) 456-7890."

John Doe Electric Co.

Licensed Electrical Contractor   No. E-12345

123 Main St, Our City, USA, 12345,   Fax (123) 456-7890

Call us   . . .   *(123) 555-6400*

Company Data Sheet—

Welcome to John Doe Electric Co,

The information contained in this letter is to acquaint you better with our company. We stand ready to assist you with your upcoming project. Just call us.

License and FEIN numbers:

Electrical license number E-12345 held by Mr. John Doe.

Federal identification number 65-0000000

Insurance:

Workers compensation and employers liability; XYZ Company, policy #407-3333-01

Agent: Independent Associates; Mr. Smith (123) 234-45678

Associations:

Electrical Council of USA

North-star Association of Electrical Contractors

John Doe Electric is a registered XYZ power and light company for Kings Counties

Operation:

The Company is licensed to operate throughout the state; however, it maintains its activities within Kings counties.

Management:

The Company manages its work through four independent branches. This method provides our customers with competitive prices, person-to-person relationships, and better job control. The branch manager is directly responsible to you for the execution of the job.

Banking:

Any-Bank 3333 Main Street, My City, USA; account manager Ms. Doris (123) 777-3434

Jobs References:

For jobs references see the attached "Jobs Reference Sheet"

John Doe Electric Co. - Reference Sheet

RESIDENTIAL

Chaney Residence	Bani Construction	(123) 555-6767
17031 Ocean Blvd.	2569 South Stewart	
Any City	Any City	

Lazo Residence	P.L. Douglas Construction	(123) 555-8856
2173 S.W. 13th Ct.	611 Medallion	
Any City	Any City	

Ladder Homes Inc.	B.C. Builders	(123) 555-9966
5205 West Hill Rd.	7788 Paris Rd.	
Any City	Any City	

COMMERCIAL

Tuscany Grill	Jankin Contractors	(123) 555-2233
1203 Main Street	40111 Atlantic Ave.	
Any City	Any City	

Baron Sports	XYZ Development Inc.	(123) 555-4510
34 Washington Street	5569 Monroe Street	
Any Town	Any City	

Merry-Go-Round	Store Builders Inc.	(123) 555-7790
2500 North Broadway	7774 Geneva Blvd.	
Any Town	Any City	

INDUSTRIAL

Morris Paint Co.	W.P. Ford Corp.	(123) 555-9999
Route 22	8934 Western Lane	
Any City	Any City	

Falcon Foundry Corp.	By Owner	(123) 555-0087
5677 Babylon Road	5677 Babylon Road	
Any City	Any City	

For further information please call John Doe at   (123) 555-6400

Printed Ad

The same guidelines as for visual impact also apply to printed ads, telephone directories, circulars, brochures, and specialty items. These guidelines, combined with marketing objectives, help create effective layouts for printed ads.

Performance

As a promotional tool, nothing has a greater lasting effect than good company performance. Perhaps the quality of your performance as a contractor will not generate a great deal more business at first, but you can be certain that in time it will become your company's hallmark.

To gain such a reputation takes a conscientious and collective effort by every member of your company. Adopt policies that will deliver quality service with integrity, and you will be on your way to success. The following topics explain how.

Punctuality

The worst feeling you can have is to have to walk into a meeting and instead of saying "Good morning," or "Good afternoon," say, "I am sorry I'm late," or make up excuses for being late. The worst part is not your feelings being hurt, but hurting your reputation as a responsible contractor. Frequent tardiness influences decision-makers adversely.

If you are a habitually tardy person and wish to experience what others feel when you are late, just think back to a situation when someone was late for an appointment with you.

As the time approached, you began to check your wristwatch. At about five minutes before the hour, you began to formulate doubtful thoughts about that person.

At the top of the hour, your thoughts became unprintable and got progressively worse with every passing minute. Fifteen minutes past the hour, you had lost considerable respect for the person and decided you couldn't take him seriously.

Once you know how others feel and think about you when you are late for an appointment, think of the effect this has on your image as a responsible contractor. No amount of "I'm sorry I'm late" will ever repair the damage. Show up on time and be considerate of other people's time.

Say it straight

When you say something, mean it and say it straight. Don't underestimate or double-talk your customer; most often, it backfires. Be a straight shooter.

Don't wait for them to call you. Get a head start.

Once we win the job, the customer expects us to take full charge and keep an eye on progress. Don't wait for the customer to call. The idle time from the award until the job goes into full swing is the best time to set up and get a head start, especially in alteration work.

Mobilize the job and do whatever work you can at your own pace. The customer is not the electrical contractor; you are. The customer will call you when he thinks the job is ready for you. By then, you will wish you had been there sooner. Staying attentive to the job's requirements prevents costly mistakes. It also builds a good working relationship with the customer.

Get timely job inspections

In contracting, passing scheduled inspections is crucial. Neglect to call for an inspection, or fail one, and the entire construction schedule goes off track.

Do this a couple of times and you will receive threatening letters from your customer asking you to shape up or ship out.

Before inspections, be certain your work is ready and you or someone from your company will meet the inspector at the job site. Inspections go more smoothly when you are available at the inspection site to answer pertinent questions.

Follow Up on Paperwork

Timely paperwork processing is as important to contract administration as passing inspections is to construction schedules. Procrastination in this area is common among failing contractors. Our efficiency directly affects job progress and collections.

Compliance with contracts, depending on the owner's requirements, can generate a great deal of paperwork. However, regardless of how much paperwork there is, it is as much a part of our contractual obligation as is the installation of conduit and wire. The only difference is that while we may get out of installing a certain conduit run, we will not get away from processing paperwork, especially if the customer needs it to satisfy the owner or a bank.

In contracting, there is no room for procrastination in any aspect of the work. Installation and contract administration are essentials to contracting. Do them both efficiently and you will have a well-balanced, performing company.

When the following items are part of our contract, they require special attention:

Submittal

Any documentation requiring evidence that the material and equipment comply with the plans and specifications, and that the contractor himself complies with the general provisions of the contract are referred to as 'submittals.'

We transmit submittals for approval to the architect through the customer (the general contractor or the owner) within the allocated number of days from the date of 'Notice of Commencement.'

The architect, in turn, has a certain number of days to either approve or reject our submission. Depending on contract requirements, this procedure can become complex and time consuming.

For example, the submissions for any one item can involve the manufacturer, the manufacturer's representative, the supplier, the contractor, the general contractor, the owner, the architect, the consulting engineers and other agencies having jurisdiction over the project.

Therefore, it behooves us to transmit our submittals promptly, and to release no work or material until we have 'physical' possession of their approvals.

Staying within deadlines despite this seemingly endless circular correspondence is a matter of survival. Its ramifications will become more apparent in later chapters.

Punctuality can affect profit. A delayed approval for certain material can disrupt shipment and, subsequently, productivity. The following is a list of the most common submittals:

- Progress Schedules

- Progress Reports

- List of Material Suppliers

- Shop Drawings

- Change Orders

- Material Samples

- Monthly Requisitions and Applicable Releases of Lien

- Payroll Reports

- Safety Report

Material Release

When you receive the approved shop drawings, promptly forward them to your supplier along with your release order. Procrastination in placing an order or in releasing approved material and equipment delays the job just as any other paper work would.

Many manufacturers and their reps shut down their entire operation for extensive periods during vacation times. Months before their scheduled vacations, they begin to restrict shipping commitments. Reflect their vacations in your job progress schedule, thus alleviating unpleasant surprises and conflicts.

If you act within the terms of your contract and meet all deadlines, there can never be any liability to you for situations beyond your control. If you fail, however, there can be enough back charges to dissipate your profit and more.

As-built Drawings

Generate as-built drawings as you carry out the work. When we neglect this important task and attempt to complete it at the end of the project, is more difficult and it will hold up final payment.

Job Site Clean-up

Job site clean up, unless otherwise stipulated in the contract, is part of the work. Failure to comply more often than not results in unexpected back charges.

In order to prevent these back charges, either we agree to a fixed charged for the service before the job starts or do it ourselves. However, under no circumstance should we neglect this work; it produces many worthless arguments.

MARKETING RESULTS

For one reason or another, many contractors reading this chapter will take exception to many of its marketing approaches, especially concerning clean up and punctuality. Their minds run off with thoughts such as, 'I always get away with that kind of stuff ... why bother?'

The fact is, however, that many contractors also go out of business because of 'stuff' like that. We could speculate that these are the same nine-out-of-ten contractors who think they can get away with that 'stuff,' and refuse to subscribe to good marketing approaches and business practices. The remainder succeeds.

In conclusion, if you want to succeed, you have to take responsibility and deliver complete jobs—including paperwork. The type of owner—private or public—indicates the extent of paperwork required for each project. To be certain, review the bidding documents beforehand.

What you gain in reputation for living up to your obligations far outweighs the few dollars you may save cheating on trivial 'stuff.' Think of it as a good marketing investment.

In contracting, you create demand by amassing as many favorable impressions as possible with those who are in position to influence others—and with those who will decide on the next job award.

When a contract is awarded to you, seize the moment. With every contract you undertake, you have the opportunity to create greater demand for your company. A contract performed on time is the ultimate and most inexpensive marketing tool. It will establish you as a competent and trustworthy electrical contractor.

SECTION III

MARKETS DEFINED

Chapter 3 Target Your Market

Conventional Markets

Market Elements

Chapter 3

TARGET YOUR MARKET

CONVENTIONAL MARKETS

The three conventional markets available to electrical contracting are:

- Residential

- Commercial

- Industrial

This chapter will help you decide what market to target and the most productive marketing method—rifle or shotgun approach.

Electrical installations, though they remain the same in principle, vary in substance from job to job. You can be installing a fifteen amperes circuit serving a light outlet in a home with non-metallic cable, plastic boxes and ordinary fittings, or you could be using rigid conduits with explosion-proof boxes and special fittings in a paint manufacturing plant. In either case, you need the knowledge of the applicable codes.

As electricians in search of employment, you seek the field for which you are best suited. First you choose the type of work—Service, Alteration, or New Work; then the category—Residential, Commercial, or Industrial. Then, according to your ability, you apply as Supers, Foremen, Journeymen, Mechanics or Helpers. If you base your choice on the principle, 'Do what you know best,' then your chances for steady work at better pay are greater.

When you stray from this rule, you lose, for you cross barriers you are not prepared to cross. If you want to cross these barriers successfully, regardless of whether you seek merely employment or a multi-million dollar job, the principles are the same—know your business.

Be aware of the advantages and pitfalls of the field you are about to enter and educate yourself to meet its challenges. Set realistic goals as part of a marketing plan that will target that field; and, in case you have to retreat, have an alternate plan of action.

To some, crossing the barrier between service work and contracting is their goal. To others, the barrier may be between residential and commercial work and any other combination of work, depending on your personal insecurities.

Nevertheless, if you want to get to the other side you must cross whatever barrier is keeping you on this side of the fence. Once you have decided to cross (expanding into other fields), whatever marketing investment you have made in time and money is lost if later you decide to retreat.

So far, we have talked about crossing the fence. However, who is to say that to be successful we must cross any fences? After all, many successful contractors hold steadfast to their field and never cross fences. Most likely, this is the secret of their success. They are good at what they do and they have expanded simply by doing more of it, which brings us to the subject of true objectives:

- Select a field of your choice, make it productive, and exploit it.

- An antidote to a popular cliché is, 'The grass is brown all over.'

In your case, you are most likely a good electrician. As you analyze the different markets, the virtually unlimited choices will become more apparent to you. Note that each choice is linked closely to a different level of electrical contracting that begs your expertise not only in the electrical field but in the business of contracting as well.

When you have mastered electrical contracting as you have mastered your electrical trade, you will be able to evaluate the strength of your operation, define your market(s), and decide on a marketing approach. You will recognize that a 'rifle' approach is the most effective.

The following definitions will help you decide through knowledge rather than guesswork:

MARKET ELEMENTS

In order to zero in on the market you want to pursue, choose one item from each of the five elements listed below. If you want your markets to be somewhat broader, choose additional items and assign them a priority level. The advantages of this method will become apparent in later chapters. In the meantime, study each element objectively and decide which market is right for you.

Element One – The Owner

The owner is the ultimate customer. The contractual obligation between the owner and you can be direct or through his agent, a general contractor, a construction manager, a property manager, or any other authorized representative. In contracting, when we refer to the 'Owner,' we refer to the project owner and his team, the architect and engineers.

The owner's financial and administrative ability to process prompt payments and other documents has a direct effect on two important variables in our formula for profit—financing cost and productivity ratio.

Another important variable, job administrative cost, is in direct proportion to the extent of the owner's operating procedures. The more paperwork, the higher the administrative cost. To handle this task, some jobs require dedicated personnel for the life of the contract. In this work, we group the different procedures into three categories: Informal, Semiformal, and Formal.

Informal

Informal procedure requires only the essentials to get the job done: a quotation, followed by a one-page contract (often your standard *Proposal/Contract)* and a permit application with the least amount of scheduled inspections. All else, with the exception of change orders, is done verbally with lots of handshakes. This procedure is most common among private owners (see definition later in this chapter).

Semiformal

Semiformal procedure goes a few steps beyond the informal procedure. To better define bid and contract documents, the owner will require: (1) a monthly requisition, with contract breakdown reflecting amounts earned and percentages; (2) releases of lien; (3) occasional shop drawings and as-built drawings; and (4) miscellaneous record keeping such as progress schedule reports and job diary. Financial institutions or other interested parties such as investors usually dictate this procedure. It is common among corporate and private owners alike.

Formal

Formal procedure requires carrying out all procedures in strict accordance with the contract documents. Its deadlines, from bidding to completion, are rigid. The contract operates on the thesis that if a deadline is broken it is due to someone's negligence. Consequently, the faulty party is liable. In this contractual relationship, comprehensive and accurate record keeping is mandatory.

Other documents not previously mentioned but included in this procedure are progress schedules, weekly payroll reports, safety reports, minority and equal employment reports, affidavits and the like. This list grows with the size of the project and the owner's internal requirements.

Formal procedure is most common among large corporations, utility companies, and taxpayer-funded projects.

In choosing your markets, therefore, it becomes evident that the owner is the first element you need to scrutinize. Can you afford to wait 30, 60, 90 or even 120 days for your money? If you feel that scenario offers a better marketplace, and you can afford to carry the job, then you should choose that kind of an owner.

However, if you cannot afford to carry such an owner, imagine, if you will, starting a job only to find out the owner pays in 60 days at best. If you think this does not happen, be assured that it puts many contractors out of business.

Since the owner of the job can influence not only the outcome of that job, but our company's overall performance, choose him carefully.

For our purposes, we can categorize owners into three different groups: Private, Corporate, and Public—each with its sub-category.

When we refer to owners as private or corporate, the terms are not mutually exclusive. A private owner can be a corporation or vice versa.

Private Owner

The private owner of a residential, commercial, or industrial project is defined here as one who manages his own work.

Usually, a private owner is a bargain hunter. If we are starting out or find ourselves in between jobs needing immediate carry-over work, the private owner is our best candidate. His procedures involve close-to-nothing paperwork and, at least initially, prompt payments. If the price is right, we can negotiate a reasonable deal, including a down payment without a 10% retainer. This is the most sought-after owner, thus making the competition fierce and our position vulnerable.

While most private owners are honorable and their projects well financed, some are unscrupulous and their projects mismanaged and undercapitalized. These owners, besides using our bid price to lure other contractors to lower theirs, quite often go over budget toward the end of the job and may be unlikely to pay you in full.

The filing of a mechanics lien will not put immediate cash in your bank account. When you ultimately collect on these liens, you will share a good part of the money with your attorney. If you fail to collect, you will be out the monies due to you plus legal costs.

Whenever possible, prevent these situations from happening. One sure way is to exclude these owners from your marketing plans (More on prevention and protections later on in this book).

Corporate Owner

This owner's operating procedure is most often dictated by the money source—the financial institution.

His operating procedures can be Formal or Semiformal. Regardless of the procedure, this owner does the work in-house or through a general contractor or a construction manager. Normally, this owner negotiates the bids within a closed circuit of pre-qualified contractors.

Before you begin estimating a job, know what to expect from the customer and what rules will govern the job. A sure way is to check the complete bidding documents, something many electrical contractors seldom do. Short of this, ask questions (see Chapter 8- Estimating).

A good rule of thumb is that large corporations such as the Fortune 500 Group as well as most publicly owned corporations operate under *Formal* procedures. Privately held corporations operate under *Semiformal* procedures.

In this book, corporations that operate under *Informal* procedures are classified as Private Owners.

Another good rule of thumb is that corporations operating under Formal or Semiformal procedures manage and finance their projects well. Their standard payment schedule is monthly. Generally, they pay a requisition submitted by the 25th day of the month within 30 days. If you count on anything short of this, you may be disappointed.

Another factor you have to take into account is the 10% retainer. It should be reduced to 5% at or about the job's midpoint.

Public Owner

The public owner is any federal, state, county, or municipal entity that wants to build or alter a project. This owner operates under *Formal* procedures. From planning to completion, the owner monitors and documents the work closely. This owner presets wages for construction workers known as Prevailing Wage Schedules, which are often in accord with local union rates and benefits.

The paperwork is extensive. The smaller the project, the higher your administration cost—a factor you must reflect in your estimate. Scheduled payments are monthly; however, you can expect your first payment to be delayed by up to 60 days, and the last one, the 10% retainer, longer.

At the halfway point of the job, if all your paperwork is in order, the retainer should be cut to 5%. The owner retains this amount until the job is declared 'done.'

A job is declared 'done' when all trades have done their work to the satisfaction of the owner. For example, you may have completed your work long before the parking lot is paved or marked. Often, you will not receive your final payment until the entire contract is closed, i.e. after the parking lot is marked. Any one trade can hold up everyone else's final payments.

Most public work requires a 5% Bid Bond, a 100% Performance Bond, and a 50% Payment Bond. If you have never dealt with surety companies, don't assume construction bonds are easy to get. Before you put your estimating tools in motion, talk to your insurance agent.

In bidding for public work, qualifying for minority and equal employment acts and the like is a prerequisite. Don't take these legislative acts lightly—the owner can cancel a job at any time, even after it starts, for lack of compliance.

Element Two – The Owner's Agent

The owner, with the exception of those who build and manage their own projects, has at least two ways to get the job done: He can hire a General Contractor or a Construction Manager.

General Contractor

The master of construction in the building industry is the general contractor. He has the expertise to deliver turnkey jobs at a fixed cost. His ability to manage contractors so that the project is completed is of value to the owner as well as to subcontractors.

Although the general contractor may have a high reputation, what draws the owner to a specific general contractor is price.

From the owner to the supplier of trivial services there is a balancing act between quality and quantity demanding some form of compromise from anyone involved.

Because the general contractor is in a position to affect the outcome of your work, consider his reputation and his administrative and financial abilities seriously.

While general contractors work with the owner's money, meaning they will pay you only after they are paid, most of them are willing to make prompt payments and advances if the price is right. In fact, that is the way most general contractors regain whatever profit they have given up in getting the job.

On the surface, your relationship with the general contractor may appear normal and accommodating, as it should be. However, when greed takes over, watch out! Check your position; most likely, you are on the losing end of the deal or, at best, you are on a lower playing field.

Construction Manager

Construction managers are usually general contractors who render their services for a fixed fee or a percentage of the cost of the job. Some construction managers go beyond general contracting; they assist the owner in planning, financing, and designing the job.

Our relationship with a construction manager is the same as that of a general contractor, but with one exception: the price-squeezing mechanism is triggered by their loyalty to the owner, rather than greed.

A construction manager, since he is not risking any of his own money, lacks the incentive to expedite the project; when a construction manager becomes complacent, watch out! You might be on the same losing end as you were with the general contractor.

Construction managers represent the owner, and as such, there is no legal bond between them and you.

Element Three – The Kind of Work

How is your shop set up? What kind of equipment do you own? Can you Hi-Pot a 4100-Volt or 115-KV device or repair a 24-Volt chime? The answers to those questions determine the kind of work you should target. In this analysis, owning a one-time hydraulic rigid bender or a hickey is as important as the high or low voltage question raised above. Know your limitations and go after the kind of work you are best equipped to do.

Low Voltage (Less than 50 Volts)

Low voltage work, also referred to as specialty contracting, includes Sound, Security, Fire Alarm, Data, Communications and similar systems. To make this work profitable requires constant personnel training and a large inventory. As opposed to conventional electrical contracting, low voltage work requires merchandising.

High Voltage (50 to 600 Volts)

High voltage work includes power and light distribution systems for most indoor and outdoor projects. This work is the kind most often referred to in the National Electrical Code and the most studied in apprenticeship classrooms. This kind of work requires little or no inventory. Journeymen are responsible for their training and continual education, thus reducing necessary personnel training to basic company procedures.

Mid to High Voltage (Over 600 Volts to 40 KV)

Light to heavy industrial and utility work is a specialty work similar to low voltage that requires personnel capable of handling high voltage work such as splices, high potential tests, grounding, discharging, etc. You need a good amount of line-work equipment.

Super High Voltage (Over 40 KV to 1,100 KV and up)

This work includes the construction of substations, switching stations and transmission lines. If you plan to do this kind of work, take into consideration that you will be assuming the role of a general contractor. You will build temporary and permanent roads and erect towers and structures made out of wood or steel. Your cable installation can stretch over miles of rural terrain and through remote towns.

Your efforts as a contractor, if you have the skills, the finances, and equipment to carry out the work, can be well compensated. While the owner supplies most materials, the payroll cash outlay can be high.

Element Four – The Category of Work

Residential

Since it appears to be easiest, residential work is where most of us start out. But if you want to succeed, don't underestimate its demands. Most often, you are dealing with an owner who is protected by an array of consumer laws.

The building of untitled dwellings such as tract homes, villas, and condominiums falls into the category of commercial work. Residential work, as defined here, consists of electrical contracting done in people's homes.

As long as you respect the properties of homeowners, you have covered the bulk of any consumer-protection act requirements that govern such areas. To be successful at this work, you must also be punctual and complete the work in its entirety, which means giving customer satisfaction. With this in place, the customer gets what he wants and you are paid in full. Residential work requires light investment. If you closely monitor collections, the cash flow is good.

Commercial

Commercial includes wiring for warehousing, shopping centers, malls, office buildings, buildings of public assembly and the like. Contractors tend to lean toward this work because it is the stepping-stone toward other electrical markets.

Commercial work requires a significant amount of tools along with maintenance and replenishing programs.

Warehousing of leftover materials from jobs and ordinary materials acquired at special discount can play a significant role in profit making. Inventory, when properly managed, can give you the extra margin to win jobs (see Chapter 27 - Warehousing).

Industrial

Industrial work is the most stable and lucrative of the three. This selective work requires personnel specially trained in control, special occupancies, and high to super high voltage wiring.

The tools required are costly. They require expensive maintenance programs and periodic replacement.

To service your industrial customer properly, an inventory of special items is necessary. In your operating costs, you must consider this slow-moving inventory and, accordingly, charge it to the customer as overhead.

While collections can be good, the industrial contractor can easily lose sight of administrative costs. He must maintain a number of employees balanced between non-productive (administrative) and productive (field) labor. The industrial contractor tends to grow complacent and neglects sales, letting production (productive labor) sag, as administrative costs remain unchanged.

Element Five – The Type of Work

Service Work

Service work is the lifeblood of a company. Very few contractors can afford to abandon it entirely, if not for financial reasons, then for the sake of properly serving the customer.

In service work, the completion of your work is rarely dependent on other trades. You are paid upon completion and cash flow is healthy, unless you choose to extend credit.

The rate of profit, if you have qualified technicians and a good administrative backup, is excellent.

Alteration

Alteration work is second to service. When you undertake this work, you cannot afford to lose sight of details. If you do, you will learn expensive lessons quickly. Consequently, this work requires mechanics you can rely on.

You can shift mechanics from one job to another as long as you return the same mechanics to complete the job they started.

Balancing workforce between work at hand and anticipated work is the never-ending task of the electrical contractor. As the saying goes, "Either you have too much work and not enough mechanics or too many mechanics and not enough work." If you adhere to the lessons in this book, you are bound to reach a happy medium and balance those two elements.

In alteration work, if you collect you money when due and stick steadfastly to the rules of good business, the profit rate is excellent.

New Work

In this book, we subdivide new work into large and small jobs and define them as follows:

A large job is the kind that can occupy at least one full-time supervisor from beginning to end,

A small job is the kind that cannot occupy a full-time supervisor from beginning to end.

In essence, starting out in new work with small projects makes it almost impossible to make profits, unless you have service and alteration work to keep your key workers busy in between the various construction stages of the new work.

Be aware that shuffling work force, tools and material can be costly, especially when you don't have a handle on the daily schedule and each job's progress.

SECTION IV

SALES

Chapter 4

CONTRACT BASICS

WHAT IS A CONTRACT

As a habitant of an area, you have implied or written rights protected by the laws of that area—city, state, federal and the world.

Whether you are ordering a cup of coffee at a restaurant or a new home from a builder, these laws protect both transactions. That is, upon delivery, one is paid in full and the other takes possession of the coffee or the house. A written contract arises when the parties wish to alter the laws that govern such transactions. We refer to these alterations as clauses or provisions.

'Providing you will do this, I will do that' and so on, is the spirit of contract writing. If you are not alert, one can take advantage of the other.

PRINCIPLES OF CONTRACT

Before you start selling your services, it is necessary to review a few basic principles that affect the closing of contracts. How a successful contract is defined—and how it comes about—is of great importance in the development of a sound marketing approach.

A successful contract is one you carry out profitably and the satisfied customer recommends you to others. The main components of this contract are:

- The customer solicits for work he needs done, called the 'Invitation to Bid'

- Our response to the solicitation, called the 'Offer' or 'Bid'

- The customer's 'Acceptance' of the Offer

When these three elements are fairly set and communicated with clarity, a fair contract arises; if not, your contract will lead to a troublesome business relationship.

The Solicitation

The solicitation or bid document details the scope of work the customer wants done. When dealing with a layperson, it is to your advantage to exercise your expertise to guide the customer toward his goal.

When quoting jobs with bidding documents prepared by experts (attorneys, architects, engineers), your focal point should be more toward the documents' fine print than the job's details.

You may discover that parts of the proposed contract don't agree with your policies, or you may not be able to comply with some of the special provisions. When this occurs, you are better off not bidding the work unless you can rework these discrepancies with your prospective customer at the start. It takes courage to walk away from potential work, but it is stupid to walk into a lion's den knowingly.

The Offer

The offer or quotation is where you define your terms. In it, you express with clarity what it is you want, for how much, and what you will or will not do.

The Acceptance

The acceptance is of reciprocal value when you and the customer sign a contract.

THE SELLING TOOLS

With the solicitation, offer, and acceptance defined, you can put together the basic tools to sell contracts. When you prepare the work order, service call, quotation, and proposal contract using the principles outlines here, these documents will protect you as well as the customer.

Business smarts dictate avoiding troublesome contracts. If you want to run a smart business, your printed forms must state your basic requirements clearly.

For clarity's sake, it is important to use written words and business forms that people can understand easily, and, when necessary, readily refresh their memory. The right paperwork is your best protection. You will be surprised how this helps you to avert temptation and how well each party performs when they are bound by a fair and valid agreement.

Proposal/Contract Form

The Proposal/Contract form shown in this chapter employs the principles explained earlier. It contains the basic elements for setting up successful contracts. This form is introduced first because it can be used for both Service and Contracting Work.

Each form's layout requires the technician to fill in the least number of blank spaces. The comments on how and why each blank space should be filled are as essential as the form itself.

Each clause requires information that, when obtained from the prospective customer, will give you the documentation necessary to carry out contracting tasks with ease.

It is therefore on this principle that you should invest the few extra minutes to fill out these forms entirely. When you do, you'll make a considerable contribution to the success of your business.

2

1

John Doe Electric Co.
Licensed Electrical Contractor E-12345

Proposal /Contract
No: _____

123 Main St, City, USA, 12345,   Fax (123) 456-7890

Call us . . . (123) 555-6400

Customer	Job
Contact:	Contact:
Name:	Name:
Add:	Add:
City/St/Zip:	City:
Phones: Hm: Wk:	Owner:
Beeper: Fax:	Job Phone:

4

John Doe Electric, referred to as "Contractor," proposes to furnish labor and material as specified herein for $_____ payable as per contract breakdown as submitted by the Contractor prior to commencing work, or as follows:

3

____ % = $ _____ down _____

____ % = $ _____ upon _____

____ % = $ _____ upon _____

6

Contractor's Rep: _____ Signature: _____ Date: _____

5

If this proposal is not accepted within 10 calendar days, then, without notice, the Contractor may withdraw it anytime thereafter.

Scope of Work

7

Install electrical wiring as per plans and specifications, if any, dated: _____ and prepared by _____ Identified as Drawings No:_____ revised on _____

1

2 **(This and other forms may be downloaded online at www.theestimatingroom.com)**

3

8

Customer Acceptance

The price, specifications, and conditions set herein are satisfactory and hereby accepted. I authorize the contractor to proceed with the work as specified herein. I shall make payment as outlined above. Unpaid balances are subject to 1. 5% per month interest until paid in full. Customer agrees to pay all of the contractor's costs related to the collection of any sum due, including legal fees and other applicable expenses.

Patching, painting, site restoration work generated by this work shall be done by others. Lamps, appliance cords, and caps shall be supplied by others. Power company charges, municipal permit fees, and contractor's processing fees, if any, are not included in this proposal. The electrical permit shall cover only the work contracted herein. The cost for removing any existing violation is not included in this proposal. The Contractor, when required, for an additional charge to the customer, shall apply for an electrical permit to cover said extra work. Changes to the scope of work shall be written as "Change Orders" and executed by both parties prior to commencing any work on said changes.

Customer please note: When this Proposal/Contract exceeds $5000, in addition to the Contractor Rep's signature it requires the Contractor's owner/president signature here: _____, Pres ___/___/ 20___ or the contract shall be considered null and void.

I _____ am authorized to accept and sign this contract because I am the customer named above, or I am acting for the customer as his agent.

Customer Signature: _____ Title:_____ Date: _____

Figure 1: Proposal/Contract

Notes to Proposal/Contract

1. Proposal/Contract Number

> A contract number is essential for cross-reference with future documents such as Change Orders, Submittals, Payment Requisitions, and other legal documents. Be consistent and use whatever numerical scheme best fits your operation.

2. Customer

> On all your forms, it is essential to identify the person responsible for paying the bill (see customer signature below) and record this data accordingly.

- Contact Name

- The contact is the person authorized to represent the customer. In corporations, a contract is signed by an officer and the work overseen by an employee or an agent—the contact person. Be aware of the contact person, for unless the customer designates him in writing, he has no authority to sign change orders or alter the terms of the contract. Therefore, it is essential to request a written statement from the customer designating their authorized representative(s) along with his limitations, if any.

- Name

- Write the name of the company, corporation, or individuals on this line.

- Address (Including zip code)

- If the customer uses a post office box, insist on an actual street address. If you ever need this information for legal purposes, it can be expensive, time consuming, and often impossible to obtain.

3. Proposal Contract Amount

Round off the amounts to the next full dollar. This method makes record keeping and billing easier.

4. Payable As Follows

Be specific about how you want to be paid. In the clause, 'We propose hereby to furnish labor and material as specified herein, for the sum of $_____ payable as follows,' the most important phrase is 'as specified herein,' meaning that no other plans or specifications apply to your price unless otherwise stated in the proposal.

- Payment Schedule

    For service work, you may choose a payment schedule that includes a down payment followed by two or three subsequent payments, as shown. If you are new to down payments, be assured that many customers, especially for service work, will be surprised if you don't ask for none. For more on this subject, see Chapter 16 - Negotiations.

    For contracting work, either use the same approach as with service work or set up a separate payment schedule, in which case it should include a clause that reads, 'Payable as the work progresses and as per the contract breakdown we submit prior to commence work.' For more details on contract breakdown, see Chapter 19 - Requisitions for Payment.

5. Proposal Withdrawal

Every offer has a beginning and an end. In this case, your proposal will end in 10 days, after which it is your choice to accept or reject the contract.

Consider the clause more of a customer motivator than a deadline.

6. Your Signature

A Proposal/Contract is a ready-made form intended to remain a proposal until signed by the parties. You should ensure that both parties sign it at the same time, because when you sign and leave the contract behind waiting for the customer's signature, you become vulnerable.

Regardless of how many copies you are holding back, you are leaving the final draft to the discretion of the customer, who can modify it into the only binding copy—something which is popular with unscrupulous customers. Unless you discover it on the spot, it may not surface until you are well into the job.

- Unsigned Proposal/Contract

This document is a limited offer for a contract-to-be if accepted and executed within a given period. If you wish to stay in tune with your competition and sign the contract before the customer does, there is a safe alternative. Present your Proposal/Contract under a signed cover sheet or letterhead indicating your willingness to sign the contract as drafted within 10 days. When you have to leave a signed Proposal/Contract for the customer to sign, take the precaution of comparing carefully your retained copy with the one the customer sends back signed before you invest money in the job.

7. Scope of Work

Be careful in writing the scope of work; don't get lazy and sacrifice clarity for easy-to-use general statements. For example, the ambiguities of the frequently used phrase 'furnish and install all electrical work as per plans and specifications' without specific reference to the scope of work or to quantities has proven costly to many contractors.

Clarity is what you want in contracts. Note the difference between the phrases 'install electrical wiring' and the wildly used 'furnish and install all electrical work.' The word 'all' has no limit and 'electrical work' includes all sorts of equipment such as magnetic starters and controlling devices, which, most likely, you have not included in the estimate.

In describing the scope of work, describe it as 'electrical wiring,' for that is what you do and sell. As to quantities and scope of work, avoid using 'all' whenever possible. Use actual quantities and refer to the architect's name, drawing numbers and dates as shown on the sample form. In the absence of plans, enumerate and describe each item of work clearly, using a logical approach beginning with the location of work, followed by quantity and definition etc.

8. Customer Acceptance

This is where you outline the terms under which you are willing to do business. Study each clause and, if necessary, modify it to serve you better. When you have finished consult your lawyer if necessary and then draft your final business policy. Since this will be your own form, it favors you. Therefore, when quoting for or contracting work, it is advantageous to use your own form whenever possible, rather than giving that edge to your customer.

When dealing with general contractors and large accounts, they will expect you to sign their contracts, which are more complex than the Proposal/Contract shown here (see Chapter 15 - The Contract).

The principal elements, however, remain the same. Read through the clutter of paragraphs and soon the true Solicitation, Offer, and Acceptance become apparent. While you are on that expedition, be certain that your   terms of doing business, as outlined in the list below, are met—or that they are at least negotiable:

- The price

- The price, specifications, and conditions set herein are satisfactory and hereby accepted. You are authorized to proceed with the work as specified herein.

- Payment

- Payment shall be made as outlined above. Unpaid balances, after due date, are subject to 1.5% per month interest rate until paid in full. The customer agrees to pay all of the Contractor's costs related to the collection of any sum due, including legal fees and applicable expenses.

- Patching, painting, site restoration

- This work shall be done by others. Lamps, appliance cords, and caps shall be supplied by others.

- Charges

- Power company charges, municipal permit fees and

processing fees, if any, are not included in this proposal.

- Electrical permit

- The electrical permit shall cover only the work contracted herein. The removal of violations is not included in this proposal. The Contractor, when required, for an additional charge to the Customer, shall apply for an electrical permit to cover said extra work.

- Change orders

- Changes to the scope of work shall be written as 'Change Orders,' each executed by both parties prior to commence work.

- Customer note

- Customer please note: When this Proposal/Contract exceeds $5000, in addition to the Contractor Rep's signature, it requires the Contractor's Owner/President signature where indicated, or the Contractor has the option to deem it null and void.

Chapter 5

SERVICE AND CONTRACTING WORK

BRANCHES OF WORK

For both branches of electrical contracting—service and contracting work—to perform at the optimum level, each has to operate under separate management.

However, because service work is a springboard to contracting, many companies keep both activities under the same managerial team. Consequently, the company requires a managerial team capable of managing both activities.

In this chapter, the tools we are most concerned with are the commonly used business forms. As with all other forms you will encounter in this book, don't be deceived by their familiar appearance.

Contracting Forms

The sample forms in this section apply to Service as well as Contracting Work.

The Service Call Form

A well laid out service calls form is the most productive tool your technician can use.

As a stand-alone instrument, the service call form is unique because it evolves from quotation to contract to invoice to release within the short time in which a service call is carried out. With this form, you can instruct your technician on a particular policy for a particular customer; for example, method of payment or how much to discount the list price.

Filling in all the blanks will improve your field and office administrative performance greatly, not to mention your collection time.

The comments following the service form below address only those items pertinent to understanding the form as a whole.

John Doe Electric Co.

Licensed Electrical Contractor E-12345

123 Main St, City, USA, 12345, Fax (123) 456-7890

JDE

Service Call
Invoice No: _____

(123) 555-6400

Customer	Job

Customer
Contact: _____
Name: _____
Add: _____
City/St/Zip: _____
Phone: Hm: _____ Wk: _____

Job
Contact: _____
Name: _____
Add: _____
Owner: _____
Phone: Job: _____ Wk: _____

Date of Order	Order Taken By	Start Date	Cust. Order No.	Invoice Date
Terms COD ( ) Charge ( ) Cash Only ( )		Paid Yes ( ) No ( )	Serviceman No	Completion Date

2

Dispatched ____:____ Arrived ____:____ Out ___:___ In___:___ Out ___:___

1

Authorization to Enter the Premises and Commence Work

I authorize the contractor and his technicians to enter my premises (home/office/plant) to repair and/or install electrical work. I also promise to pay for all work performed in accordance with the terms and schedule rates shown below.

CUSTOMER SIGNATURE: _____ DATE: _____

3

Service Call: (Includes travel time to and from job site.)

	Rates	Invoice
A. Regular time	$49	$ ____
B. Sunday and Holidays	$65	$ ____
C. Any day between 6:00 pm and 11:00 pm	$65	$ ____
D. Any day between 11:00 pm and 8:00 am	$85	$ ____

4

5

Labor Rates per each 1/2 hour unit or part thereof:

A. Regular time	$35 Ea x ___	units	=	$ ____
B. Sunday and Holidays	$45 Ea x	units	=	$ ____
C. Any day between 6:00 pm &11:00	$45 Ea x	units	=	$ ____
D. Any day between 11:00 pm & 8:00	$55 Ea x	units	=	$ ____
E. 3 hours and over quoted at	$ P/hr x	hours	=	$ ____

6

Labor Total (a) $ ____
Material and Direct Job Expenses (b) $ ____

Please Pay

Invoice Total (a + b) $ ____

Customer's Acceptance of Work

7

I hereby acknowledge the satisfactory completion of the work described herein. I agree to pay all of the contractor's costs related to the collection of any sums due, including legal fees and expenses. Patching, painting, and site restoration, if required, shall be done by others.

CUSTOMER SIGNATURE: _____ Title: _____ Date: _____

For C.O.D. please fill the following:
PRINTED Name: _____ Dr. Lic. # _____ State:___ Exp. Date: _____

8

Work Description

_____
_____
_____

Form G-120-rev05 ©2005 The Estimating Room™ Inc.

Figure 2: Service Call

Notes

1. Authorization to Enter Premises and Commence Work

This clause, aside from giving you permission to enter and commence work, establishes the foundation of a binding contract. The customer accepts your offer to do work at your scheduled rates and promises to pay in accordance with your terms and conditions.

2. Dispatched

Here you and the customer agree to and document the amount of time you spent for his job. Notice 'for his job' and not 'at his job.' 'For his job' includes travel time to the job and to suppliers. This information must be entered prior to having the customer sign the "Acceptance of Work" clause. If there is any dispute, especially with charge account customers, the best time to resolve it is before your technician leaves the job, and not later when you are trying to collect your money and important details have been forgotten.

3. Rates

You may refer to this column as your list price and offer a discount to better customers, which you will reflect in 'This Invoice' column.

4. This Invoice

In this column, you extend the charges earned. You can calculate them at a full or discounted rate.

5. Labor Rate and Units of Work

In this form, the labor rate is set at $35 per one ½-hour unit or portion thereof. Therefore, if you complete the work in 40 minutes, you are entitled to two units, or $70.

6. Hourly

For any service work that exceeds 3 hours, convert the charges to hourly rates. The hourly rate should be posted here prior to the customer signing the "Authorization to Commence Work" clause.

7. Customer Acceptance

By signing this clause, the customer releases you and accepts your collection terms. For cash customers paying by check, you will need their driver's license information as well as their signature.

8. Work Description

Identify the work performed and any other work conditions. For example, when you come across a violation or a hazardous condition, write it down in the work description space as well as pointing it out to the customer.

The purpose of this form is clarity and legal protection, especially with first-time customers.

When we put our service call policy and our labor rates in print, we give the customer the opportunity to accept or reject our service, thus avoiding misunderstanding and disputes. Most customers welcome this candid approach.

Nowadays, attaining the customer's acceptance of work first is becoming conventional wisdom.

The Work Order Form

A work order form, as the title implies, is an order to carry out work on existing contracts, change orders, or just undertake a day's work for a given customer. Its purpose is to record clearly the work done in a format that will make billing easy and enable the customer to review the charges.

In the form that follows, each line is self-explanatory and, as with all other forms, filling it out completely will assist the field crew as well as your own billing and collection.

Read the explanatory notes following the form.

John Doe Electric Co.

Licensed Electrical Contractor E-12345

123 Main St, City, USA, 12345, Fax (123) 456-7890

Work Order

Invoice No: _____

(123) 555-6400

Customer	Job

1

Contact:

Name:

Addr:

Citv/St/Zip:

Phone: Hm: W

Contact:

Name:

Addr:

Owner:

Phone: Job: Wk:

Contract Work ( ) Extra Work ( ) for Job No. _____C.O. #____ Ticket #_____ Daywork ( )

Date of Order	Order Taken By	Starting Date	Cust. Order No.	Invoice Date

	Terms		Paid	Serviceman	No.	Completion Date

COD ( )   Charge ()   Cash Only ( )   Yes ( )   No ( )

Dispatched ____:____   Arrived ____:____   Out ___:___   In ___:____   Out ____:____

2

Date	Day of Week	Workman / Crew	Hrs Worked	Hourly Rate	Amount
				$	$
				$	$
				$	$
				$	$
				$	$
				$	$
				Labor Total	$
			Material and Direct Job Expenses		$

Please Pay

Invoice Total $

Work Description

(This and other forms may be downloaded online at www.theestimatingroom.com)

Customer Acceptance of Work

I hereby acknowledge the satisfactory completion of the work described herein. I agree to pay all of the contractor's costs related to the collection of any sums due, including legal fees and expenses. Patching, painting, and site restoration, when required, shall be done by others. By signing this document, I accept the terms and conditions set herein.

CUSTOMER SIGNATURE: _____ Title: _____ Date: _____

PRINTED Name: _____Dr. Lic#_____ State:___ Exp. Date:_____

Form EG-110-rev05   ©2005 The Estimating Room™ Inc.

Figure 3: Work Order Form

Notes

1. Work order defined

   In this line, you check the type of work you are ordering:

   * Contract Work ( )

   A check mark in this box indicates the order is for an existing contract, such as a punch list or repair. The checkmark also indicates not to charge the customer.

   * Extra Work ( )

   A check mark in this box indicates the order pertains to a specific change to an existing contract. In the blank spaces, insert the Job and Change Order numbers. We keep the Ticket numbers in sequential order; for example, for three days work on C.O. No. 3 for Job No. 08-1210 the ticket numbers would be 01, 02, and 03, while the C.O. and Job numbers remain constant.

   If the customer wants you to support the charges and you want your verifications approved for every day's work, just fill out a different Work Order for each day.

   * Day-work ( )

   A check mark in this box indicates a short-term job from one to a few crew-days, usually ordered by house-account customers. The work is done with no written contract payable upon completion or invoiced.

2. Material and Direct Job Expenses

   Insert a lump sum amount here. If required, list materials cost including markups on a separate sheet.

The Change Order Form

The scope of work of a contract is bound to change. On such occasions, you should detail the changes before you add or delete work and get a written approval from the customer. You do this with a change order form similar to the following to reflect cost and time changes (see Chapter 18 - Contract Management).

John Doe Electric Co.
Licensed Electrical Contractor E-12345
123 Main St, City, USA, 12345,   Fax (123) 456-7890

Change Order

No: ___

Date:___/__/___

Customer	Job
Contact:	Job Name:
Name:	Contract No. Dated:___/__/
Add,	Add.
City/St/Zip:	
Home: Wk:	Owner:
Beeper: Fax:	Job Phone:

Terms   Paid   Charge To

C.O.D. ( )   Cash Only ( )   Yes ( )   No ( )   Cust/GC: ( )   Others:

Documentation

No ( )   Not Applicable ( )   Will Follow ( )   Yes ( )   No of Sheets:

The Contractor and the Customer agree to make change(s) as specified below for: $ _____

Previous Contract Amount including all previous Change Orders: $ _____

Revised Contract Amount: $

With this Change Order, the contractor requests _____ day(s) extension to the project completion date. No work shall commence on the work covered by this Change Order until both parties execute it.

Contractor's Rep: _____Signature: _____Date: _____

Changes To Original Contract

(This and other forms may be downloaded online at www.theestimatingroom.com)

Customer Acceptance

The price and conditions set forth are satisfactory and are hereby accepted. The contractor is not be responsible for redesigning or upgrading any existing power distribution system that might be affected by the added electrical load of this change. This Change Order, upon its execution, becomes part of and conforms to the terms and conditions of the existing contract as identified above.

I (Print name) _____ am authorized to accept and sign this Change Order because I am the customer named above, or I am acting for the customer as his agent.

Customer Signature: _____Title: _____Date: _____

Form EG-130   ©2005 The Estimating Room™ Inc.

Figure 4: Change Order Form

Notes

1. Contract No. & Date

    Insert the job contract number and date to tie the terms and conditions of the contract to the change orders.

2. Terms

    On some jobs, you may want to be paid in cash for extra work. Check the appropriate box.

3. Documentation

    Some changes require backup paperwork; for the record, check the applicable box.

4. Extension of Time

    Changes that require labor hours to perform the work entitle you to an extension of time on the contract completion date. When requesting the approval of a change order you should request the appropriate extension of time along with outlining the costs. Do this by converting the estimated labor hours into days or fractions of a day (¼, ½, or ¾).

    You will appreciate the value of this, especially toward the end of the contract, when you may wish you had accumulated more extensions of time.

5. Customer Acceptance

    Unauthorized personnel, especially on large jobs, tend to fill the shoes of those who are authorized. Here, the change order form questions and commits them to their claim in writing. When in doubt, check their status with the customer.

Contracting Work

So far, we've been in control of most transactions when doing service work because we've been able to use our own forms. In contracting work, however, as we work for general contractors, home improvement companies, property managers and the like, we will discover that our standard forms are less acceptable. For example, most prospective customers use their own contract forms. If we want their jobs, we will have to use theirs.

While this is true in most cases, quote your price on your own proposal/contract form (written documents favor the writer) even when you think it will not be used as the final contract document. There are two basic reasons for doing this:

- Never assume that the customer will not sign your proposal, even if it is a general contractor. If your proposal is well written, don't be surprised if the customer seizes the opportunity and, either to save paperwork or to expedite the job signs our contract on the spot, just the way we submitted it.

- In case of a conflict between your proposal and the final contract, you can refer to your proposal and prove the initial intent. In fact, when you sign others' contracts, besides reading and comparing them carefully to the original proposal, always attempt to make the proposal part of the final contract document either by reference or as an exhibit to it.

In private work, we should mostly be aware of two widely accepted practices, for they are not likely to change:

- The bidding of a job with an incomplete set of drawings, usually the electrical set only. The problem arises when the customer expects you to sign a contract listing an array of drawings and documents you didn't know existed and showing more work than you estimated.

- The acceptance of a verbal contract not knowing its terms and conditions until you receive it in the mail, usually well after you have started the job.

The evolution of these practices stems from the customer's (sometimes intentional) procrastination in preparing the final contract document and the contractor's fear of losing the job if he rocks the boat. Regardless, due to a lack of clear understanding, both parties stand to lose from the outset.

To protect your interests, don't build up undue expectations even when in possession of a letter of intent. Before you commit yourself to permit applications, purchases, and equipment, negotiate, agree to, and sign the contract first.

Ironically, as long as contractors fail to review the contract documents and take precautions before they bid the job, a majority of unfair and lopsided contracts will be signed, with most of them ending up in litigation.

Before we bid a job we should know the full scope of work, including the customer's lopsided terms and conditions. Only then can we decide whether to bid the job and, if necessary, add the extra cost associated with the lopsidedness into our estimate (see Chapter 11 - Compiling the Bid).

In contracting, what will hurt us most are the unknown and hidden costs. The road to successfully completing a job is very narrow and usually left in the hands and opinions of others. For sample contracts and more discussion on this subject, (see Chapter 15 - The Contract).

Chapter 6

THE STARTING POINT

WHERE IT ALL STARTS

It all starts with a sales lead. Regardless of the marketing methods employed in promoting your business, the result should always be a lead to potential work.

Each sales lead is a new starting point whose outcome is dependent on your decision to accept or reject it; and you should reject it unless you are ready to carry it out to the end. Accepting a sales lead is to invest your resources into something that will become progressively more costly with the extent of your involvement.

Taking on a sales lead is the start of a new business transaction, a 'loop' that is worthless unless it has the potential to close into a good sale. Anytime its potential declines, close the loop quickly. If you hesitate, you will increase cost and disappointment with every passing moment. For example, abandoning a sales lead three quarters of the way into its loop when you could have done so at the start is wasteful and distracting to all parties concerned, including your staff.

To get your business on the road to success, there is no better way than to evaluate each sales lead before taking it on. Sales leads are the seeds of your business: a lead develops into a job, and a job into a customer. Your customers' quality determines your company's quality, and thus the degree of your success.

The knowledge gained on the many aspects of prospective customers and job procedures will assist you in evaluating sales leads so you can invest your resources (time, energy, and money) in productive business rather than chasing wasteful dead-end prospects.

Before you follow up a sales lead, ask yourself:

- How will I be paid for the work?

- Who is the customer?

- Can I successfully deal with this customer?

- Do I have the resources and workforce to deliver the job?

- Who is my competition?

- Can I be competitive and still make a profit?

If you decide to take on the sales lead, use the best resources and go at it wholeheartedly; if not, no matter how attractive the lead or whatever justifiable reasons you come up with, don't second-guess yourself—just walk away. If it hurts, it will only be for a couple of days or until you find a better lead (see Estimating and Bidding).

VULNERABILITY

To reinforce the importance of evaluating sales leads, here are a few compelling thoughts on the subject of vulnerability.

The ranks of contractors include individuals whose optimism seems boundless. They believe things will get better after every devastating blow they receive. For example, if the building collapses, they believe they will make more money from the insurance claim; and, if the scope of work is changed, they will make more money from the extra work, and so on.

No matter how often these individuals fall, they always rebound thinking that the next customer is their best friend with their best interests at heart and is ready to pay in full for every job they do. In essence, they have the ability to put aside bad experiences, trust newcomers, and treat a new job as a new start. But, like gamblers, they start from scratch every time they lose and never learn how to do business based on facts rather than feelings.

Anyone can call such individuals for a quote and, most likely, they will invest their last dollar in doing the job without ever questioning the customer's ability to pay. They work on the assumption, especially when they have received one or two partial payments that they will be paid in full, for they have a signed 'standard contract'— whatever that means.

If you think this is an exaggerated claim, think again. It is a daily occurrence in our industry. The following short story will enlighten you:

A few days into demolition, a construction manager for a national chain restaurant uses the yellow pages to invite several contractors to a pre-construction meeting and job site tour to bid the job.

At the meeting, each contractor heard promising answers to his technical questions. After a two-hour Q & A session, you could feel the excitement in the air. If they had been asked, each contractor would have been ready to go to work on the spot.

What makes this story compelling is that none of the contractors asked the most important question: How do you pay? When one contractor finally did ask, neither the construction manager nor the owner's representative could answer the question readily. As to the other contractors, they thought the question was impertinent, for they assumed that payment schedules were standard procedures. However, a deafening silence fell into the room as if a cardinal rule had been broken. When asked again, the construction manager had to call the owner, proving that neither he nor the owner's representative had given much thought to payment.

This is not to insinuate that owners or construction managers put out jobs for bid with no intention of paying, even though our carelessness in that regard creates a huge temptation for them; this is merely a reminder of how easily enthusiasm can lead to bad investments.

Either by rule of thumb or by checking the lead, each contractor could have avoided the problem. Those that declined the invitation suffered no losses and went on to better jobs. The optimists are still waiting for their payments, not to mention profits.

When attending pre-construction meetings, pay attention to the other contractors. Their line of questioning can tell you a great deal about them and the type of cooperation you can expect on the job. The expertise and cooperation of other trades in carrying out the work diligently can affect your work greatly. For example, a bad masonry or mechanical contractor can upset the progress of the job and drastically decrease your productivity.

Assessing other contractors' reputations is part of contracting. When asked to bid jobs, don't hesitate to ask who the other subs are. You might avoid major problems down the road.

WHO IS THE CUSTOMER?

The customer is the person who purchases goods or services from you. If you do a job at City Hall for a general contractor, your customer is the general contractor, not City Hall. The customer is the individual or entity that hires you to do the work and with whom you have a contract, whether written, verbal, or implied. In all your dealings, you should never lose sight of this relationship. In this example, if you want to maintain a legal, moral, and ethical standing, you cannot bypass the general contractor and deal with City Hall directly.

Anyone you deal with directly—a homeowner, a property manager, or a general contractor—is the customer. The most prominent customer you are bound to deal with is the general contractor, and therefore you should learn all you can about this relationship.

Workable Relationship

The relationship between the general contractor and subcontractor has to be straightforward, for both parties have a common goal—make a profit in the construction of the project they've contracted.

However, for each to earn a profit, the one depends on the ability of the other to carry out the work. Each must do what he does best; that is, using the tools of his trade in the most productive way.

For our purposes, we refer to this kind of relationship as a 'workable relationship.' In this relationship, neither should feel threatened by the other's actions when dispatching their duties, especially when they fall within the contract's legal framework and the industry's standards.

The Scrupulous General Contractor

The scrupulous general contractor undertakes contracts to deliver complete projects at a fixed cost within an allotted time. His position is relatively risky and demands the respect and support of his subcontractors.

This general contractor often has to make concessions to the owner to secure a contract. In a workable relationship, subcontractors share the burden of the concession.

The Subcontractor

The subcontractor carries out a portion of the general contractor's work. He uses his business and managerial skills to make the most profit while respecting the general contractor's position.

The subcontractor provides the general contractor with the tools for getting his extra work and materials approved. In most instances, the subcontractor cannot expect the general contractor to prepare his submissions or do the legwork for the approval of those requests.

Getting materials approved is the work of our supplier or the manufacturer rep. They have the resources, expertise, and interest to make things happen. When those approvals depend on you, do them yourself.

This is the gist of a fair and balanced relationship between general contractor and subcontractor. There are no plausible excuses for knowingly entering into a lopsided relationship. If for no other reason, you should be selective regarding the general contractor you choose to work with, for he will have influence over the endgame—profit.

Non-workable Relationship

In this work, non-workable relationships are those you will quite often live to regret for a long time. These relationships have a tendency to plunge bank accounts to dangerously low levels.

In theory, if your estimate is true to costs and you can carry out the work, then you can call the job good. Moreover, if both you and the general contractor pay steadfast attention to what was agreed, the relationship is good and workable. This is the theoretical aspect of a good job and a workable relationship. Workable, that is, until the unscrupulous human element takes over.

The introduction of this human element into the equation requires you to be alert. Today, more then ever, you should concern yourself with the following two elements:

The Unscrupulous General Contractor

The unscrupulous general contractor (GC) will eventually cross your path. His predatory behavior is frequently encouraged if you are in a seemingly weak financial position.

The following is a list of unscrupulous contracting methods. Occasionally, these practices arise inadvertently, sometimes deliberately:

- The GC requests a quote based on an incomplete set of drawings.

- The GC withholds bidding documents from the bidding package.

- The GC uses a lopsided contract form that *looks* like an industry-accepted contract.

- The GC shows others' bid prices to lure us into lowering our price.

- The GC withholds a 10% retainer from our payment when it should be 5% or lower.

- The GC cuts down our monthly requisition unduly.

- The GC evades and delays issuance of bona fide directives and change orders.

- The GC signs documents improperly.

- The GC withholds completion of work, thus delaying our final inspection and final payment.

- The GC refuses certified mail.

- The GC clutters the work areas with building materials and fixtures hindering the free rolling of scaffolds, ladders, and lifting equipment.

- The GC improperly supervises and coordinates the trades.

The Unscrupulous Plans and Specifications Writers

Conflicts between plans, specifications, and contract documents are usually accidental, but are still costly when they go undetected by the estimator. However, accidental conflicts that are generated by designers, specification writers, and project managers due to negligence are also classified as unscrupulous contracting. (For more on this subject and how to prevent it, see Chapter 17- Protecting the Job).

Chapter 7

WHERE TO LOOK FOR WORK

FORESIGHT

Whether we are green or seasoned electrical contractors, if you subscribe to the methods shown in the previous chapters, you should be eager and confident of choosing customers and jobs at will. Moreover, if the conditions don't fit your bill, you should have the conviction to walk away, for that is how you should feel by now—eager and confident.

However, to live by your convictions you must look at the overall contracting market and forecast where you want to go. When you are happy with it, not only will you be able to live by your convictions, but you will also become a focused electrical contractor with one purpose only— success.

This foresight will help you find the kind of work that fits your marketing plan best. If you restrict yourself through undue   limitations   or   you   are   not   aware   of   the opportunities around you, then you are doomed to fail, or at best struggle along just making ends meet.

If you want a clear demonstration of this, make a small investment. On a clear night take a short helicopter ride over your city, and suddenly you will see and feel very clearly all the prospective work awaiting you.

You will see the street lighting, the sports fields, the cinemas, the malls, the shopping centers, the sewer treatment plant, the substations and switching stations, the hospitals, the churches, the government center, and the empty lots people will build on. You will see the extent of your prospective work and you will see why you can afford to be choosy, for you have the talent to sell and the expertise to repair, maintain, alter and install all that you see.

With this in mind, we present the following methods and approaches to help you in choosing prospective customers and jobs. If you ever need to re-focus, revisit this list of opportunities to keep your goal vivid.

SERVICE WORK

Service work is most common with commercial and residential accounts. It is the most sought-after work by start-up contractors. Service work entails repair, adding to, altering, and maintaining existing installations. You can generate this type of work either from the private sector (realtors, property managers, home and business owners) or from federal, state, county, and municipal agencies. Regardless of the category, most service work comes through customers' referrals. Each satisfied customer earns you a referral, which is the foundation of service work.

THE ESTABLISHMENT

In recent years, both private and public markets have been switching from total patronage of service companies to a three-bid system.

While this method creates more opportunities for competition, it also imposes on your daily schedule. Unless you screen and evaluate your sales leads, as discussed in the previous chapter, you will be giving bids all day long with little or no success.

No matter how much a customer likes you, or how much work you have done for him, his next job award is still predicated on price first. In other words, you must possess all the qualities a customer looks for in a reliable contractor, with price being at the top of the list.

PRIVATE SECTOR

To generate service work from the private sector, the approach is different from contracting. Here are some suggested methods:

Directories

Directories such as Yellow Pages or Community Industrial Listings are comparable to the helicopter ride mentioned earlier for giving you an overview. You may shop for your business markets through their pages.

For example, if you are a one-man shop just starting out and want to create an immediate clientele with good cash flow, choose retailers of lighting fixtures, paddle fans, heat pumps, exhaust fans, spas, and major appliances and then call on them personally for their electrical needs on a regular basis.

If you are beyond starting out and wish to expand your service, choose home improvement contractors, interior decorators, heating and air conditioning contractors, etc.

If you are an established electrical contractor with a service work quota to fill, get your sales force to shop through the industrial pages. There, they will find suppliers of specialty equipment for offices and business such as automotive spray booths, electric car lifters, electronic systems, moveable partitions installers, computer network specialists—and don't forget the insurance adjuster for flood and fire damage—and offer them your expertise.

Use your imagination and exploit these directories to your advantage—they contain a wealth of markets for the electrical contractor. They are the most informative and inexpensive way to either start up or boost your business, especially when you apply your marketing skills with enthusiasm and determination, for they will pyramid into endless opportunities.

Yellow Pages and Local Directories

In some areas, ads placed in Yellow Pages and local directories do not generate as much service work as they used to before the do-it-yourself concept was popularized by Home Depots and building-supply stores. The cost of non-productive ads, especially in long-term commitments, can overrun your advertising budgets.

After you have considered the pros and cons but still feel you must advertise in these directories, do so on a trial basis. Use a dedicated telephone number for each locality in which you wish to advertise. This method will allow you to cancel your monthly charges as soon as you shut off the telephone number used in the ad. With some publishers, this might cost you a couple of months; work out a deal with them before you sign on the dotted line.

Do not use your advertised telephone number for any other purpose. Your business card and stationery should have your company's operating telephone numbers, thus directing your new customers to your office over those lines. Later on, you will be able to retain whatever customers you paid for if you decide to shut down the ad.

Other hints to consider:

- Size of Ad
  Large or largest is not necessarily better. Look into four or five back issues (the library has them) of the directory you want to advertise in and check how many ads of the size you are contemplating have survived more than two or three issues. If the ad is three quarters of a page or larger, economics will most likely restrict this size to no more than two years.

- Stay with the Crowd
  In any one directory there is always a largest, a smallest, and many in-between ads. The last one is where the crowd is most likely to shop. Consumer habits will force the shopper to flip to the next pages for more choices. The page with only one ad will make the consumer feel cornered and too scared of price gouging. After flipping over the page, the consumer will tend to stop in the middle, where there are the most choices. If the middle has one-quarter page ads, the customer will be faced with eight choices and will totally forget page one and the others in between, no matter what their messages are.

- The Ad Layout
  Keep it simple and free of clutter. For cost-effective ads, review the specifications in Chapter 2 and use them as guidelines here. Use words that sell.

- The Calls

  These ads will generate telephone calls only; it is up to you and your staff to receive these calls and turn them into jobs.

Knocking on Doors

This method can begin with your next-door neighbor and end at the doorstep of the largest corporations. It all depends on how ambitious you are and how far you are willing to travel.

Regardless of your goal, this method has passed the test of time. In a sense, it could be called business politics at its best. You simply mingle with and lobby those who are most apt to give you work.

For a list of who's who, their contact names, mailing addresses, telephone numbers and all other pertinent information, subscribe to specialist publications. This endeavor focuses on national chain stores, restaurants, fast-food stations, banks, department stores and the like that are still entertaining the concept of service contracts for their outlets.

PUBLIC SECTOR

No electrical contractor should be in business without seeking a share of public work. Our participation in public works, especially service work, is as essential as joining the local chamber of commerce or any electrical association. Doing work for local municipal agencies, besides enhancing our image as reliable contractors, generates steady work for our company—a sort of security blanket for when the private market slows down. We must cultivate these markets always, for they are the bedrock of our business.

It is a common temptation to abandon all efforts toward public work as soon as we get busy with private work. But this demonstrates that we haven't considered properly the consequences of quitting public work.

Many public agencies send invitations to bid only to active bidders. To stay on these lists, we must respond to their invitations. If not, they will drop us.

The process of being posted on the active bidders list of the various agencies is time consuming and a feat of perseverance and politics—or luck, in the case of the so-called lottery or rotation systems.

As in the private sector we must build a solid reputation for dependability when doing service work for public agencies. If we pay close attention to their needs and complete the work on time and as specified, contract administrators will begin to favor us in their next round of invitations. In other words, they will pull out of the list of active bidders and post in the preferred list of responsive and dependable contractors. When that occurs, we have closed a marketing loop successfully, for work will be looking for us, instead of us looking for work.

This is the service work that we are looking for in the public sector—where most agencies are authorized to award work without competitive bids up to a certain amount. Find out what that amount is with each agency.

You need not visit any of these agencies in person to apply. You can begin by calling the purchasing agent or the contracting administrator of the specific agency you are interested in and have them send you the necessary documents to place you on their bidder's list. Study the material from each agency. Each operates under a different set of rules.

Public Agencies

For a complete list of public agencies within your area, start with the white pages of your telephone directories and end at the Small Business Administration office. The following lists will steer you in the right direction. Investigate any other areas or agencies that interest you.

Federal Agencies

Within taxpayer-funded departments there are numerous agencies and sub-agencies you can call on. The following is a list of the most prominent that are likely to provide service work:

- General Service Administration (GSA)
  (Manages all properties owned and leased by the US Government such as post offices, office buildings, etc.)

- Federal Aviation Administration (FAA)
  (Responsible for all navigation and landing systems for airports, including structures that house these systems.)

- US Army Corps of Engineers

- US Navy

- Housing and Urban Development (HUD)

State Agencies

- Department of Transportation

- General Service Administration

- Department of State

County Agencies

- Board of Education

- Public Library

- Treatment Plants

- Hospitals

Municipal Agencies

- Public Works

- Recreational Facilities

- Housing Authorities

- Utilities

CONTRACTING WORK

Construction Reports

On any given day, all sorts of prospective work is contained in construction reports funneled right to your doorstep or to your desktop computer.

Through these reports, you can feel the pulse of the industry in any geographic area. The price tag for these services varies with frequency, age, style, territory, and immediacy of the leads. These services, when properly tailored to our business, must never exceed the cost of sending our sales force into the field.

On a daily or weekly basis, the report will reveal who is planning and designing what, who is building where and when, or who won and lost yesterday's bid. If we wish to bid for work, it will provide us with the list of bidders for any given project, along with their phone and fax numbers, email addresses, and all other pertinent information.

While these reports are available to us through private companies and governmental agencies, the final result is the same—sales leads, which should be investigated before we put our wheels in motion.

Sales Approach

Cold calls are seldom productive. In contracting, cold calls made at the wrong time of the day are never productive.

The most effective time to contact a prospective customer, especially a general contractor who is on the go, is between 7:00 and 10:00 a.m.

That is the time when people are thinking the most clearly and are most receptive to doing business. In this industry, you must make the most of your deals at that time of the day. The rest of the day is spent on job management and negotiations with those we have called early in the morning.

Knocking at a general contractor's door at two in the afternoon on a fishing expedition for work—without even a job name to get your foot in the door—will greatly decrease your chances. This is a cold and wasteful sales call.

When looking for work, consider two things: the time of day you are making the call and the knowledge of the job you are calling about: the latter is the most vital. The more you know about the job, the more confident your prospective customer will feel about your capabilities and the better your chances of getting the job.

In short, look for contracting work with whatever means available, then continue from designing to bidding stages. Obtain the list of bidders and find the right time to contact those you wish to work with. Once you have gotten your commitments, enter the race by estimating and bidding the job to your prospective customers.

This process depends on your sales lead analysis and your intuition for calling on general contractors with the same level of interest in the job as you have.

Contracting with Public Agencies

In some areas, mechanical trades for public jobs are bid through general contractors and in others to the owner directly. However, regardless of the system adopted in your area, the basic bidding principle is the same.

If you don't want to subscribe to paid reports, follow the same guidelines laid out earlier in the Service Work section and apply with the various agencies for a place on their bidders list, then bid directly to the owner.

When to Look for Work

Look for work when you are busy. Don't fall for the 'I am too busy to look for work' syndrome, and don't get distracted by the first job you get. Eventually, it will be completed and you will be looking for work again. This time it will be under pressure, for you will have lost momentum.

SECTION V

ESTIMATING

Chapter 8

ESTIMATING

ESTIMATING ACCURACY

In electrical contracting, if there is something more elusive than electrons it has to be estimating. How one can bid a job at a fixed cost based on what we know is at best an approximate summation of labor and material costs and without the certainty of favorable weather and job conditions for when the work is scheduled?

How can we estimate the cost of these factors accurately? Amazingly, estimators have mastered the art of predicting and bidding jobs with no less certainty than has a banker approving non-collateral loans.

In this section, we will discover ways of estimating and bidding jobs that will keep us competitive while carrying the least amount of risk. We will discover the elements that compose an accurate estimate. We will also discover how to account for unpredictable items of work.

The reliability of the estimate is dependent on our ability to visualize the scope of work and to anticipate what the design fails to show. It is also dependent on the accuracy of our quantity takeoff.

The estimate can only be as accurate as our interpretation of the bidding documents in conjunction with good common sense and our own contracting experience.

To begin, we must define 'estimate' and 'bid.' Estimate, also known as prime cost for the purposes of this book, is the anticipated cost of all labor and materials for the job. Bid is the amount quoted to the customer, which includes the estimated costs plus markups.

Many contractors have learned the art of wearing both hats at once. With no prejudice, they estimate the job as an estimator would; then, objectively and remotely, they summarize it into a bid as a businessperson would.

MANUAL OR COMPUTERIZED ESTIMATES

To a proficient estimator, the choice between manual and computerized estimating, notwithstanding speed, should be no different than choosing between two different pencils. The estimator will feel at home with either one, for the final product will be the same—a bid price.

Unless or until you are proficient in your estimating program and it becomes second nature, you shouldn't lose concentration by worrying about what command-key does what; estimate your jobs manually.

Estimating is a craft; as such, you need to master its different aspects and techniques independently of the tools you will ultimately use. The materials in these chapters comprise the fundamentals of estimating and bidding the job. The example shown reflects a manual estimate done with the simplest tool—the pencil. Be patient in learning this, for it will give you the foundation to understand and work with any computer program that comes your way.

ESTIMATING CRITERIA

To deliver consistent estimates, an estimator must base his estimates on consistent formulas.

For example, one formula is to apply the same discount on all standard material list prices. Another is to apply the same footage allowance for wire slacks, conduit drops and elbows on takeoff quantities for branch circuits and feeders. A third one might entail labor-hours, labor rates, and productivity ratios for specific job conditions.

Consistent takeoffs are important to establish estimating criteria that will be as close as possible to true prime costs, thus building confidence in the working relationship between the estimator and the decision-makers—a must for successful bidding.

In agreement with management, the estimator should create and update a template of formulas that reflect the company's estimating policies, and apply them consistently to the entire estimating process—both estimates and bids. Without a disciplined policy, the tendency among those involved in the process is to add a little here and there, just to play safe.

The estimator, short of confidence regarding the takeoff quantities, will compensate by adding a little more here and there. The boss, usually remote from the nuts and bolts details of the estimate, also adds a little more here and there. The result? An out of the ballpark bid with a bunch of decision-makers trying to figure out what went wrong.

In bidding a job, confidence in the estimate is paramount. Without it, no reasonable contractor can consciously submit a competitive bid; nor can he make a convincing argument to defend his price.

Over the following few chapters, we introduce first the different estimating methods, then the estimating forms and tools, and, lastly, the actual estimating process.

Estimating Prime Cost

There are three basic methods for reaching an estimated electrical prime cost:

- Detailed

- Units Count (Openings Count)

- Combined (Detailed and Units Count)

Detailed Method

A detailed method lists and prices the conduit and wire and equipment, including every type of lock nut, bushing, strap, wire-nut and the like for a complete electrical installation.

The process begins by taking off quantities of the same groups of materials and posting them on takeoff sheets. For example, feeders, branch circuits, light fixtures, devices and other similar items.

Summarize these takeoff sheets and transpose their totals onto pricing sheets, where you then apply and extend material and labor units.

In turn, summarize each pricing sheet within its category of work and transpose each category and its total onto the estimate recap sheet; then multiply the labor-hours by their labor rates. By adding these prime costs, you produce the estimate prime cost.

Due to its detailed material count, this method delivers the most reliable prime cost you can derive from a set of drawings. The size of the job, its intricacy, and your estimating preferences determine its application.

Units Count (Openings) Method

Units count, or openings, is a widely used system for residential and most commercial work. When properly applied, it is a very productive estimating method.

Unit Prices, which include labor, material, and, most often, overhead and profit, are based on an average cost or selling price for a specific group of items. Uncontrolled, it brings about unacceptable estimating practices, for the groups are often composed of unrelated items with disproportional price structures.

For example, an average hearsay-price per opening, which should include items of the same category such as 110-volt wall receptacles, ceiling outlets, wall switches, and telephone and TV outlets may include the wiring of large appliances, or even the complete installation of the electric service and distribution equipment—all unbeknownst to the user.

These hearsay prices can cost you either the job or money.

How we compute average unit prices is a preference more than a science—but a preference that must employ good estimating practices so the final product remains consistent among similar jobs (see Chapter 12 - Computing Average Unit Prices).

When using average unit prices you did not develop, consider their make-up. What do they include or exclude from the average?

Combined Method

The combined method is a combination of detailed and unit count methods. It is valuable for estimating jobs with extensive power distribution systems and relatively uniform lighting and power circuits.

A detailed takeoff of the power distribution—feeders and panel-boards—and a count of all devices that make up the per-opening unit price produces the estimate prime cost. All branch circuits, except those listed in the detailed takeoff sheets, are included in the average unit prices.

When using this method, make a clear distinction between cost and selling price. If our average unit price is a selling price, which includes profit and overhead, then its extended price belongs at the tail end of the bid. If not, then treat it as subtotal and add it to your estimate prime cost.

ESTIMATING VARIABLES

If you want to turn estimates into reliable and successful bids, you must analyze the essentials that control the bidding process before you discuss estimating details.

Out of the five components—quantity, material cost, labor, overhead, and profit—only three are 'alive,' that is, have a life of their own that you are able to change.

Labor units can change with your perception of the work, material cost with your company's buying power, and overhead with your company's operating efficiency. These three variables, therefore—labor units, material cost, and overhead, which reflect your company's strength and expertise—are the only items you should compete for, because all other factors are generally fixed.

How you arrive at the numbers that make up these variables is perhaps the most important factor in your estimating success.

These numbers are the life of the business and you should make it your business to develop your own set, rather than depending on databases or labor units books that are developed for general purposes.

If you choose published labor units, the least you should do is to study and understand their structure and adjust them to your particular needs.

To some, the making up of labor units is unfortunately either a mystery or only the result of long years of extensive work, thus unattainable anywhere but in books and computer databases.

If you are a proficient electrician and a master of your trade, you are the best estimator for your business, a fact you must always remember and believe. Yes, you can have others taking off quantities and extending them, but, in your company, you remain the ultimate estimator.

To let this notion sink in deeper, we can say that the electrician-owner is the best and only estimator for his business. If there is anything missing that might further complement your estimating skills, perhaps it is the mechanics of how to turn knowledge into units of labor, and ultimately into extended costs that will help translate the estimate into a bid.

Because you are the pacesetter for your company's production mode, when push comes to shove, you are the ultimate labor-units producer for your company. Therefore, base all labor units on your perceptions of the work and on your company's level of productivity, a call that only you can make.

Unless and until you develop a database detailing such experience for others in the organization to plug into, you will remain the party responsible for your own estimating and bidding success.

The setting of your own estimating units and bidding markups is the method employed by most successful contractors. They are also successful because they stay within their financial and productive means.

For example, estimating a job with labor units that are below your productivity level is an unrealistic challenge. Unless you are willing to re-tool and motivate everyone in your organization to meet that challenge, you will undertake a job that is beyond your capacity.

Until you have learned how to incorporate realistic variables into your estimating process, you cannot estimate jobs with confidence; nor can you reflect your true expertise in your bids.

To understand the true meaning of these factors, consider the work of moving contractors:

To move a built-in-place wall unit that is too large to fit in an elevator from one penthouse to another across the city, different movers may give different estimates based on their perception of the work. One mover may think of using the stairs at both sites then trucking it across town. One may think to use ropes and tackles, or a crane, to lower it down and up again at the other end. Another, who owns a large helicopter, may use it. The last, using efficient equipment, submits a winning bid, which most likely has the largest profit margin of the three.

Contracting is full of similar situations, where tools, buying power, and expertise combined with good marketing techniques often give you the winning edge. Having said that, why would you surrender your estimating skills to others, especially when each job is different?

Chapter 9

HOW TO DEVELOP YOUR OWN NUMBERS

UNITS OF COST

For an estimator—in fact, for any company—the development of consistent units of cost is the only road to successful bidding. The units we are most concerned with in this chapter are:

- Labor units in hours

- Hourly-rate average

- Material cost

- Overhead markup

Standard Measurement Units

Electrical contracting has its own measurement units. For example, labor units per hour, conduit per hundred feet, wire per thousand feet, and all others are expressed per each. In addition, it is a good practice to round off material extensions to the nearest dollar.

The following form is a typical estimating pricing sheet reflecting these

PRICING SHEET

| Job Name: | | Job # | | | | Date | | | |

Items of Work From:			Material Cost			Labor Hours			
		Quantity	Price	Per	Extend	Unit	Multi plier	Per	Extend
1	1/2" EMT in bar joists	450'	14 50	C	65	3.45		C	14 18
2	#12 THHN Cu stranded wire	2363'	44.00	M	104	2.00		M	4.73
3	30A disconnect switch fused nema 1	3	18.50	E	56	0.75		E	2.25
4									
5									
6									
7									
8									
9									
10									
11									
12									
13									
14	**(This and other forms may be downloaded online at www.theestimatingroom.com)**								
15									
16									
17									
18									
19									
20									
21									
22									
23									
24									
Totals: This page( ) System Set ( )					225				21 16

System: #____ Number of sheets in the system:_____   Sheet #____ of _____

Form EE-310-rev05 ©2005The Estimating Room™ Inc.

Figure 5: Pricing Sheet

Labor units

To develop a labor unit for an item of work we conduct a detailed time study of its installation. The following will introduce you to the basics of such a time study.

LABOR UNITS WORKSHEET						

Item of Work: 1/2" EMT conduit **Item No. EMT 1255**

Type of Work

New (**X**)	Alteration (**X**)	Residential ( )	Commercial ( )	Industrial ( )

Installation

Bar Joist ( )	Concrete Exposed (**X**)	U/G ( )	Slab ( )	Ceiling Height: **14'**

Other:

Labor Breakdown In Man Hours

	Bill of Material Based On: 500Ft run exposed on masonry wall	Quant	A Receive	B Mobilize	C Install	D Clean-up	Total Hours
1	1/2" EMT conduit including fittings. Estimated installation time 6 hours for two men.	500'	0.50	0.75	12.00		13.25
2	Junction boxes and fasteners	6			1.00		1.00
3	Pick-up and clean-up	1 lot				1.00	1.00
4							
5							
6							
7							
8							
9							

(This and other forms may be downloaded online at www.theestimatingroom.com)

						Totals Hours	15.25

Formula

Total Hours		Quantity		Unit		Labor Unit	Per
15.25	÷	500	**X**	1( ) 100(x) 1000( )	=	3.15 hours	E ( ) C (x) M ( )

Form EE-370-rev05 ©2005 The Estimating Room™ Inc.

Figure 6: Labor units Time Study

The labor-hours used in computing the labor units are the author's estimates. You are encouraged not only to substitute them with your own, but also to create as many time studies as possible, for this is the chief objective of this chapter.

The objective is to introduce you to the nuts and bolts of estimating. As you develop your own labor units, you will also improve your understanding of published labor units, thus taking control of your estimates.

The Worksheet shown above is applicable to most items of work. You input data in the 'Type of Work' and 'Installation' lines will set up the scenario for computing the labor unit you are seeking.

The 'Labor Breakdown' section is where you lay out the various increments of work on a step-by-step basis.

Each step is subdivided into Receive, Mobilize, Install, and Clean-up—identified as A, B, C, and D.

A. Receive – this includes the estimated time for one man or a crew to receive the material.

B. Mobilize – this includes the estimated time a) to relocate the material from the received area to the installation site; and b) to set up tools, materials, and equipment for the installation.

C. Install – this includes the estimated time to install that particular item of work listed in the Bill of Material.

D. Clean-up – this includes the estimated time to remove tools, equipment, and leftover material, leaving the installation site ready for the next phase of work.

In essence, the process can be broken down into small and easy to estimate steps.

Receiving the material, moving it to the working area, installing it, and pick-up and cleaning are the logical steps needed to carry out the work.

Each step, analyzed in terms of its elapsed time, leads to a fixed number. We convert time, logic, and experience into labor-hours and, ultimately, into labor units.

At this level of estimating, because you are dealing with the basics, there are no magic formulas or reference tables, only experience and imagination.

Here, we are using all-new data. However, if you are working on an item with which you have no experience and you need to obtain your base numbers, either consult a publication such as a pricing manual or database, or pick the brain of someone who has experience with that particular item of work.

Complex work should be broken down into smaller portions. The more logical the steps that we create, the more accurate your labor units will be.

The following samples are meant to unleash your imagination. The format employed is one of many used for this purpose. As long as you keep the time study principles in mind, you can and should experiment with any format in which you feel comfortable.

LABOR UNITS WORKSHEET

Item of Work:*3-1/2" EMT conduit*	Item No. *EMT 351255*

Type of Work

New **(x)**	Alteration ( )	Residential ( )	Commercial **(X)**	Industrial ( )

Installation

Bar Joist **(X)**	Concrete Exposed ( )	U/G ( )	Slab ( )	Ceiling Height:**14'**

Other:

Labor Breakdown In Man Hours

	Bill of Material Based On: *300-Ft run*	Quant	A Receive	B Mobilize	C Install	D Clean-up	Total Hours
1	3-1/2" EMT including fittings. Estimated time to install each length of conduit 0.25 hour x 30 lengths = 7.5 hours x 2 men = 15labor-hours.	300'	0.75	1.50	15.00		17.25
2	Beam clamps and straps estimated time 0.10 each x 58 units = 5.8 hours x 2 men = 11.6 labor-hours	58	w/item #1	w/item #1	11.60		11.60
3	J.B. 18" x 20" x 6"	3	w/item #1	w/item #1	3.00		3.00
4	3-1/2" elbows and fittings	2	w/item #1	w/item #1	1.00		1.00
5	Clean-up	1 lot				2.00	2.00
6							
7							
8							
9							

(This and other forms may be downloaded online at www.theestimatingroom.com)

							Totals Hours	34.85

Formula

Total Hours		Quantity		Unit		Labor Unit	Per
34.85	÷	*300-Ft*	**X**	1( ) 100(x) 1000( )	**=**	*11.62 Labor-hours*	E( ) C(x) M( )

Form EE-370-2-rev05 ©2005 The Estimating Room™ Inc.

Figure 7: Labor Units Time Study

LABOR UNITS WORKSHEET

Item of Work: 4 #500 MCM THHN Cu. in 3-1/2" conduit	Item No. THHN 501255

Type of Work

New (x)	Alteration ( )	Residential ( )	Commercial (x)	Industrial ( )

Installation

Bar Joist ( )	Concrete Exposed ( )	U/G ( )	Slab ( )	Ceiling Height:

Other:

Labor Breakdown In Man Hours

	Bill of Material Based On: *250-Ft run + 10% slack*	Quant	A Receive	B Mobilize	C Install	D Clean-up	Total Hours
1	500 MCM Cu. in 4 reels each with 315 Ft of pre-cut wire. Unload, receive, and place reels: 0.50 hour each x 4 reels x 2 men = 4 labor-hours.	1100'	4.00				4.00
2	Set up reels on jacks: 0.25 hour per reel x 4 reels x 4 men = 4 labor-hours.	4 reels		4.00			4.00
3	Set up wire pulling machine	1 set-up	1.00				1.00
4	Install pulling rope	1 set-up	2.00				2.00
5	Strip and make-up wires in pulling basket 2 men x 0.75 hour =	1 set-up	1.50				1.50
6	Pull wires in conduit and through 3 pass-through pull boxes 4 men x 5 hours = 20 labor-hours.	1 pull			20.00		20.00
7	Pick-up &clean-up 4 men x 1 hour	1 lot				4.00	4.00
8							
9							

(This and other forms may be downloaded online at www.theestimatingroom.com)

						Totals Hours	36.50

Formula

Total Hours		Quantity		Unit			Labor Unit	Per
36.50	÷	*1100'*	**X**	1( )	100( )	1000(x)	= *33.18 labor-hours*	E ( ) C ( ) M (x)

Form EE-370-2-rev05 ©2005 The Estimating Room™ Inc.

Figure 8: Labor Units Time Study

In computing or assessing labor-units, the following three items should be given special consideration:

Wire Pulling

Not knowing the quantity upon which the labor unit is based can deceive you, especially when it pertains to parallel pulls. A disproportionate labor unit can influence the outcome of a bid adversely. For example, the labor unit required to pull 4-500MCM in a 100 ft. run is greater than that required to pull the same conductors in a 1000 ft. run; and the labor unit required to pull 6-500MCM is indirectly proportional to that required for 4-500MCM in a run of the same length.

The controlling factor in both examples is the set-up time versus the actual pulling time. How to compensate for these variables is the concern of many estimators. Aside from compiling individual units for each instance, the most practical approach is to conduct your own time study and develop a table based on the most common length-increments for common combinations, similar to the one below, from which you can interpolate comparable wire labor-units:

WIRE PULL: Base 16 Ft. Height Method: Winch wirepuller.					
Wire Size & Number of Conductors		Production	Labor unit per M (1000' of wire)		
1	500MCM Cu. In Rigid Conduit	Scale	100 Ft Run	250 Ft Run	500 Ft Run
	(*)Base unit for: 2 conductors	100%	37.50	22.27	20.00
	3 conductors	- 20%	45.00	26.72	24.00
	4 conductors	- 25%	56.25	33.41	30.00
	6 conductors	- 35%	73.62	43.43	39.00
2	350MCM Cu In Rigid Conduit				
	(*) Base unit for: 2 conductors	100%	29.54	19.00	17.00
	3 conductors	- 20%	35.45	22.80	20.40
	4 conductors	- 25%	38.40	28.50	25.50
	6 conductors	- 35%	57.62	36.65	33.15
FORMULA for pulls with more than 2 parallel conductors: *(*) Base Unit ÷ 2 x Number of conductors - Production scale % (See Figure 10) = Labor unit*					

Figure 9: Wire Pulling Labor Units example

Notes to Wire Pull Labor Units

The base units entail the pulling of two parallel conductors in the same raceway. When more than two conductors at a time are pulled, then the appropriate percentage shown in Figure 10 should be deducted from the estimated base-unit (see Figure 9 for examples and formula).

Wire terminations to circuit breakers, panel boards, equipment, and splices are combined with the labor of the equipment they serve. For example, in estimating the eight wire-terminations of a 4-wire feeder, charge four terminations to the Main Distribution Panel, four to the Power Panel, and none to the feeder itself.

Drops and Risers: When taking off wire quantities, it is important to allow for wire drops to the equipment.

If the wire pull is less than 100 feet, a special allowance should be made for drops into distribution panels and motor control centers. Each of these drops can vary from a 10- to a 40-foot run. This is a significant factor, even in 250-foot runs, especially where large conductors are involved.

The computed labor units shown in Figure 9 are in labor-hours per 1,000 feet of wire used in the run, including slack and drops. For example, the distance between MDP and PP-A is a 200-foot plus a 20-foot drop with 4-350MCM. The computed wire total is 880 feet. To compute the total labor-hours, the '250 Ft. Run' column in Figure 9 shows the labor unit at 28.50 per 1000 feet of wire installed; thus, the total estimated labor-hours required to install 880 feet of wire is 25.08 or 880 ft. x 28.50 ÷1000.

If a more accurate labor unit is desired, then instead of using the value shown in the '250-Ft. Run' column, interpolate the labor units between the 100-Ft. and 250-Ft. Run and pick the value at the 220-Ft. increment, in which case the total is 30.48 labor-hours per M (1000 feet).

Conductors. Installation --- Paralleling Production Scale			
From 750MCM to #1/0AWG		From #1 to #14AWG	
# of conductors	Group discount	# of conductors	Group discount
3	20%	3-5	25%
4	25%	6-10	30%
5	30%	11-14	35%
6	35%	14 & Up	40%
7 & Up	40%		

Figure 10: Paralleling Production Scale

Conduit Labor Units – What is included

Labor units for conduit installation can also be deceptive, especially when they include fittings and fasteners. To develop labor units into reliable rates, you must know what's included in their assembly and at what production rate. By using published labor units, it is possible to double the labor-hours for the installation of said fittings and fasteners.

For example, when a publication lists the labor-hours for individual conduits, fittings, and fasteners and it does not state readily that the conduit labor-unit includes fittings and fasteners, then an estimator can make a wrong assumption and duplicate his labor by applying it to each individual fitting and fastener in the takeoff sheet.

Such an event affects the estimate. When we list fittings and fasteners individually, as we should, for lack of base quantity, their labor unit is high and disproportionate to the conduit installation itself.

For instance, to find the labor-unit of 0.75 (45 minutes) to install a set of 3½" fiber bushing or 0.50 (30 minutes) for a 3½" strap, and so on for every bolt and nut, is customary with some publications. This example should persuade you to assess labor units produced by others.

When estimating jobs with an extensive conduit network, your estimate is more realistic if you include the installation of fittings and fasteners with the conduit labor unit. If the publication does not allow you to combine these items, then you may create a table of labor units for different lengths and sizes from which you can interpolate the units you need.

One thing worth mentioning is that while labor should be combined with conduit, material—fittings, fasteners, and conduit—is priced individually.

Efficiency Level and Other Units

In assessing labor-units, in addition to wire and conduit, allow for job conditions, labor efficiency, work-breaks and non-productive labor, for these are all part of the prime cost.

Of the three, efficiency is the most important. We often expect others to produce the same as we do or would and allow no labor hours for items such as receiving and moving material about the job site, mobilization, work layout time, and clean-up.

In some cases, efficiency can drop as low as 60% or lower, i.e. for every hour spent, only 60% is applied to actual installation, with the remainder spent on preparatory or non-productive tasks.

What *you* are capable of doing is not necessarily what others are able or willing to do for you.

HOURLY RATE - AVERAGE

To average labor rates for estimating purposes, base them on the make-up of the crew that will do the work. You can make up crews for a specific item of work, system, phase, or for the entire job.

For easy reference, assign each crew a category for its specific class. For example, you may assign category I to residential work, II to commercial, III to industrial, IV to special, and so on. The list can be as elaborate as you wish to make it.

You should also make up crews based on: (1) your perception of the work; (2) who's best suited for the work, (3) local ordinance for journeymen-to-apprentices ratio; and (4) labor agreements and the like.

You can summarize the estimate into total labor-hours or break it down into as many systems or phases you wish. If you break it down you can price each increment at its average rate, which defines cost more accurately.

However, before we examine the different rates and methods of pricing labor, we must define 'total labor-hours' and 'labor-units rate.'

Estimated total labor-hours, regardless of whether it pertains to a single system or to the job total, represents the number of hours 'one' person will spend doing the estimated work. All labor units are based on this principle.

Therefore, considering 160 labor-hours, this can represent four 40-hour weeks for one person or one 40-hour week for four persons. If only one person is employed to do the work, then the equation for calculating labor cost is 160 hours times whatever hourly rate the man costs—say $20—resulting in an extended labor cost of $3200.

The equation can become complicated when you want the job and the customer demands the work be completed in one week at a competitive price. In this case, you may have to put together a four-man crew with each man paid at a different rate. To calculate labor cost, multiply each man's rate by 40 hours and then add the results. The calculation should look something like this:

1 Supervisor	40 Hours	@ $22	$ 880
1 Mechanic	40 Hours	@ $20	$ 800
2 Helpers	80 Hours	@ $ 9	$ 720
Total Labor Cost			$2,400

This method works fine for small jobs and service work. However, in jobs with crews of different categories, it is necessary to convert it into an average method.

For example, you can average the labor rate in the above example using two different equations, with each having the same result.

a) $2400 ÷ 160 Hours = $15
b) Total per hour rate $22 + $20 + $9 + $9 = $60 ÷ 4 men = $15

While the method is the result of the estimate, it does not apply to job estimates where we apply different crews to different tasks.

We estimate average hourly rates in direct proportion to each crew's make-up, as in the case of one supervisor running two crews or one journeyman with a crew of two apprentices. To charge each of these crews proportionally to the total estimated labor-hours, you need to define your rates further by reflecting the percentage cost of each crewmember into the hourly rate average.

We can convert our example to this formula as noted. The crew being 100% and the number of crewmembers being four, we calculate that each crewmember represents 25% of the crew. Thus, the hourly rate average can be obtained as laid out in the following two steps (To facilitate this task, we may use the 'Average Hourly Rate Computation Sheet' as shown in Figure 11):

Step #1 - Crew Make-Up

Crew	(a)	(b)	(c)	(d)
Category IV	Supervisors	Mechanics	Helpers	Members Total (a + b + c)
Crewmember(s)	1	1	2	4
Crewmember(s) %	25%	25%	50%	100%

Step #2 - Labor Rate Distribution

	Supervisor	Mechanic	Helper	Average Hourly Rate
Cost per Hour	$22.00	$20.00	$9	
% Charged to crew	25%	25%	50%	100%
Per hour cost	$5.50	$5.00	$4.50	$15.00

Because labor units are crew-hours converted into labor-hours, 'true' labor cost can be estimated only by converting the process to the average hourly rate at the summary of each increment.

In our example, if we bid the job with the estimated labor cost of $3200, we show a great anticipated profit on paper, but we have a greater chance of losing the job.

These inflated and wishful bids carry a great deal of hidden fat (fake profits) that often throws off good estimates, explaining why some contractors cannot add profit to their estimated cost and remain competitive.

Another conventional method is the across-the-board labor adjustment. When applied to our example it looks like this:

> Total estimated labor-hours: 160
> Percentages applied:
> Foreman 25% = 40 Hours at $22 $880
> Journeyman 25% = 40 Hours at $20 $800
> Helper 40%= 80 Hours at $9 $720

This method may appear the same as the one above, since it has the same results; but it lacks flexibility.

In this example, we are matching the results of the previous one because the percentages applied are the same. It is erroneous to carry the same percentages from one estimate to another.

Had this not been the case, most likely we would have estimated the supervisor at 10%, the mechanic 20%, and the helper at 70%—or used some other gut feeling combination, thus giving us different results. However, aside from this guessing game, the across-the-board system does not allow for adjustments in individual bid increments.

In our sample job in Chapter 10, the system employed offers a great deal of flexibility. We use Category II crew at $16.23 per hour for the main portion of the work and Category IV crew at $12.11 per hour for trimming work. We cannot calculate this properly with the across-the-board adjustment. Using the most accurate of applicable methods can be the difference between winning and losing bids.

The following 'Hourly Rate Computation Sheet' reflects the make-up of these crews and their respective average rates. The labor rates and percentages used in the computation are introduced for the sole purpose of walking you through the mechanics. If you have to develop hourly rate averages, you must apply rates that are applicable to your area.

HOURLY RATE WORKSHEET

Prepared by:		Checked by:				Date:

	Description	Supervisor	Journeyman	Mechanic	Apprentice	Updates
1	Hourly Rate	17.00	16.00	12.00	8.00	/
2	Hourly Rate Benefits: Annuity, Disability, etc.					/
3	Hourly Rate Expenses: Crew Leader, Travel	1.00	0.50			/
4	Hourly Rate Other:					/
5	Payroll Taxes: %					/
6	S S & Medicare 7.650					/
7	Fed & State Unemployment 0.035					
	(This form and others may be download online at www.theestimatingroom.com)					
8	Insurance:					
9	Workmen Comp 14.600					
10	General Liability 2.600					
11	Medical & Others					
12	Labor Burden Total 24.885					
13	Subtotal	18.00	16.50	12.00	8.00	
14	Labor Burden: (24.885 %) = line 12 x line 13	4.48	4.11	2.99	1.99	
15	Cost Per Hour (Line 13 +14)	22.48	20.61	14.99	9.99	

Crew Make-Up — Cost % Applied to Crew

Crew	(a) Supervisor	(b) Jrmn	(c) Mech	(d) Apprent	(e) # of:	(f) a+b+c+d+e	(g) Foreman %*	(g) $**	(h) Journeyman %*	(h) $**	(i) Mechanic %*	(i) $**	(j) Apprentice %*	(j) $**	(Average Rate) %	(g+h+i+j+k) $
I		1	2	1		4	25.00		25.00	5.15	50.00	7.50	25.00	2.50	100	15.15
II	1	2	2	2		7	14.28	3.21	28.56	5.89	28.56	4.28	28.56	2.85	100	16.23
III	1	6	4	4		11	9.10	11.25	54.50	11.35	36.40		36.40	3.67	100	16.96
IV		1		4		5			20.00	4.12			80.00	7.99	100	12.11

(*) % = 100 ÷ Column (f) x # of workers for that class (Choose column a, b, c, d, or e for column g, h, i, j or k) (**) $ = % x Line 18 (Cost per hour)

Form EE-375 ©2005 The Estimating Room™ Inc

Figure 11: Hourly Rate Work Sheet

MATERIAL COST

The material cost is a variable controlled by your buying power. If your relationship with the suppliers is fluent and you discount the bills, your buying power should be the same or better than that of your competition. If not, spot and correct this problem area. Afterward, re-assert your position with each supplier. You will get better discounts and more insights.

OPERATING OVERHEAD

Overhead, expressed in percentages for any given period, is the business operating cost inversely proportioned to sales. Because each business operates differently, there are no fixed overhead rates. In fact, overhead fluctuates with every business transaction.

In computing bids, we can work with 'experienced' or 'projected' overhead. Experienced overhead is based on actual sales, usually made in the last business period. Projected overhead is based on projected sales versus anticipated operating expenses for the next business period.

For example, if last year sales were $500,000 and your operating cost was $125,000, the experienced overhead is 25% ($125,000 ÷ $500,000). In essence, your ability to increase or decrease operating expenses and sales determines your overhead rate. The most desirable rates are usually in single digits for large companies and in the teens for the smaller and most cost-conscious companies.

Conceivably, you can have a high overhead rate—well in excess of 30% or 40%—which, if applied to your bids, makes it impossible for you to compete.

Usually the remedy is to increase sales while maintaining the same operating expenses or decrease operating expenses while maintaining the same sales. Short of that, you will quickly face financial problems.

The following is a list of the most common overhead items to review:

- Rent for offices and warehouses

- Utilities

- Communication equipment: Land and Mobile

- Administrative salaries: Officers and Partners

- Clerical salaries

- Non-productive labor

- Office expenses

- Equipment rentals / leasing

- Automobiles

- Trucks

- Depreciation

- Advertising

- Subscriptions

- Travel and entertainment

- Special Services

Analyze the cost-effectiveness of each item listed above. Trim and retain those you think are necessary to run your business effectively. If the new computed overhead rate is still out of the competitive market, then your only alternative if you want to stay competitive is to start a new business period based on a projected overhead rate not to exceed 20%.

Be aware that from the moment you convert to projected-overhead, the new rate determines the sales quota you must meet for that new period.

For example, if your operating expenses are fixed at $90,000 per year with a projected overhead of 20%, your sales for the same period cannot be less than $450,000. For more information, see Section X, General Administration.

Here, instead of a straight line, the bottom line is a circle. The more efficiently you run your business, the lower your overhead rate is and the higher your sales. Higher sales breed lower rates, thus creating a better growth cycle.

Chapter 10

ESTIMATING THE JOB

A Must in Estimating:

To deliver reliable estimates, we must first grasp the full scope of work and clearly perceive the environment in which we will do the work. This requires four essential steps:

Step #1 – The Checklist

In competitive bidding, where time is of the essence and accuracy is paramount, we employ a checklist as soon as we receive the bidding documents. Then, if we need clarifications or miss parts of the documents, we will have ample time to get them. This preliminary check verifies the completeness of each document. For thorough follow-up, scan through the basics, take a page-count inventory, and record any discrepancies.

While this checklist is an absolute necessity, many fail to put it into practice. To stay on the cutting edge of estimating, we must have a place to record and maintain critical information at our fingertips. The few minutes it takes to fill out a checklist like the one shown below will pay off many times over at bid-closing time.

PRE-TAKEOFF CHECKLIST						
Job Name:				Job No:	Sheet 1 of 2	
Address:					Bid Due: / /	
Location:					Time:	
Quote To:			Phone:		Fax:	

Bidding Information

Performance Bond: %	Payment Bond: %		Bid Bond %	Certified check for $		
Prevailing Wages	Yes( )	No( )	Liquidated Damages		Yes( )	No( )
Set Aside for Minority	Yes( )	No( )				
Lump Sum Bid ( )		No. of Alternates:	Unit Pricing ( )	Other:		

Documents Reviewed & Pages Count

Specifications	Yes	No	Checked by	Comments
General Conditions				
Special Conditions				
Special Provisions				
Other				
HVAC				
Plumbing				
Electrical				

Drawings

Architectural				
Structural				
HVAC				
Plumbing				
Electrical				
Others:				

Special Scope of Work

	Furnished by:			Furnished by:	
Items of Work	Electric	Others	Items of work	Electric	Others
Trenching			Back-filling		
Concrete work			Precast Items		
Core Boring			Patching & Painting		
Site Restoration			Garbage Removal		
Hoisting Material			Storage		
Temp Light & Power			Utility Charges		
Maintain of Temp L /P					

Form EE-301-1-rev05 ©2005 The Estimating Room™ Inc

Figure 12: Pre-takeoff Checklist - Sheet 1 of 2

PRE-TAKEOFF CHECKLIST

Project:	Job No:	Sheet 2 of 2

Special Equipment

CODE: F = Furnished   I = Installed   C = Connect   R = Remove

Items of Work	Contractor								Items of Work	Contractor							
	Electrical				Others					Electrical				Others			
	F	I	C	R	F	I	C	R		F	I	C	R	F	I	C	R
Lighting Fixtures									Light Poles								
Lamps									Batteries								
Switching Gear									Emerg. Generator								

Inclusions and Exclusions from Bid Price

Items of Work	In	Out	Items of Work	In	Out
1			2		
3			4		
5			6		

Addendum Received

Addenda Number	Date	Posted by	Addenda Number	Date	Posted by
1			2		
3			4		
5			6		

Comments

(This and other forms may be downloaded online at www. theestimatingroom.com)

Form EE-301-2-rev05 ©2005 The Estimating Room™ Inc.

Figure 13: Pre-takeoff Checklist Sheet - 2 of 2

Step #2 – The Job Visit

Most bidding documents will contain statements like this:

> 'The contractor shall bear the sole responsibility to visit and acquaint himself with the existing conditions of the job...'

> 'Wherever existing wiring, materials, devices, or equipment are encountered which serve functions or equipment to remain, the contractor shall inspect the installation and correct, repair or replace the existing work to establish code conformance.'

> 'In submitting this bid the contractor certifies to have visited the job site and to have familiarized himself with all aspects of the existing work.'

These and similar statements are included in the bidding documents to entice the bidder to visit the job prior to submitting a bid and to hold him responsible for any existing conditions adverse to the owner. Yet many contractors, in spite of these warnings, estimate the work without such a jobsite visit and blindly submit their bid.

To comprehend the full scope of work, nothing is more important than a jobsite visit. In fact, for alteration work and most new jobs it is imperative. A jobsite inspection reveals technical conditions and field environment that are impossible to envision, even through drawings.

The most effective time to conduct such a visit is after you have reviewed the bidding documents and before starting the takeoff.

This in-between time is when you are most open-minded about the job. In addition, the knowledge you acquire about the job simplifies the estimating task, for you are able to visualize the full scope of work and see what the designer may have failed to show. In other words, assume nothing.

New Work Inspection

- Job Accessibility – Check roads leading to the job site for low overpasses, small bridges, narrow tunnels, tonnage limits and the like. In addition, take into consideration tolls and other road fees.

- Ground Conditions – A set of drawings for a new job, especially electrical drawings, will rarely show existing conditions that can be either adverse or beneficial to the job.

- Adverse conditions – There may be abandoned parking lots, railroad tracks, fuel tanks, light pole pedestals and the like under which you may have to install conduits.

- Favorable conditions – These include available temporary power, nearby suppliers, easy access to electric service, easy to dig ground, secure storage area, and a safe neighborhood.

Alteration Work Inspection

These items are common to most jobs and introduced as guidelines only. You should adapt the list to each job you bid.

- Job accessibility

- Available utilities

- Ceiling heights

- Floor conditions – Are they level? Can you roll scaffolds on them? Are they crowded with furniture and the like?

- Doorways – Are they wide enough for your equipment?

- Safe storage area

- Existing electric meter room and power distribution – Are they different than specified? Is there room for the new equipment? Are there any existing violations?

- Existing grounding system – Is it adequate?

- Hallways and demising walls – Are they made of concrete, cinder blocks, or sheetrock?

- Telephone, security, and other systems – Are they existing or furnished by others?

Step #3 – The Estimating Folder

To avert errors and chaos at bid closing, you must manage your estimating material wisely. This begins with setting up an estimating folder and ends with counting all the pages that make up the estimate. Flipping large drawings sheets can produce enough draft to airlift estimating pages into wastebaskets.

Generally, an estimate consists of takeoff, summary, and pricing sheets. Based on its size, you can estimate a job on pricing sheets only, or on a combination of takeoff and pricing sheets. If a job has too many takeoff sheets, they should be compiled into a summary sheet, thus reducing the number of pricing sheets.

To control your paperwork, estimate the number of sheets you anticipate using for a particular set, estimate, or system.

For example, say you anticipate using a five pricing sheet set. To play safe, make up a set of 7 pricing sheets with the job name written on each sheet and each page sequentially numbered as Sheet #1 of 7, Sheet #2 of 7, Sheet #3 of 7, etc. What is important is not how many sheets you set aside, but how you identify and bind each set.

The number of pricing sheets you ultimately use does not affect the estimate page control. Suppose the takeoff is complete and only six of the seven sheets have been used. You can mark the unused sheet "Void" or remove it from the set and renumber the rest as Sheet #1 of 6, Sheet #2 of 6, Sheet #3 of 6, and so on. Using a pencil makes erasures easy.

Based on the intricacy, a job can be taken off on a single pricing sheet set or in several different sets. The objective is to control the paperwork and the record keeping of critical information. The better you get, the more reliable are your estimates.

One safe way to achieve this is to set up your systems ahead of time and two-hole punch and secure them in an estimating folder. Loose sheets floating on estimating tables, besides standing a good chance of getting lost, keep your estimate in a constant state of disarray. An estimating folder should hold these sheets:

- Feeder Takeoff

- Branch Circuits Takeoff

- Lighting Fixture Takeoff

- Fire Alarm (System) Takeoff

- Summary

- Pricing

- Recapitulation Sheet

Of these sheets, the recap sheet is the most valuable. This is where all totals converge. Post each system's totals (standard and quoted materials, labor-hours including the number of pages in the system) in their respective lines and columns, and then summarize them into the sought-after prime cost.

The recap sheet becomes the 'Table of Contents' of your estimating folder. In this sheet, you outline the estimate by inserting a cross (X) in the 'In' column next to the active systems. This mark, along with the number of pages listed in the '#Pgs' column, gives us a dependable control system.

In addition to page control, the recap sheet lets you spot check any system by tracking it back through a paper trail, to its takeoff sheets and drawings.

The recap sheet shown below lists 20 standard electrical systems that can be identified readily, for they represent the most common electrical installations. You may adopt the recap sheet as laid out and check off only those systems you intend to use for a particular job, or create your own set of systems.

If you win the job, the list of systems you use in the recap sheet can be used in your requisitions breakdown for billing purposes (see Chapter 19 - Requisitions for Payment).

A well thought out recap sheet answers the most important question in business right from the start. Therefore, when you lay it out, think in terms of how you want to be paid.

ESTIMATE RECAP SHEET

Job Name: Sample Job 1, Warehouse   Job # 02-1231

ESTIMATE BREAKDOWN

	Systems' Title	Systems Control		Material		Labor				Systems' prime cost (a+b+f)
		In	# of Pgs	(a) Standard	(b) Quote	(c) Hours	(d) Crew	(e) $-Rate	(f) Extended	(g)
1	Mobilization (DJE)	xx								
2	Temp. Light & Power									
	Site Work									
3	Excavation & Back Fill									
4	Substation/ Transformer									
5	Precast & Concrete									
6	Primary Feeders									
7	Branch Circuits									
8	Light Poles & Fixtures									
	Work In Building									
9	Service									
10	Secondary Feeders									
11	Switching Gear									
12	Branch Circuits									
13	Lighting Fixtures									
14	Wiring Devices									
15	Equipment Connections									
16	Emergency Generator									
17	Telephone									
18	Sound/ Clock/ TV									
19	Security									
20	Fire Alarm									
21	**(This form and others may be downloaded online at www. theestimatingroom.com)**									
22										
	Totals									

Form EE-305-1-rev05 ©2005 The Estimating Room™ Inc.

Figure 14: Recap Sheet

To detail your requisitions further, you may want to expand certain systems by dividing them into two or more items of work. For example, you can divide as follows:

Standard System			Split System		
6	Primary Feeder		6a	Primary Feeder-------------	Conduit
			6b	Primary Feeder-------------	Wire
8	Light Poles & Fixtures		8a	Light Poles & Fixtures----	On Site
			8b	Light Poles & Fixtures ---	Installed
10	Secondary Feeders		10a	Secondary Feeders --------	Conduit
			10b	Secondary Feeders --------	Wire
11	Switching Gear		11a	Switching Gear-------------	On Site
			11b	Switching Gear ------------	Installed
12	Branch Circuits		12a	Branch Circuits ------------	Conduit
			12b	Branch Circuits -----------	Wire
13	Lighting Fixtures		13a	Lighting Fixtures ----------	On Site
			13b	Lighting Fixtures ----------	Installed

Figure 15: Systems Split

We subdivide systems for better billing control. For example, if the conduit installation for branch circuits is complete and you want to get paid before the wires are pulled in, or if you want to get paid for lighting fixtures on site, there is no better time to establish that criteria than when you are setting up the systems for the estimate.

Perhaps you want to subdivide the branch circuit conduit further into branch circuit conduit for lighting and branch circuit conduit for power and so on for every other system, then use these criteria instead as your contract breakdown for monthly requisitions.

To undervalue the importance of this method is to affect your cash flow adversely.

The recap sheet check and balance format gives us control over the calculations. To prove your additions and extensions, add columns (a), (b), and (f); this total must equal that of column (g). If it doesn't, there is an error in your calculations. You can prove each line the same way.

Step #4 – Setting Up the Estimate

For most estimates, manual or computerized, control your paperwork by setting up a six-section, reusable, legal-size folder and label it as follows:

- Section 1 – Checklists
- Section 2 – Takeoff Sheets
- Section 3 – Summary Sheets
- Section 4 – Pricing Sheets
- Section 5 – Recap and Bid Sheets
- Section 6 – Proposals to Prospective Bidders

Before you roll up your sleeves and start estimating, you should get the following tasks out of the way, for they are essential to the finished product.

- Record Addenda – Addenda are documents issued by the architect listing corrections to the bidding documents. Record their changes onto the related plans and specs. They are part of the contract documents.

- Set up the Estimating Folder as shown above.

- Pre-Takeoff Checklist - read the specifications. Insert all pertinent information on this sheet and update it as new information becomes available.

- Scales - Highlight all scales in drawings, especially when they change from sheet to sheet.

- Read all notes in the drawings – Highlight those

that pertain to your work and checkmark all others. Marking all notes minimizes anxiety and builds your confidence and that of those checking the work. When you look at a drawing, you want to see each note either check marked or highlighted. To ensure good estimating control, complete this task before you start taking off quantities.

- Lighting Fixtures – Send lighting fixture specs and counts to your supplier or lighting representative. Preferably, send this package to your local lighting rep. Most suppliers will just turn your package over to the same rep you would; the difference is that while you are not tied down to one supplier you will get whatever technical information you need quickly and straight from the rep.

  Another reason is that you will accommodate the supplier's busy schedule. A good practice when it comes to lighting fixture counts is never to accept other people's counts nor mark their quantities or prices on the drawing's schedule. There are no short cuts; using the proper takeoff sheet is the shortest distance to good estimating.

- Switching Gear – Send switching gear specs and layout drawings to your supplier or manufacturer's rep. The same rules that apply to lighting fixtures apply to switching gear and distribution equipment.

- Low Voltage System – Send specs and related drawings for systems such as fire alarm, security, sound, TV, emergency to whomever you work with. Again, the same rules that apply to lighting fixtures also apply here.

- List of Bidders – Obtain a list of bidders from the architect, the owner, or construction reports and decide whom you want to quote your price. Once you have made your choice, set your position early with each bidder by letting him know you are bidding the work.

Handle these items promptly, for they represent a substantial part of the estimate. Directly and indirectly, you enlist the aid of others to estimate a job. In return, the least you can do is to give them ample time to help you put the bid together.

To get prices, don't wait until the last minute or you will wind up guessing most of them. If you cannot execute this step in a timely fashion, you are better off not bidding the job. Calling your suppliers and reps in the early stages of the estimate strengthens your relationship and allows you to keep a finger on the pulse of the industry.

ESTIMATING THE JOB

The basic steps for estimating a job are takeoff, summary, and pricing. The sample estimate that follows will walk us through that process in detail.

The job is an 8000 sq. ft. warehouse shell with a small office and a future welding station. The electric service, 600 amps 120/240 volts 3 phase, is designed to accommodate a future conversion of 2000 sq. ft. of warehousing into a manufacturing area; thus, the power distribution system includes a main distribution panel and two 225 amps 3 phase 42-circuit panels. There is also a two-zone fire alarm system.

Quantity Takeoff

The simplest and most comprehensive way for taking off an electrical job is to begin at the power source and end at the outlets.

To record and track the progress of the estimate, start with the recap sheet (see figure 16), where all the systems that make up the estimate are check marked in the 'In' column. As each system is completed, add a second check mark. Thus, a box with two check marks indicates that the system is part of the estimate and the takeoff is completed.

While most systems are taken off on a special takeoff sheet, 'System #9 - Service' is taken off directly on two pricing sheets (see Figures 17 and 18).

Through the estimate, the extended material cost is rounded off to the nearest dollar.

The 'Multiplier' column allows you to adjust labor units for degree of difficulty as you proceed with the estimate rather than at the end when your recollection is not as sharp. A multiplier can add or deduct a percentage from the standard unit.

For example, 1.25 multiplier adds 25%, while 0.80 deducts 20% from the labor unit (see Figure 18, line 5). Here, the estimator feels that 3 hours per hundred feet labor unit is too low for such a small quantity; he therefore increases the unit to 300%, 3 times its original value; conversely, on Figure 19, line 11, the labor unit is cut by 15%, or 0.85 of its original value.

Adjusting labor units on a line-by-line basis 'where and when' they're due, rather than at the end in a lump sum format across the board, produces truer estimates.

Column (g), 'Systems Prime Cost,' of the recap sheet reflects the prime cost of each system, which, ultimately, becomes the contract breakdown for billing.

In working with this sample estimate, focus more on understanding the process of compiling the estimate than on the different labor and material unit costs. These units are examples and you should determine the units that are most applicable to your work.

The estimating methods shown here are the essentials of estimating. You should acquaint yourself with their workings, for this will simplify whatever other system you choose to use, whether manual or computerized.

The sheets in the following estimate are in the order in which they should appear in your estimating folder.

As noted earlier, your Table of Contents is the Recap Sheet.

ESTIMATE RECAP SHEET

Job Name: Sample Job 1, Warehouse   Job # 02-1231   Date

ESTIMATE BREAKDOWN

			Material		Labor				(g)
	Control		(a)	(b)	(c)	(d)	(e)	(f)	Systems Prime Cost (a+b+f)
Title	In	#Pgs	Standard	Quotes	Labor-hrs	Crew	$-Rate	Extended	
1 Mobilization (DJE)	xx								
2 Temp. Light & Power									
Site Work									
3 Excavation & Back Fill									
4 Substation/ Transformer	.								
5 Precast & Concrete									
6 Primary Feeders									
7 Branch Circuits									
8 Light Poles & Fixtures									
Work In Building									
9 Service	xx	2	2,588		49.30	II	15.49	764	3.352
10 Secondary Feeders	xx	2	2,844		68.68	II	15.49	1,033	3,877
11 Switching Gear	xx	1	60	3,055	17.35	II	15.49	269	3,384
12 Branch Circuits	xx	3	1,303		85.74	II	15.49	1,328	2,631
13 Lighting Fixtures	xx	1	102	3,250	54.50	IV	12 11	660	4,012
14 Wiring Devices	xx	1	268		14.03	IV	12.11	170	438
15 Equipment Connections	xx	1	400		4.87	II	15 49	75	475
16 Emergency Generator									
17 Telephone									
18 Sound/ Clock/ TV									
19 Security									
20 Fire Alarm	xx	2	298	1,650	57.44	II	15.49	890	2,838
21									
22									
Totals		13	7,863	7,955	351,91			5,189	21,007

Form EE-305-2-rev05 ©2005 The Estimating Room™ Inc.

Figure 16: Sample Job 1, Recap Sheet

PRICING SHEET

Job Name: Sample job 1, Warehouse — Job #02-1231 — Date

	Items of Work	Quantity	Material Cost			Labor Hours			
	From:		Price	Per	Extend	Unit	Multip	Per	Extend
1	Trench & back-fill 36"x18"	60'	3.00	Ft	180	L.S			2 00
2	Primary Feeder from Utility Co.								
3	Xfmr to MDP via CT cabinet:	Note							
4	3 1/2" PVC Sc 40 2 runs of 70' Ea.	140'	195.00	C	273	5.00		C	7.00
5	3 1/2" PVC elbows	2	14.50	E	29				-0-
6	3 1/2" PVC couplings	4	2.90	E	12				-0-
7	3 1/2" PVC end-bells	2	3 45	E	7				-0-
8	3 1/2" male adapters	6	4 10	E	25				-0-
9	3 1/2" luck-nuts	6	4.05	E	24				-0-
10	3 1/2" bushings	6	2.90	E	17				-0-
11	350MCM THW Cu w slacks & Loop								
12	Trough CT Cabinet;Small Meter Rm								
13	add 50% efficiency factor to labor								
14	8 run at 95' each	760'	2,540	M	1,930	29.00	1.50	M	33.05
15	350 MCM Wire terminate. MDP only	6	-0-		-0-	0.30		E	1.80
16	10 Point watt meter cabinet	1			F.B.O	1.50		E	1.50
17	1" RGC	10'	112.00	C	11	4.50		C	0 45
18	1" luck-nuts	4	0.29	E	1				-0-
19	1" bushing	2	1.35	E	3				-0-
20	1" strap	3	1.64	E	5				-0-
21	#10/10C cable	15'			F.B.O.	F.B.O.			-0-
22	600A CT cabinet	1			F.B.O	F.B.O.			-0-
23									
24									
	Totals: This page(X) System Set ( )				2,517				45.80

System: # 9 Service - Number of sheets in the system: 2 — Sheet # 1 of 2

From EE-310-1-rev05 © 2005The Estimating Room™ Inc.

Figure 17 Sample Job 1, Service - Pricing Sheet

PRICING SHEET

Job Name: Sample job 1, Warehouse   Job #02-1231   Date

	Items of Work		Material Cost				Labor Hours			
	From:	Quantity	Price	Per	Extend	Unit	Multip	Per	Extend
1	Grounding:								
2	5/8" x10 Ft ground rod	2	13.85	E	28	0.50		E	1.00
3	5/8" ground rod clamp	2	2.85	E	6	0.30		E	0.60
4	1" water pipe clamp	1	4.90	E	5	0.50		E	0.50
5	3/4" pvc sch 40 (ssmall quantity)	10	24.00	C	2	3.00	3.00	C	0.90
6	3/4" straps	4	18	C	1				-0-
7	#1 THW Cu wire	15	730	M	11	L.S			0 50
8	Hardware for CT & meter	1-lot		E	18				-0-
9									
10									
11									
12									
13									
14									
15									
16									
17									
18									
19									
20									
21	Total (this) sheet #2				71				3.50
22	Total sheet #1				2,517				45.80
23									
24									
	Totals: This page( ) System Set				2,588				49.30

System: #9 Service   Number of sheets in the system: 2   Sheet #2 of 2

Form EE-310-2-rev05 ©2005 The Estimating Room™ Inc.

Figure 18: Sample Job 1, Service - Pricing Sheet

PRICING SHEET

Job Name: Sample job 1, Warehouse   Job #02-1231   Date

Items of Work		Material Cost				Labor Hours			
From: Feeder takeoff sheet #2 of 2 for panel MDP	Quantity	Price	Per	Extend	Unit	Multip	Per	Extend
1	2" EMT (Add 15% to Labor)	180'	83.00	C	149	9 00	1 15	C	18.63
2	2" EMT	90'	83 00	C	75	9 00		C	8.10
3	2" EMT elbows	4	4 25	E	17				-0-
4	2" EMT couplings DC SS	24	2.25	E	54				-0-
5	2" EMT insulated Connectors DC SS	6	3 95	E	24				-0-
6	2" EMT bushings	6	0.90	E	5				-0-
7	2" straps	48	1.05	E	50				-0-
8	3/8" beam clamps	48	1.75	E	84				-0-
9	18" x 12" x 6" pull box with cover	1	21 00	E	21	1.00		E	1.00
10	12" x 24" trench and back fill	160'	1.25	FT	200	L.S.			4.00
11	1" PVC Sch 40 in trench (less 10%)	170'	32	C	54	3.90	0.85	C	5.64
12	1" PVC elbows	2	1.15	E	2				-0-
13	1" PVC couplings	16	0.41	E	7				-0-
14	1" PVC male adapters	2	0.48	E	1				-0-
15	1" luck-nuts	2	0.25	E	1				-0-
16	1" bushings	2	0.26	E	1				-0-
17	1" LB condulet with cover	1	8.62	E	9	0.30			0.30
18	#4/0 THHN Cu wire	970'	1,680.00	M	1,630	20.00		M	19.10
19	#2/0 THHN Cu Wire	190'	995.00	M	189	17.00		M	3.23
20	#2 THHN Cu Wire	540'	490	M	265	9.00		M	4.86
21	Wire pulling lubricant	1Qt	6.00	E	6				-0-
22	#4/0 wire terminations	14			-0-	0.20		E	2 80
23	#2/0 wire terminations	2			-0-	0.18		E	0.36
24	#2 wire terminations	6			-0-	0.11		E	0.66
Totals: This page(x) System Set (x)				2,844				68.68

System: #10 Secondary Feeders - Number of sheets in the system:2   Sheet #1 of 2

Form EE-310-3-rev05 ©2005 The Estimating Room™   Inc

Figure 19: Sample Job 1, Secondary Feeders - Pricing Sheet

FEEDERS TAKEOFF SHEET

Job Name: Sample job 1, Warehouse Date:

Panel ID: MDP Description 600A 3 Phase 120/240 V 4 Wires MLO Loc: Meter Room

| C | Number of Circuits: 6 |
| O | Active: 3 Spare: 3 |

	Frame Amp	Trip Amp	Poles	Ckt #
D/E	225	225	3	1
	225	200	3	2
	100	90	3	3

Conduit

Code	2" EMT Length	90s	Term	1 1/2" EMT Length	90s	Term	1 1/4" EMT Length	90s	Term	1" PVC Length	90s	Term
B	180'	2	4									
B	90'	2	2							170'	2	2
T										170'	2	2

Wire: THHN CU

#4/0 Length	Wires	Term	#2/0 Length	Wires	Term	#2 Length	Wires	Term
570'	3	6	190'	1	2			
400'	4	8						
						540'	3	6

Intermediate — Pull boxes, Manholes, Others / **Serving** — Panel board, Devices Disconnects, Others

Intermediate	Serving
1 18x12x6 Pull	Panel "A"
	Panel "B"
1 1"LB conduit	Welding station / 100A 3p NF WP

Notes:

		2" EMT	1 1/2" EMT	1 1/4" EMT	1" PVC	#4/0	#2/0	#2
Total Conduit	Code: B = Bar Joist	270'			170'			
Total Conduit	Code: T = Trench							
Total Conduit	Code.							
Total Elbows (90)		4			2			
Total Termination (Term)		6			2	14	2	6
Total Wire						970'	190'	540'

Conduit Installation Codes: T = Trench D = Duct-bank S = Slab B = Bar Joist E = Exposed H = Hung ceiling

System: #10 Secondary Feeders Number of takeoff sheets in the system: 2

Prepared by: DWG #E-1, E-2 Sheet #2 of 2

Form EE-315-rev05 ©2005 The Estimating Room™ Inc.

Figure 20: Sample Job 1, Feeders -Takeoff Sheet

PRICING SHEET

Job Name: Sample job 1, Warehouse **Job #02-1231** Date

	Items of Work **From:** Riser diagram & panels schedule	Quantity	Material Cost				Labor Hours			
			Price	Per	Extend	Unit	Multip	Per	Extend
1	MDP 600A 120/240 4 W 6-ckt, MLO N1				Quote	6.00		E	6.00
2	with. 225A 3 poles C/B	1			Quote	0.35		E	0.35
3	200A 3 poles C/B	1			Quote	0.35		E	0.35
4	90A 3 poles C/B	1			Quote	0.20		E	0.20
5									
6	Panel A & B· 225A 120/240 4W 42-Ckts	2			Quote	4.00		E	4.00
7	with. 20A 1 pole C/B	5			Quote	0.15		E	0.75
8	30A 2 poles C/B	1			Quote	0.25		E	0.25
9	50A 2 poles C/B	1			Quote	0.25		E	0.25
10	30A 3 poles C/B	2			Quote	0.30		E	0.60
11	40A 3 poles C/B	2			Quote	0.30		E	0.60
12									
13	Mounting hardware	1-lot			60.00	L S.			4.00
14									
15									
16									
17									
18									
19									
20									
21									
22									
23									
24									
	Totals· This page(x) System Set (x)				60				17.35

System: #11 Switching Gear   Number of sheets in the system: 1 Sheet #1 of 1

Form EE-310-4-rev05 ©2005 The Estimating Room™ Inc

Figure 21: Sample Job 1, Switching Gear - Price Sheet

PRICING SHEET

Job Name: Sample job 1, Warehouse   Job #02-1231   Date

	Items of Work		Quantity	Material Cost				Labor Hours			
	Branch circuits & devices from take-off sheets #2 & #3 for panels A & B		Quantity	Price	Per	Extend	Unit	Multip	Per	Extend
1	1/2" EMT	Bar joist	880'	15.90	C	140	2.50		C	22.00
2	1/2" EMT	Exposed	150'	15.90	C	24	3 15	1.30	C	6.14
3	1/2" EMT	Hung cel	610'	15.90	C	97	2.00		C	12.20
4	3/4" EMT	Bar joist	380'	25.30	C	96	3.00		C	11.40
5	1" EMT	Bar joist	90'	41 50	C	37	3.75		C	3.38
6	1/2" EMT couplings DC SS		98	0.29	E	28				-0-
7	3/4" EMT couplings DC SS		36	0.47	E	17				-0-
8	1" EMT couplings DC SS		8	0.74	E	6				-0-
9	1/2" EMT connectors DC SS		128	0.25	E	32				-0-
10	3/4" EMT connectors DC SS		6	0 41	E	3				-0-
11	1" EMT connectors DC SS		2	0.68	E	1				-0-
12	1" EMT bushings		2	0.22	E	1				-0-
13	1/2" EMT straps		125	0.14	E	18				-0-
14	1/2" EMT caddy clips		250	0.42	E	105				-0-
15	3/4" EMT caddy clips		150	0 45	E	68				-0-
16	1/4" EMT beam clamps		18	0.40	E	7				-0-
17	1/2" - 3/4" JB combo		2	1.52	E	3	0.15		E	0.30
18	4" square boxes with cover		10	1.60	E	16	0.10		E	1.00
19	4" round boxes with cover		34	1.18	E	40	0.10		E	3.40
20	#12 THHN Cu str wire		5377'	57.50	M	309	3.00		M	16.13
21	#10 THHN Cu str wire		1281'	93.60	M	120	3.50		M	4.48
22	#8 THHN Cu str wire		1008'	115.20	M	116	4 00		M	4.03
23	#6 THHN Cu str wire		189'	102.30	M	19	4 50	1.50	M	1.28
24										
	Totals: This page( ) System Set (X)					1,303				85.74

System: #12 Branch Circuits - Number of sheets in the system: 3	Sheet #1 of 3

Form EE-310-rev05 ©2005 The Estimating Room™ Inc.

Figure 22: Sample Job 1, Branch Circuits - Pricing Sheet

HOME RUNS AND BRANCH CIRCUITS TAKEOFF SHEET

Job Name: Sample job 1, Warehouse   **Job #02-1231**   **Date:**

Panel ID: "A"   **Description: 225A 120/240V 4-wire Nema 1**   **Location: East wing**

Number of Ckts: Active: 12   Spare: 30

Wire: THHN Cu

C/O/D/E	Ckt #	Trip Amp	# of Poles	1/2" EMT Length (90s)	1/2" EMT Term	3/4" EMT Length (90s)	3/4" EMT Term	#12 Length (Wires)	#12 Term	#10 Length (Wires)	#10 Term	#8 Length (Wires)	#8 Term	Line	Devices ⊕	Devices ⊖	JB	S	S3	Others A/C
B	1,2,3	40	3			120'	2	126' (1)				378' (3)		Line 1						
														Line 2		1				
B	2,4,6	30	3	300'	2					945' (3)				Line 1						
														Line 2						1
B	7,9,11	40	3			200'	2	210' (1)				630' (3)		Line 1		1				
														Line 2						
B	8	20	1	60'	2			378' (6)						Line 1						
														Line 2			1			
B	8	–	–	380'	48			1197' (3)						Line 1	6					
														Line 2	4			4	2	
B	10	20	1	200'	40			1260' (6)						Line 1	6	8				
														Line 2	4			3		
E	12	20	1	100'	2			315' (3)						Line 1			1			
														Line 2						1
Totals														Line 1	12	2	1	7		
														Line 2	9	14	1		2	1

Total Conduit Code: H   1/2" EMT: 880'
Total Conduit Code: B   1/2" EMT: 100'; 3/4" EMT: 380'
Total Conduit Code: E
Total Elbows (90): 6
Total Terminations: 1/2" EMT 92; 3/4" EMT 6
Total Wire: #12 3,486'; #10 945'; #8 1,008'

Conduit Installation Codes: T = Trench   D = Duct-bank   S = Slab   B = Bar Joist   E = Exposed   H = Flung ceiling

System: #12 Branch Circuits & System #14 Wiring Devices   Number of takeoff sheets in the system: 2

Prepared by: DWG # E-1   Sheet #2 of 3

Form EE-320-1-rev05 © 2005 The Estimating Room™ Inc.

Figure 23: Sample Job 1, Branch Circuits/Devices - Takeoff Sheet

HOME RUNS AND BRANCH CIRCUITS TAKEOFF SHEET

Job Name: Sample job 1, Warehouse Date:

Panel ID: "B" Location: West wing

Description: 225A 120/240V 4-wire Nema 1 Job #02-1231

Number of Ckts: Active: 10 Spare: 32

Wire: THHN Cu

Ckt #	Trip Am	Poles	1/2" EMT Length	90s	Term	3/4" EMT Length	90s	Ter	1" EMT Length	90s	Term	#12 Length	Wires	Term	#10 Length	Wires	Term	#6 Length	Wires	Term	Devices		S / S3	Others A/C / WH
1	20	1	250'	32								788'	3								Line 1			
																					Line 2			WH 1
2	20	1	300'	12								945'	3								Line 1	6		
																					Line 2	16	S3 4	
3,5	30	2	60'	2								63'	1		126'	2					Line 1	2		
																					Line 2	4	S3 2	
4,6	50	2							90'	2		95'	1					189'	2		Line 1	1		A/C 1
																					Line 2			
7,9,11	30	3	50'	2											210'	4					Line 1	1		A/C 1
																					Line 2			
Total Conduit Code: H			610'						90'												Totals			
Total Conduit Code: B			50'								2										Line 1	6 / 1		A/C 1
Total Conduit Code:																					Line 2	2 / 20	S3 6	WH 1
Total Elbows (90)																								
Total Terminations			48								2													
Total Wire												1,891			336'			189'						

Conduit Installation Codes: T = Trench D = Duct-bank S = Slab B = Bar Joist E = Exposed H = Hung ceiling

System: #12 Branch Circuits & System #14 Wiring Devices Number of takeoff sheets in the system: 2

Prepared by: DWG # E-1 Sheet #3 of 3

Form EE-320-2-rev05 ©2005 The Estimating Room™ Inc.

Figure 24: Sample Job 1 - Warehouse Branch Takeoff Sheet

PRICING SHEET

Job Name: Sample job 1, Warehouse **Job #02-1231** **Date**

Items of Work	Quantity	Material Cost				Labor Hours			
From: Lighting	Quantity	Price	Per	Extend	Unit	Multip	Per	Extend
1 2 x 4 Lay-in flour. fixtures	20			Quote	040		E	8.00
2 2/ 96 strips (40% factor high ceiling)	30			Quote	0.75	1.40	E	31.50
3 Exit lights with battery back-up	5			Quote	1.00		E	5.00
4 2 heads emergency lights	2			Quote	1.00		E	2.00
5 100 watt wall mounted incand. fixtures	5			Quote	0.60		E	3.00
6 F-40 CW lamps	40			Quote				-0-
7 F-96 CW lamps	60			Quote				-0-
8 100 watt incandescent lamps	5			Quote				-0-
9 6-Ft whips	20	3.45	E	69.00	0.15		E	3.00
10 Disaster clips	40	0.15	E	6.00	0.05		E	2 00
11 Toggle bolts and fender washers	60	0.30	E	18.00				-0-
12 Yellow wire-nuts	171	0.05	E	9 00				-0-
13								
14								
15								
16								
17								
18								
19								
20								
21								
22								
23								
24								
Totals. This page(X) System Set ( )				102				54.50

System: #13 Lighting Fixtures - Number of sheets in the system: 1   **Sheet #1 of 1**

Form EE-310-6-rev05 ©2005 The Estimating Room™ Inc

Figure 25: Sample Job 1, Lighting Fixtures - Pricing Sheet

PRICING SHEET

Job Name: Sample job 1, Warehouse   Job #02-1231   Date

Items of Work		Material Cost				Labor Hours			
From:	Quantity	Price	Per	Extend	Unit	Multip	Per	Extend
1 20A 125V duplex receptacles	18	3.05	E	55	0.15		E	2.70
2 20A 125V single receptacles	11	2.75	E	30	0.15		E	1.65
3 30/40A 250V 4 wire receptacles	3	5.75	E	17	0.25		E	.75
4 20A 125V 1P toggle switches	13	2.75	E	36	0.20		E	2.60
5 20A 125V 3-way switches	2	4.25	E	9	0.30		E	0.60
6								
7 Device metal boxes 1-1/2" deep	31	1.42	E	44	0.08		E	2.48
8 Device metal boxes 2-1/8" deep	3	2.30	E	7	0.08		E	0.24
9 Mud-rings 1 gang 1/2" deep	31	0.71	E	22	0.04		E	1.24
10 Mud-rings 2 gang 1/2" deep	7	1.10	E	8	0.04		E	0.28
11 Duplex industrial covers 1 gang	8	1.45	E	12	0.04		E	0.32
12 Single gang industrial covers	3	1.73	E	5	0.04		E	0.12
13 2 gang industrial switch covers	4	1.90	E	8	0.05		E	0.20
14 Duplex ivory plates	10	0.53	E	5	0.03		E	0.30
15 Single receptacle ivory plates	9	0.30	E	3	0.03		E	0.27
16 Single switch ivory plate	7	0.23	E	2	0.04		E	0.28
17 Red wire-nuts	130	0.07	E	9				-0-
18 Yellow wire-nuts	60	0.05	E	3				-0-
19								
20								
21								
22								
23								
24								
Totals: This page(x) System Set (x)				268				14.03

System: #14 Wiring Devices - Number of sheets in the system: 1	Sheet #1 of 1

From EE-310-7rev05 ©2005 The Estimating Room™ Inc

Figure 26: Sample Job 1, Wiring Devices - Pricing Sheet

PRICING SHEET

Job Name: Sample job 1, Warehouse				Job #02-1231			Date	

Items of Work		Material Cost				Labor Hours			
From: Branch circuits/Devices take-off sheets #2 &3 for panels A & B	Quantity	Price	Per	Extend	Unit	Multip	Per	Extend
1	30A 3P 250V N3 fused disc. sw. for a/c	1	63 25	E	63	0.80		E	0.80
2	30A 2P 250V N3 fused pull-out for a/c	1	18 50	E	19	0.50		E	0 50
3	1/2" liquid tight	10'	130.00	C	13	1 80	3.00	E	0.54
4	1/2" liquid tight straight connectors	2	2.13	E	4				-0-
5	1/2" liquid tight 90 connectors	2	3.93	E	8				-0-
6	#10 THHN Cu wire	49'	93.60	M	5				-0-
7	Red wire-nuts	5	0.07	E	-0-				-0-
8									
9	50A 2P 250V N1 NF sw/ Water Heater	1	32.50	E	33	0.65		E	0 65
10	1" flex metal conduit	3'	75.00	C	2	12.00	3 00	C	1.08
11	1" flex metal connectors	2	5 85	E	12				-0-
12	#6 THHN Cu wire	8'	169 00	M	1				-0-
13	#12 THHN Cu wire	4'	57.50	M	-0-				-0-
14									
15	100A 3P 250V N3R switch for welding								
16	station. Wire only to disconnect	1	182.00	E	182	1.30		E	1 30
17	Fuses: 90A 250V RK5 TD	3	9.35	E	28				-0-
18	30A 250V RK5 TD	5	1.93	E	10				-0-
19									
20	Mounting hardware	1-lot			20				-0-
21									
22									
23									
24									
Totals. This page(x) System Set (x)				400				4 87

System: #15 Equipment Connection - Number of sheets in the system: 1	Sheet #1 of 1

Form EE-310-8-rev05 ©2005 The Estimating Room™ Inc

Figure 27: Sample Job 1, Equipment Connection - Pricing Sheet

PRICING SHEET

Job Name: Sample job 1, Warehouse   Job #02-1231   Date

Items of Work From: System takeoff sheets Fire Alarm	Quantity	Material Cost			Labor Hours			
		Price	Per	Extend	Unit	Multip	Per	Extend
1 ½"EMT conduit with fittings	920'	15 90	C	146	2.6		C	23.92
2								
3 Wire								
4 THHN #16 Stranded	630'	42 50	M	27	2 5		M	1.58
5 THHN #14 Stranded	830'	47 50	M	39	2 5		M	2.08
6 2/16 pair	500'	172 00	M	86	2 5		M	1.25
7								
8 Device: Packaged with Panel	1		LS	1,650			LS	15 61
9 HS	6				.50		E	3 00
10 SL	2				.50		E	1.00
11 SD	8				.50		E	4.00
12 DD	2				.50		E	1 00
13 PS	6				.50		E	3.00
14 FS	1				.50		E	.50
15 TS	1				50		E	.50
16								
17								
18 Material. Quoted $1,650 00								
19 Material Standard $298 00								
20								
21								
22								
23								
24								
Totals: This page(x) System Set (x)				1,948				57.44

System: #20 Fire Alarm -   Number of sheets in the system: 2 | **Sheet #1   of 2**

Form EE-310-9-rev05 © 2005 The Estimating Room™ Inc.

Figure 28: Sample Job 1, Fire Alarm - Pricing Sheet

SYSTEM TAKEOFF SHEET

Job Name: Sample job 1, Warehouse **Job #02-1231** **Date:**

Panel ID: "F.A." **Description.** Two zones fire alarm **Location:** Office

C O	Number of Active 2 Spare 0 Zones 0	D E	From (via)	To (via)	Ckt #	Conduit 1/2" EMT Length	90s	Term	3/4" EMT Length	90s	Term	Length	90	Term	Wire: THHN Cu #16 Length Wire	Term	#14 Length Wire	Term	2/16 Pair Length Wire	Term		Serving Devices	HS FS	SL TS	SD	DD	PS	Others
B					Zone 1	300'	16								2 / 630'		2 / 630'				Line 1		6	2				
																					Line 2							
B					Zone	480'	32												1 / 500'		Line 1				8	2	6	
																					Line 2							
B					Phone	50'	2														Line 1							
																					Line 2							
B					Ded. Ckt	90'	4										2 / 200'				Line 1		1	1				
																					Line 2		1					
					Totals																Line 1		6	2	8	2	6	
																					Line 2		1	1				

Total Conduit Code B 920'

Total Conduit Code:

Total Conduit Code:

Total Elbows (90) 54

Total Terminations

Total Wire #16 630' #14 830' 2/16 Pair 500'

Conduit Installation Codes: T = Trench D = Duct-bank S = Slab B = Bar Joist E = Exposed H = Hung ceiling

System: # Fire Alarm   Number of takeoff sheets in the system: 2

Prepared by   DWG # E-1   Sheet #2 of 2

Form EE-325-1-rev05 ©2005 The Estimating Room™ Inc.

Figure 29: Sample Job 1, Fire Alarm - Takeoff Sheet

Chapter 11

COMPILING THE BID

BID RECAP

Now that we have estimated the labor and material costs for our sample job, it is time to wear a businessperson's hat and transfer those costs from the Estimate Recap Sheet to the Bid Recap Sheet.

To get a better handle on the following notes, see Figure 33 for the recap sheet. You can photocopy and use it for quick reference as you read this material.

Line 1 – Standard Material

Here you can adjust the estimated material cost either by a lump sum amount or by a percentage plus applicable sales taxes. No prior adjustments were made in the estimate.

Standard material, usually priced from 'Column 3' of trade-price publications was adequate to get you to this point.

For the first time in the estimate, you can discount the standard material. This percentage is determined by your buying power. In many cases, you can discount 'Column 3' prices by 50% or more.

For this job, first discount the material by 10%, and then add 6% sales tax. Thus, compute $7,863 x 0.90 + 6% = $ 7,502.

Line 2 – Quoted Material

This total is obtained either from the estimate recap sheet or from a quote worksheet (Figure 34), if you have set one up.

The quote worksheet is convenient. Without affecting the bid recap sheet, it allows you to record last minutes price changes. If the price changes are relevant to the bid, then you only need to change one number in the recap sheet.

Regardless of its makeup, quoted material is adjusted the same as standard material. In this job, due to a last-minute revision, it is credited $255.

Line 4 – Labor

As opposed to material, labor is adjusted during the estimating process. You may use this line to make additional adjustments.

Line 5 – Other

Allows further labor additions or deductions.

Line 14 – Non-Productive Labor

Non-productive labor covers work that is not related to any material installation. For example, a 'gofer' is non-productive labor. Because this labor can be charged to several jobs, you may charge a portion to each job he serves.

Line 15 – Supervision

Although this cost is often included under Operating Overhead, you can charge a proportion as Direct Job Expense (DJE) to each job supervised. Supervision does not include supervisors and working supervisors. Their cost is included in the Labor Rate Average (see Chapter 9 - Labor Rate Average).

In this job, the supervision is set at 5% of the total labor hours at an arbitrary rate of $40 per hour. Adjust both figures to reflect your cost.

Line 18 – Profit

This line allow you to apply either a lump-sum markup or, for better control, four different markups.

Profit markup, if not proportionally applied, can win or lose a bid. Here you must control greed and apply realistic markups that will keep you competitive without jeopardizing profit.

Although profit is computed by percentages, it helps to look at it as a lump-sum amount. To average it out to a true percentage, you'll need to base it on sales. In this job, that percentage is $3,719 profit divided by $30,711 sale price, times 100 equals 12.11%.

Line 25 – Contingencies

In our (lean) method of estimating, contingency is an important item to consider. Up to now, we have totaled our bid into an amount (line 24) that, as stated earlier, is free of fat and guesswork.

Therefore, based on the intricacy of the job, you may apply a contingency factor. You can apply it to Prime Cost (Line 17) to cover unforeseen items of work, or to the Bid Subtotal (Line 24) to cover unforeseen costs for the whole contract. In the example it is applied to Line 24.

The percentage varies with each job. It may range from 2% to 8%. To determine a fair rate, invoke your trade and business skills and analyze each job objectively.

Line 27 – Operating Overhead

To justify this item and the markup method employed to compute its value, you will need to clarify two points (For an in-depth discussion, see Operating Overhead under Efficiency Level and Others, Chapter 9 and Chapter 19):

- Applying operating overhead to the bid grand total (Line 26) serves a distinct purpose—it can be applied as a markup rather than a percentage with no effect on your estimated profit.

- Markup is an equating method that allows you to cover your operating overhead in full, which is based on a percentage of sales.
  Therefore, when you apply this percentage to your bid total, unless it is converted to a markup, its value will not cover your cost.

  For instance, converting the 12% overhead into a 1.136 multiplier allocates an operating overhead of $3,677 (Line 27 less line 26). To check if the amount is adequate, apply 12% to the $30,711 sale price and you come up with an acceptable amount of $3,685.

  However, using the straight percentage method, the

allocated amount is less than the estimated operating cost—a deficit that grows progressively worse as the overhead increases. This fallacy becomes clearer in the three comparison charts that follow. To emphasize the point, each is computed at a different rate—the first at 12%, the next at 20% and the third at 30%.

Comparison Chart at 12%

Line	Description	Method Applied			
		Multiplier		Percentage	
a	Bid Grand Total (Bid Recap Sheet Line 26)		27,034		27,034
b	Sale Price = Line a + overhead	@ 1.136	30,711	@12%	30,279
c	Allocated Overhead = Line b - a		3,677		3,245
d	Overhead @ 12% of Sales = Line b x 12%		3,685		3,633
e	Overhead surplus or deficit = Line c - d		+8		-388
f	Deficit Percentage Rate = Line e ÷ d x 100				10.67%

Figure 30: Overhead Comparison Chart at 12% Rate

Comparison Chart at 20%

Line	Description	Method Applied			
		Multiplier		Percentage	
a	Bid Grand Total (Bid Recap Sheet Line 26)		27,034		27,034
b	Sale Price= Line a + overhead	@ 1.250	33,7922	@20%	32,441
c	Allocated Overhead= Line b - a		6,758		5,407
d	Overhead @ 20% of Sales = Line b x 20%		6,758		6,488
e	Overhead surplus or deficit = Line c - d		-0-		-1,081
f	Deficit Percentage Rate = Line e ÷ d x 100				16.70%

Figure 31: Overhead Comparison Chart at 20% Rate

Comparison Chart at 30%

Line	Description	Method Applied	
		Multiplier	**Percentage**
a	Bid Grand Total (Bid Recap Sheet Line 26)	27,034	27,034
b	Sale Price= Line a + overhead	@ 1.43 38,659	@30% 35,144
c	Allocated Overhead= Line b - a	12,625	8,110
d	Overhead @ 30% of Sales= Line b x 30%	11,599	10,543
e	Overhead surplus or deficit = Line c - d	+26	-2,433
f	Deficit Percentage Rate = Line e ÷ d x 100		23.08%

Figure 32: Overhead Comparison Chart at 30%

Since the overhead allowance is the only item paying for your operating expenses, and all else in the bid being true and lean, because your experienced or projected overhead is the product of the sales price, you cannot compromise nor apply it as a straight percentage.

You must always convert your operating overhead rate into a multiplier. If not, you'll be cutting into profit and, if you're too excessive, into cost.

Out of all the revelations from these three charts, the most important is the 'deficit factor.' A mystery to many contractors, it preys on their business success constantly.

For example, if your operating expenses for the year are fixed at $90,000 and your projected sales quota is $450,000, your operating overhead is also fixed at 20%, or a 1.25 markup.

At that rate, for your jobs to cover the cost, you will have to earn at least $90,000 for the year. However, if you use, as many do, the conventional straight percentage method and sell $450,000 in contracts, rest assured that at the end of the year the overhead budget will be $15,030 short, or 16.7% (see Figure 31)—a position that rarely breeds success.

Before we analyze the Bid Recap Sheet, we should know that percentages, whether we use them to compute a bid or a work order, can be deceptive. When not properly applied, they can lead us into believing that all is well until the avalanche hits, and when it does, we won't have much time to recover.

BID RECAP SHEET

Job Name: Sample job 1, Warehouse   **Job #02-1231**

Bid Compiled by. MS   Bid To: Owner   Bid Due Date: 12/30/94   Time: 10:30 EST

	Description	Estimate Amount	Adjustment Flat Amount +/-	Adjustment Multiplier	Sales Tax	Extended Bid Items
1	Standard Material	7,863		0.90	6%	7,502
2	Quoted Material	7,955	-255		6%	8,162
	Bid Recap Sheet(x) Quotation Sheet ( )					
3	Material Total Lines 1, 2					15,664
4	Labor: From Estimate Recap Sheet	5,189				5,189
5	Other:					0.00
6	Labor Total Lines 4, 5					5,189
7	Direct Job Expenses (DJE):					
8	Office Trailer	0.00				00
9	Storage	100				100
10	Utilities	125				125
11	Permit Fees	250				250
12	Rentals	00				00
13	Others: Per Attached Breakdown	00				00
14	Non-Productive Labor Estimated 40 Man-hour @ $12.00 Per Hour					480
15	Supervision 5% of 359 =18 hours @ $40.00 Per Hour					720
16	DJE Lines 8, 9, 10, 11, 12, 13, 14, 15					1,675
17	Prime Cost Lines 3, 6,16					22,528
18	Profit: (Apply it either a lump-sum markup to line 17 on this line, or as % on the following lines)					00
19	20% on Standard Material, Line 1					1,573
20	10% on Quoted Material, Line 2					816
21	25% on Labor, Line 6					1,297
22	5% on DJE, Line 16					84
23	Total Profit Line 18 Or Lines 19, 20, 21, 22					3,770
24	Bid Subtotal Lines 17,23					26,298
25	3% Contingencies, Line 24					789
26	Bid Total Lines 24, 25					27,087
27	Prime Bid 12% OH Line 26 x1 136 Markup					30,771
28	_% Performance / Payment Bond Line 27					-0-
	Markup Formula: 100 ÷ (100 - %) = Markup	**Sale Price** Lines 27, 28 OK'd By:_____				$ 30,771

Form EE-350-rev05 ©2005 The Estimating Room™ Inc.   .

Figure 33: Sample Job 1, Bid Recap Sheet

Finally, regarding estimating and bidding jobs, consider the following:

- Bid jobs to win them. Don't waste your resources on wishful and over-inflated bids, for you will only open the floodgates of competition.

- Know all your costs—no guessing—and apply your profit knowing we have done the best you can do.

- From this point on, any bid you lose is not your doing, nor is it due to some mysterious formula others use. It is just part of the business.

- Bid jobs with confidence, for as long as you stay true to your principles, you will get your share of profitable work.

QUOTE WORKSHEET

Project:

Bid Due Date:

Sheet #   of

Items of Work		QUOTE #1		QUOTE #2		QUOTE #3		USED IN BID	
		Vendor	Amount	Vendor	Amount	Vendor	Amount	Vendor	Amount
Lighting Fixtures	Base Price								
	Alternate 1								
	Alternate 2								
Switching Gear	Base Price								
	Alternate 1								
	Alternate 2								
Fire Alarm	Base Price								
	Alternate 1								
	Alternate 2								
Precast Products	Base Price								
	Alternate 1								
	Alternate 2								
	Base Price								
	Alternate 1								
	Alternate 2								
	Base Price								
	Alternate 1								
	Alternate 2								

(This and other forms may be downloaded online at www.theestimatingroom.com)

From EE-360 –rev05 ©1994 The Estimating Room™ Inc.

Figure 34: Quote Work Sheet

Chapter 12

COMPUTING AVERAGE UNIT PRICES

PER-OPENING UNIT PRICE

We use per-opening unit prices for estimating residential as well as some commercial work. These unit prices include items of work that are closely related in function, installation, and cost. While per-opening unit prices make estimating easy, we should know their common denominators and what they include.

For example, in a typical residential unit price, the following can be included:

- Duplex receptacles, 110-Volt 15 and 20-Amp

- Single receptacles, 110-Volt 15 and 20-Amp for small appliances such as refrigerator, dishwasher, disposal, and washing machine

- GFI receptacles counted as duplex receptacles; the cost of the GFI receptacles themselves or GFI circuit breakers are added separately as special equipment

- Single pole, 3- and 4-way wall switches

- Ceiling and wall outlets for lighting

- Branch circuits 15- and 20-Amp of 40-ft. average run

- Branch circuits 15- and 20-Amp of 70-ft. average run

- TV outlets, phone outlets

- Bell or chimes and push buttons

Once you average the per-opening price to estimate the cost for the 'general wiring' of a house, multiply the unit price by the number of openings shown on the drawings. When using this method, bear in mind three things:

- Electric dryers, water heaters, ranges, cook-tops, ovens, stoves, air conditioners, service, panel boards, lighting fixtures, lamps, and GFI devices should not be counted as openings. You should price each one separately and then add it to the 'general wiring' cost.

- Per-opening unit prices are applicable only to jobs comparable in category and substance—category being residential or commercial and substance being wiring methods such as non-metallic cable or conduit and buildings with similar structural characteristics such as ceiling heights, wall construction, etc.

- The result of your per-opening price is an estimated prime cost. As with all estimates, convert it into a selling price using the Bid Recap Sheet.

Per-opening Price Assembly

To compute average unit prices, first estimate the cost of each component and then assemble and price each part of that component's installation.

The following example shows the first step in that process, i.e. how to list assemblies in pricing sheets and the various pricing options. Detailed pricing for items of work listed above are based on the same principle and are therefore not shown in the example.

The intent is to show how to develop workable unit prices that can facilitate speedy estimating for residential and some commercial work.

Use this pricing sheet form as a template to develop a library of per-opening unit prices in conjunction with your own or published material cost and labor units.

PRICING SHEET

Job Name: Sample Unit Price **Job #02-1231** **Date**

Items of Work		Material Cost				Labor Hours			
110V 20A Duplex outlet assembly with 10Ft 12/2 NMC w/ground	Quantity	Price	Per	Extend	Unit	Multi	Per	Extend
1	12/2 NMC w/ground	10'	0.27	Ft	2.70	0 01		Ft	0.10
2	NMC box 2-1/2" deep	1	1.73	E	1 73	0.11		E	0 11
3	Duplex receptacles 110V 20A	1	3.28	E	3 28	0 16		E	0 16
4	Duplex plate	1	0.33	E	0.33	0.05		E	0.05
5	Misc: Staples, wire-nuts, etc.	1-lot			0 50				-0-
6									
Totals: This page(x System Set ( )				8 54				0.42
System: #	**Number of sheets in the system:**				**Sheet # of**			

Form EE-310-1-rev05 © 2005 The Estimating Room™ Inc.

Figure 35: Units Cost

Openings Average Cost

Having assembled and priced each item as shown in the pricing sheet above, compute your averages by listing their cost in the "Openings Average Worksheet as follows:

	OPENINGS AVERAGE WORKSHEET								

Category of Work: Residential, one family home, one story structure, metal studs, ceiling average height 9 Ft, one cathedral ceiling.

Wiring method: NMC Copper   Standards as per NEC Devices standard grade

Prepared by: Checked by: Date: 00/00/00

	Items of Work Included in the average	## of Openings	Material Cost			Labor Hours		
			Price	Per	Extend	Unit	Per	Extend
1	Duplex wall recept. 110 V 15 A	90	6.85	E	616.50	0.42	E	37.80
2	Duplex wall recept. 110 V 20 A	4	8.54	E	34 16	0 42	E	1 68
3	GFI 15 A (without devices)	4	6.50	E	26.00	0.54	E	2.16
4	Appliance Recept. 110 V 20 A each	5	15 60	E	78.00	0.50	E	2.50
5	Single pole wall switches 15 A	30	6.14	E	184.20	0.40	E	12 00
6	3 way wall switches	6	8 67	E	52 02	0 40	E	2 40
7	Ceiling outlets for light	16	8.80	E	52 80	1 34	E	8.04
8	Wall outlets for light	6	9 60	E	57.60	1 50	E	9.00
9	20 A Branch circuits at 40 Ft average	6	10 97	E	65.82	0.36	E	2.16
10	20 A Branch circuits at 70 Ft average	4	19 20	E	76.80	0.63	E	2 52
11	15 A Branch circuits at 40 Ft average	8	7 62	E	38 40	0 36	E	1 81
12	15 A Branch circuits at 70 Ft average	6	13.32	E	79 92	0.63	E	3.78
13	TV and Phone Outlets	12	5.90	E	70.80	0.45	E	5.40
14	Doorbell and push button	3	14 00	E	42.00	0.75	E	2.25
15								

(This and other forms may be downloaded online at www.theestimatingroom.com)

Totals	200			1475.02			93.50

Formula

Average material cost per opening = Total material $1,475 ÷ 200 openings = $7.38

Average labor hour per opening = Total labor-hours 93.50 ÷ 200 openings = 0.47Hr.

Form EE-390-rev05 ©2005 The Estimating Room™ Inc.

Figure 36: Openings Average Cost Computation

ELECTRICAL CONTRACTING

After the per-opening computation, use the 'Estimate Recap Sheet' to quickly quote any job. In the following example, the sample job is a house with 158 openings and a 200 A. overhead Service.

ESTIMATE RECAP SHEET

Job Name: Single Family Residence — Job # 02-1231

ESTIMATE BREAKDOWN

		Control		Material		Labor				(g) Prime Cost
		In	#Pg	(a) Standard	(b) Quotes	(c) Hours	(d) Crew	(e) Rate $	(f) Extended	Per System (a+b+f)
General wiring 158 openings										
1.	Material:158 @ $7.38 Ea.			1,166						
2.	Labor: 158 @ $0.47 each	xx	1			74.26	I	15.62	1,160	2,326
	(Cost per opening$14.72)									
4.	Service, feeders, panels	xx	1	1,785		38.00	I	15.62	594	2,379
5.	Air conditioner	xx		145		6.00	I	15.62	109	254
6.	Lighting fixture and lamps	xx		25	975	12.00	V	13.50	162	1,162
7.	GFI, devices, and misc.	xx		75		-0-			-0-	75
	Totals		2	3,196	975	130 26			2,025	6,196

Form EE-305-rev05 ©2005 The Estimating Room™ Inc.

Figure 37: Estimate Recap Sheet

Note to Per-opening Average Price

The method shown here is safer than conventional methods for you can convert these numbers to single unit prices inclusive of profit, overhead, and all other applicable markups. However, if it is not used in accordance with the various job conditions you will defeat its purpose and ultimately lose control of the unit price, for it will tend to inflate or deflate.

To prevent this, monitor average unit prices and adjust them when necessary to meet the conditions of the job at hand.

To convert the number shown in the above Recap Sheet into a single number, divide $2,326 (Line 1) by 158 (# of openings). The result, $14.72, is the per-unit cost as shown in Line 2.

Don't divide the prime cost, or—worse yet—the sale price by the number of openings to get a unit price for estimating other jobs. This would work only if all factors on the other jobs were equal to that of the job for which we were developing the unit price. If all things are equal, then you need not repeat the estimating process, just calculate the sale price based on the per-opening method shown in this chapter—but always with caution.

Compiling the Bid

The next and final step is to compile the bid. However, first note that the unit costs used above are arbitrary and most likely not applicable to your job. The labor rates are averages based on two different crew make-ups. As always, use your own numbers and estimate each item of work on its own pricing sheet. Without further shortcuts, we transfer our totals to the Bid Recap Sheet as shown below, in Figure 38.

BID RECAP SHEET

Job Name: Single Family Home   Job #02-1022

Bid Compiled by: MS   Bid To: Owner   Bid Due Date: 12 /30 /__   Time: 10:30 EST

	Description	Estimate Amount	Adjustment Lump-sum	Adjustment Multiplier	Sales Tax	Bid Items
1	**Standard Material**	3196		0.90	6%	3,388.00
2	**Quoted Material**	975	-255		6%	1,034.00
3		Material Total Lines 1, 2				4,63.00
4	**Labor: From Estimate Recap Sheet**	2,025				2,025.00
5	Other:					0.00
6		Labor Total Lines 4, 5				5,189.00
7	**Mobilization/Direct Job Expenses (DJE):**					
8	Office Trailer					
9	Storage					
10	Utilities					
11	Permit Fees	300				300.00
12	Rentals					
13	Others: Per Attached Breakdown					
14	Non-Productive Labor Estimated 4 Man-hour @ $14.00 Per Hour					56.00
15	Supervision 5% of 137 =6.85 hours @ $25.00 Per Hour					171.25
16	DJE Lines 8, 9, 10, 11, 12, 13, 14, 15					527.25
17	**Prime Cost** Lines 3, 6,16					6,915.25
18	**Profit:**(Apply it either a lump-sum markup to line 17 on this line, or as % on the following lines)					0.00
19	15% on Standard Material, Line 1 3,388.00					508.20
20	10% on Quoted Material, Line 2 1,034					103.40
21	25% on Labor, Line 6 2,025.00					506.25
22	5% on DJE, Line 16 527.25					52.73
23	Total Profit Line 18 Or Lines 19, 20, 21, 22					1,170.58
24	Bid Subtotal Lines 17,23					8,85.83
25	2% Contingencies, Line 24					161.72
26	Bid Total Lines 24, 25					8,247.55
27	Prime Bid 14% OH Line 26 x1.136 Markup					9,591.90
28	_% Performance / Payment Bond Line 27					-0-
	Markup Formula: 100 ÷ (100 - %) = Markup **Sale Price** Lines 27, 28 OK'd By:_____					$ 9,591.90

Form EE-350-rev05 ©2005 The Estimating Room™ Inc.

Figure 38: Bid Recap Sheet

Chapter 13

THE ESTIMATING ROOM

THE ESTIMATOR

The Estimating Room is where we generate costs and keep them for future reference. Ask any successful marketer and he, or she, will tell you that in sales, knowing the true cost of what you sell is the first step toward closing contracts.

In contracting, the estimator is responsible for delivering cost estimates free of guesswork. He must estimate his work objectively and leave speculation to others. When items of work lack clear definition, the estimator is responsible for getting those clarifications from the architect or owner. If that fails, then the estimator must list them as exceptions to the scope of work.

The estimator's skills must inspire confidence in those responsible for converting his estimate into a sale price.

LIBRARY

Building a unit prices library is another responsibility of the estimator. You may begin your library with a three-ring binder with at least six dividers, labeled as follows:

- Labor Rates Average – Make up crews that are most appropriate for your business using the Hourly Rate Worksheet as shown in Chapter 9.

- Wire Labor Units – See Chapter 9

- Conduit Labor Units – See Chapter 9

- Special Items Labor Units – For any unusual item of work refer to Chapter 9, How to Develop Your Own Numbers.

- Per-opening Cost – See Chapter 12

- Bid Markups – A Bid Recap Sheet reflecting your markups is the best choice here. Keep different sheets for different jobs or update the existing one – See Chapter 11

When maintained properly, this is the most valuable tool in The Estimating Room. Besides supporting the different aspects of your estimating process and minimizing errors, it saves countless research hours.

ESTIMATING TOOLS

Calculators

Regardless of how extensively you use hand-held calculators always carry a tape calculator for estimating. When adding long columns with such a calculator, round off all entries to the nearest dollar whenever practical.

Scale Ruler

Scale rulers—the stick type with three sides and multiple scales—are also indispensable. For those new at using the wheel, a word of caution—they tend to skip on certain types of paper, thereby computing faulty measurements.

Schedule Board – Bidding and Estimating

The most important tool in The Estimating Room is the Schedule Board.

On this board are displayed jobs scheduled for bid with their names, bid due date, and time.

With some ingenuity, you can use the same board for contracted jobs as well. At a glance, the board shows what material quotes are needed for what job, how many quotes have been scheduled for each item of work, and how many quotes are due or already received.

You can also schedule other information pertinent to bid bonds and bidding documents on this board. See Figure 39 below.

The board is based on the placement of three different color pushpins in the column and box where each job function intersects. These colors—red, yellow, and green—signify stop, wait, and go, just like traffic lights. For each job displayed there are two columns marked, "Takeoff" and "Quotes."

The Takeoff Column

- Red Pushpin – A red pushpin placed in this column indicates which items of work are included in that job. When you first lay out a job for estimating, the pushpins in this column should all be red.

- Yellow Pushpin – Indicates that the item of work is in progress. Replace the red with yellow when you begin or assign the takeoff of that item to others.

- Green Pushpin – Indicates the item is posted in the estimate recap sheet.

This 'Takeoff Column' is very useful, especially when working on large projects and more than one estimator is working on compiling the estimate. At a glance, it shows everyone's progress.

In the 'Takeoff Column,' you can include special items using the same color principle, such as getting the bid bond or filling out bidding documents. Don't overlook the last line: 'Visit the job before you close the estimate.

Quotes Column

- Red Pushpin – A red pushpin indicates the quotations needed for each item of work. Each pin in the same box indicates the number of quotes sought for that specific item.

- Yellow Pushpin – Each red pin replaced by a yellow pin indicates the number of quotes committed/in progress. For example, if you want three different quotations on lighting fixtures, insert three red pins when you first place the job on the board, one for each quote you seek in the lighting fixtures box. As you call your suppliers, replace one red pin with a yellow one for each committed quote. Every yellow pin indicates the calls you have made and the quotes you can expect to receive before the bid due date. If you want to be more specific, a supplier's I.D. on the yellow pins would tell you who has promised the quote.

- Green Pushpin – Indicates the number of quotations received for that specific item of work.

- Board overview – The advantages of having the bidding and estimating schedule board in The Estimating Room are many; it's a reminder for getting quotes and a tool for preventing duplicate phone calls as well as a visual record keeper for tracking down quotes and other items related to the estimate. With this board clearly visible, you can see at a glance what jobs to discuss when a vendor calls.

You can build a board similar to the sample shown below on a 24" x 16" corkboard or larger. The index cards pegged on the board are 2½" x 3" cards.

As mentioned earlier, you can also use the board for contracted jobs. You can double the size of the one you are building or just build two boards, one for estimating and one for active work.

BIDDING & ESTIMATING SCHEDULE

Legend

Pushpins Color Code	Takeoff	Quote
☞		
(R) = Red Pin	Included	Get a Quote
(Y) = Yellow Pin	Started	Promised
(G) = Green Pin	Done	Received

#	Systems Titles	#02-1231 Warehouse Due 11/22/00 14:00 EST — Takeoff	— Quote	#06-0222 City Hall Due 1/25/00 10 30 EST — Takeoff	— Quote	Job # — Takeoff	— Quote	Job # — Takeoff	— Quote
1	Bid Bond /Certified Check	(Y)		(R)					
2	Bidding Documents Review /Fill out			(R)					
	Site Work								
3	Excavation and Back-filling			(R)	(R) (R)				
4	Substation /Transformer								
5	Precast and Concrete Work			(R)					
6	Primary Feeders			(G)					
7	Branch Circuits			(R)	(R) (R) (Y)				
8	Light Poles and Fixtures			(R)					
	Work in Building								
9	Service	(G)		(R)					
10	Secondary Feeders	(G)		(Y)					
11	Switching Gear	(G)	(G) (G)	(G)					
12	Branch Circuits	(G)		(G)					
13	Lighting Fixtures	(G)	(G) (G) (G)	(G)	(R) (R) (G)				
14	Wiring Devices	(G)		(R)					
15	Equipment Connections	(G)		(R)					
16	Fire Alarm		(G) (Y) (Y)	(R)	(R) (G) (Y)				
17									
18	Jobsite Visit	(G)		(R)					

Form CDEE-700 © 2005 The Estimating Room™ Inc.

Figure 39: Bidding and Estimating Schedule Board

Security

Estimating room security is important for successful bidding. Many visitors can read documents upside down. In a busy environment, bidding documents, estimates, and other pertinent confidential documents abound on takeoff tables and desks.

The best method of securing your information is to keep another room set aside for vendors. The next best thing is to keep all your bidding material out of sight in closed folders.

In estimating, news can travel as fast as an unscrupulous vendor can make a phone call. Unbeknownst to vendors, many estimators use that media to disseminate unfavorable information to their competition.

Chapter 14

THE BID PRICE

PRESENTATION

Now that you've compiled the bid, it would be disastrous to lose the job simply due to a weak presentation. This is the hallmark of those who lack confidence in their estimates and consequently in their bid prices. They reflect this weakness all the way into their proposal and presentation. The fact that you've burned the midnight candle to produce the bid or you know the customer well does not exempt you from presenting a businesslike proposal.

A clear-cut proposal (see Chapter 4 - Basics of Contract, and Notes to Proposal/Contract Form) is the hallmark of a successful businessperson who radiates confidence, which is the foundation of a sound business relationship. Most of us would like to know, in the least number of words possible, what we are getting for our money. When certainty is lacking, so is confidence.

For example, 'The work will cost us between $2000 and $3000' is a sure loser to 'The work will cost us $2700 with the following exceptions,' complemented by a clear list of exceptions. Even if the first statement is well meant and the ultimate cost may be less than $2700, the second statement wins because it delivers certainty; it satisfies the customer's objective—knowing where he or she stands beforehand.

When people invite you to bid a job, they want firm prices. If you are not sure about the job and need to add some contingencies into your price, do it—regardless of consequences. When you show uncertainty, you are telling the customer that you don't really know what you are doing. While this is an innate syndrome with some contractors, it can occur sometimes with others. Every now and then, it creeps up on them just in time to kill a few good jobs. Review your pattern and if you are guilty of it, take corrective measures.

Pricing Structure

The hardest barrier to overcome is the psychological effect the less-than-a-dollar pricing structure has over the consumer. For instance, $1.99 is not $2.00, just as $99,999.99 is not $100,000.00. If we adopt this rule to bid pricing and change orders, it increases sales.

When bidding jobs, we want the price to deliver the most favorable impact and getting the most dollars without losing the job.

If the bid adds up to $10,050.25, make it $10,050—it's easier to read. Although you've made it easier to read, it still doesn't favor you. According to our rule, the number is $51 too high—an amount most contractors will shave off gladly just to get the job.

The bid price should be $9,999 or, if you feel funny about all the nines, $9,995. No matter how you look at it, psychologically, the revised price appears to be far cheaper than it really is and more appealing than $10,050.25

This rule breaks the barrier between $10,000 and $9,000, where the in-between numbers from 9,001 to 9,999 or 10,001 to 10,999 have little or no effect on initial price-impact.

For example, unless facing fierce competition, bidding the job at $9,250 or $9,450 or $9,750 or $9,999 or any other number in the $9,000 range will not take you out of the customer's $9,000 cost-perception. The $9,000 becomes the leading number and any other bid above its max, even by a dollar, will fall into the next plateau—the $10,000 cost-perception. Therefore, if you write the proposal with certainty and clarity, the odds will be in your favor.

One further point to ponder—once you have decided on the plateau for bidding the job, cutting the price further or staying at the bottom end of that plateau does not greatly enhance your chances of getting the job. In fact, you can speculate all the way down to nothing and still have no chance. Knowledge of the competition and of the customer is always your best tool.

However, it is worth noting that if you contract eight jobs per month and drop an average of $500 per job, you need not speculate about the effect this will have on your bottom line. Being a low bidder is what contracting is about, but being too low a bidder is usually an unnecessary burden.

Be attentive to this subtle rule. Corporations use it in their national campaigns to create a lower price perception while using the higher end of their pricing structure.

What Are the Odds?

Why should your bid be favored over another? The odds are what you make them. Conventional wisdom tells us price and perseverance lead the pack, with reputation in tow.

If you follow the development of a bid and support the customer diligently through the bidding process, then you are placing the odds in your favor. By support, we mean attending pre-construction meetings, having a genuine concern for the job, and making a timely submission of the quote.

You may submit to all prospective bidders, short of price, a proposal outlining our scope of work and its exceptions long before the bid date, giving them ample time to digest the bulk of your bid. At bid date, the only thing left for you to do is to call in your price. This method enforces strong ties.

Changing the Basic Price Structure

In this chapter, the subject of fine-tuning the bid price— for example, from one plateau to another—should not be confused with the fundamentals of estimating. Developing a pricing structure that keeps you competitive and profitable is the result of a painstaking estimating process. Once developed, it becomes your company's foremost resource and exempt from any tampering or speculation.

Compute bid prices by adding your markups to prime costs and not on hearsay numbers. Pursuing inflated bids destroys your ability to compete in a real world, thus keeping you out of the mainstream.

Chapter 15

THE CONTRACT

STANDARD CONTRACT FORMS

The multitude of standard contract forms used today makes it impractical—if not impossible—to list them all in a single chapter. While most were fair and impartial at one time, thanks to the imagination of the overprotective or unscrupulous customer, they have evolved into detrimental legal instruments.

Following is a collection of contract clauses you are likely to encounter. They are transcribed verbatim as they appeared in various executed contracts. We refer to each contract as abstract. Key words or phrases that adversely affect the spirit of the clause are printed in bold and followed by comments.

Abstract 'A'

Payments

> If the Owner does not pay the Contractor **for any reason**, including the Owner's insolvency, the Contractor has no obligation to pay the Subcontractor.

Comment: If the contractor does not carry out the work, should he be exonerated?

Change Orders

> Only changes authorized in writing and agreed to in amount prior to performance by the Contractor will be paid. It is agreed that if such change involves an order, directive, act or omission of the Owner, or any other third party, then the Subcontractor shall be limited in recovery to the amount received by the Contractor from said third party, **less its costs, mark-up, expenses, and attorney fees**.

Comment: It appears the general contractor wants to make his profit and more, but won't allow the sub to make his. In fact, he's going to charge the sub all expenses plus legal fees, even if he only chooses to consult his lawyer for whatever reason.

Completion

> Work will be completed on or before 00/00/00. **Time is of the essence.**

Comment: When you encounter the phrase 'Time is of the essence,' bells should ring in your head, for it has a legal significance. The customer is alerting you that the satisfactory completion and acceptance of the contract is contingent on the completion of the work in time. If you don't complete the work on time, then the contract has no existence or value.

Termination

(a) Should there be any work stoppage or slowdown caused by a strike, picketing, boycott, or any other voluntary or involuntary cessation, delay or interference of work by the Subcontractor, or the Subcontractor's suppliers, or any of them for any reason, and which, in the judgment of the Contractor *is causing or* **is likely to cause** delay in the progress of the work to be done by the Subcontractor, the Contractor shall have the right to declare this Agreement in default in accordance with the procedures outlined in Sub-Paragraph (c) of this Paragraph 4."

(b) All work under this subcontract shall conform to all applicable laws, rules, regulations and codes. Wherever the specifications or drawings conflict with such documents, **work shall be performed in compliance therewith at no extra cost.** Subcontractor further agrees that [it] shall comply with the Occupational Safety and Health Act of 1970 as amended and all rules, regulations, standards and orders issued there under. If any act or failure by the Subcontractor results in the assessment of a civil penalty against the Contractor, Subcontractor shall reimburse Contractor the amount paid by Contractor on demand by Contractor. **If, in the opinion of Contractor,** Subcontractor is in violation of any standard, rules, regulations, or code requirements of said OSHA Act, Contractor shall have the right to declare this Agreement in default in accordance with the procedures outlined in Sub-paragraph (c) of this Paragraph 4."

(c) In the event that Contractor **desires** to declare this Agreement in default for any reasons stated in Sub-Paragraph (a) or (b) above, or in the event that Subcontractor threatens to or fails in any manner to properly or timely perform any obligation on its part to be performed under this Agreement, Contractor shall have the right to declare this Agreement in default after giving the subcontractor twenty-four hours notice of the intention of the Contractor to claim such default. . . .

Comment: These clauses, which unfortunately are common, should be read very carefully, especially the bold typeface writing, before you decide how far you are willing to go.

Subcontractor Representation

The Subcontractor shall have a representative competent in the field of work covered under this Agreement on the job site at all times work under this Agreement is being performed. Said representative shall have full authority to act on Subcontractor's behalf and **shall not be changed without written consent of the Contractor**.

Subcontractor agrees to indemnify and hold Contractor harmless from any and all liability, claims and damages, including attorney fees, which any party might seek or claim against the Contractor, or which it may incur, and which directly or indirectly, actively or passively, was caused by Subcontractor or one in its employ, contract, or for whom the Subcontractor might be responsible. Subcontractor's liability and indemnification shall be valid whether or not the Contractor was directly or indirectly responsible for the damage or was otherwise liable to the third party.

Comment: Just read and meditate on this for future consumption.

Abstract 'B'

Contractor-Subcontractor Relationship

Contractor shall have the same rights and privileges as against the Subcontractor herein as the Owner in the General Contract has against the Contractor.

Subcontractor acknowledges that he has read the General Contract and all drawings and specifications, and is familiar therewith and agrees to comply with and perform all provisions thereof applicable to the Subcontractor.

The Subcontractor agrees to indemnify and hold harmless the Contractor and the Owner from and against any and all suits, claims, actions, losses, costs, penalties, and damages of whatever damage kind or nature, **including attorney's fees arising** out of, in connection with, or incident to the Subcontractor's performance of the subcontract work.

Comment: While this 'Hold Harmless' clause appears to be milder than the one in Abstract "A", it is very bold when you consider it is part of a $1500 contract—a steep liability to assume when the cost of attorney's fees for any claim could well be ten times your anticipated profit.

As subcontractor, you must keep these clauses in perspective with the contract amount and the anticipated profit.

How can you prevent anyone from suing the owner for a defective device you did not manufacture? How can you then indemnify the owner and the contractor from something that is specified by the owner and manufactured by someone you don't control? You make the final call.

In the event that any work fails to conform to the requirements of the contract, the same shall be corrected by the Subcontractor immediately upon its discovery; further, in the event that defects due to faulty materials or workmanship appear within one year from **useful occupancy,** the Subcontractor shall at his own expense correct the same and this applies to work done by his Subcontractor(s), his employees and those working by, through, or under him.

The work covered by this contract shall be commenced within three (3) days after written notice to the

Subcontractor by the Contractor, and completed within 60 days from date of commencement: **time being of the essence** of this contract. Loss of time on account of materials or work being condemned will not be considered as a cause for an extension of the contract time. In the event the Subcontractor fails to complete on time, he shall pay the Contractor by way of liquidating damages the sum of $300.00 per day for each and every day the work remains incomplete unless the cause for delay is caused by strikes not caused by Subcontractor, fire, governmental regulations, or acts of God, in which case the time for completion shall be extended for the actual time of such delay. Said liquidated damages shall be deducted as such from balance due the Subcontractor. Should damages exceed the sum due, or to become due, the Subcontractor, then in that event, shall be liable unto the Contractor for such difference.

Comment: Again, the penalty is $300 per day on a $1500 contract.

Should the Subcontractor fail to do or perform the work required hereunder, thereby in the **opinion** of the Contractor causing or threatening to cause delay in the general progress of the work, Contractor shall have the right to declare this Contract to be breached by the Subcontractor and cancel this Contract by notice to him in writing and to re-negotiate and re-execute contract(s) for the completion of the work required to be done under their Contract with such persons, firms, or corporations as shall in the **opinion** of the Contractor be necessary. In the event Contractor cancels the Contract, as hereinabove provided, it shall pay to the Subcontractor only for work completed to the date of the cancellation and the Subcontractor shall not be entitled to profits of any kind or character, anticipated or otherwise, or compensation for materials and labor unfurnished. Further, all losses, damages, and expenses, including attorney's fees in the prosecution or defense of any action or suit incurred by or resulting to Contractor on the above account shall be borne by and charged against Subcontractor, the Contractor may recover on said bond, and both Subcontractor and/or his surety agree to pay Contractor immediately such losses, damages, expenses, and attorney's fees.

Comment: The clause is contingent on the customer's opinion and not on accepted business practice.

The Contractor shall not be responsible or accountable for any losses or damages that shall or may happen to the Subcontractor's work, materials tools, or equipment employed during construction until **all work is completed and accepted by Owner.**

Comment: What does "until completed" mean? Would he then pay for damages?

The Subcontractor shall put himself in communication with other subcontractors whose work may affect his, so as to promote harmony of work. In the event Subcontractor, its agents, employees, or subcontractors commits or allows to be committed any act or acts, or does or allows to be done any thing(s) which tends to create or creates disharmony, a work slowdown, work stoppage, or strike, then and in that event **the Contractor shall have the absolute right to immediately cancel this Contract** and complete same in accordance with breach of contract procedure as set forth in Section 10.

All labor employed by the Subcontractor upon the job-site will be subject to the Contractor's approval and in the event the Contractor finds fault with any employee **for any reason whatsoever**, said employee shall immediately be removed from the job-site and replaced.

Comments: For any reason "whatsoever," meaning he can chase your workers off the job. Can you afford that?

The work shall be done subject to the final approval of Contractor and Architect, if any, and their decision as to the performance of the work in accordance with the drawings and specifications and the true construction and meaning of same shall be final.

Food for Thought Clauses

Payment Sample 1

The Contractor shall submit to the Owner's Representative, before the Owner's Representative shall be required to make any payments, an application for each payment and receipts or vouchers showing his payments for materials and labor and a schedule of the various parts, including quantities, and supported by such evidence as to its correctness as the Owner's Representative may require; and the Owner shall at all times be entitled to retain 10% of all moneys due and owing to the Contractor as part security for the faithful performance of this agreement, said 10% so withheld shall not be paid to the Contractor until 30 days after final acceptance of the work or materials **shall have been made by the owner.**

Comment: What do you do if the owner never accepts the work?

Payment Sample 2

Project is to be invoiced at completion of project. A notarized Waiver of Lien must be submitted with Subcontractor's invoice. Approved Change Orders are to be invoiced separate from the contract amount and a separate lien waive must be submitted. **No invoice will be processed for payment until a lien waiver** and certificate of insurance is received. Two payments will be issued: first for 90% of the contract amount and second for retention and approved Change Orders. Payment for properly submitted invoices will be made within five (5) days after Contractor's receipt of payment from Owner.

Comment: If you must release your rights to lien in order to be paid, then why bother with lien laws in the first place?

Working Conditions :

Working hours are 12AM to 12PM or as approved by the superintendent.

Comments: Under this clause, we will have a tough time collecting overtime or premium time.

Possession Prior Completion

Whenever it may be useful or necessary for the Contractor to do so, **the Contractor shall be permitted to occupy and/or use any portion of the work** which has been either partially or fully completed by the Subcontractor before final inspection and acceptance thereof by the Owner, but such use and/or occupation shall not relieve the Subcontractor of his guarantee of said work and materials nor of his obligation to make good at his own expense any defect in materials and/or workmanship which may occur or develop prior to Contractor's release from responsibility to the Owner. Provided, however, the Subcontractor shall not be responsible for the maintenance or such portion of the work as may be used and/or occupied by the Contractor, nor for any damage thereto that is due to or caused by the negligence of the Contractor during such period of use or occupancy.

Comment: The ceiling electrical rough is complete and the owner ships the wall units long before the ceiling grid is up. He invokes this clause and stores them on the floor beneath, occupying most of the working space. If the contractor asks us to install the lighting fixtures before the units are moved out of the way, which usually is the case, our crew will not be able to use rolling scaffolds, having to work off stepladders instead.

In this case, any claim for loss of productivity has no merit.

You can prevent this only if you are aware of its existence; in which case, have it struck it out or negotiate a fair compromise.

Owner's Furnished Materials

Subcontractor shall be responsible for unloading, storing, maintaining, and inventorying any Owner supplied material and equipment pertinent to his trade. Written notice shall be given to the Contractor within 24 hours of any shortages or damage of Owner supplied material and equipment. **Failure to notify Contractor of shortage or damage within 24 hours** constitutes acceptance by the Subcontractor and the Subcontractor will assume responsibility for shortage and damage.

Comment: The only problem with this clause is that most owner-supplied materials arrive well in advance of schedule and the contractor or the owner doesn't want any boxes opened until it is time to install the materials. Have this clause struck out or the '24-hour' deadline extended to installation time.

Extra Work Clauses :

If the Owner requests changes by altering, adding or deducting from the work to be performed under this contract, the Contractor shall give the Owner's Representative a written proposal outlining work to be performed, including cost of the labor, materials and equipment, which shall be approved by the Owner's Representative, in writing, before the Contractor proceeds to execute the work, and in any event the Contractor shall not be entitled to any claims of extras unless approved by Owner's Representative in writing. **Extra charges shall not be claimed by the Contractor due to weather conditions or job scheduling.**

Comments: The last sentence takes away the spirit of the clause, which is fair compensation for extra charges. If the Contractor chooses to schedule work in ways that impair productivity, should he compensate you?

Legal Advice

These are suggestions based on principles that most courts of law accept. For specific legal advice, always consult a lawyer.

Construction Drawings

When we receive a set of drawings, there is an implied guarantee from the owner that the drawings are correct and suitable to carry out the work. This is the reason we cannot hold the architect, the engineer, or other professionals liable—just the owner.

The only time we can hold the architect or other professionals liable is when the damage involves injuries to others or to property. Other losses such as money loss, contractors' loss of productivity, etc., are not bound to their performance.

Architects

Most architects are supervisory in nature and have limited control. Before we try to sue an architect, it is wise to know that in most cases recourse to professionals is a limited right and the 'economic loss rule' applies. The owner is liable for defective design.

Judges

Clarity of contract is the best prevention. Most judges are not construction people and construction disputes can be complex.

Beneficiary to the Contract

Find out if there is any beneficiary to the contract. There can be some nasty surprises if the beneficiary is not the person you thought you were dealing with.

Right to Stop Work

Negotiate this clause into your contract. 'If not paid within 7 days the subcontractor (you) has the right to stop work.' Then, if the owner breaks his promise, you can stop work without consequence.

Requisition

Contract breakdown for requisition (see Chapter 19) by virtue of their clarity supports breach of contract. In that format, the amount due is better defined. It gives the owner less excuse not to pay and eliminates ambiguity, which is the main cause of disputes.

Arbitration rather than Court

When reviewing a contract, look for this provision. Is it for general arbitration or just for a specific dispute?

The difference between court and arbitration is that the court will allow us to call anyone we want or that has anything to do with the case or dispute. In arbitration, the contract will specify how to dispute. If the contract calls for arbitration, you as the subcontractor will be subject to arbitration. Arbitration is final; we can appeal court decisions.

Termination and Specifics

When giving notices, you have to follow the contract procedures to the letter if you want to preserve your rights.

Other Contracts

Check what other contracts or documents are made part of the contract.

Final Payment

For the release of the final payment, negotiate how many punch lists and determine whose you will be subjected to.

Signatures

Photocopied or faxed signatures are okay until challenged.

Conclusion

Before you enter a contractual obligation, you must have a clear perspective about elements that can entrap the unwary contractor. The danger of running into dishonest dealers is there always.

A common flaw among unwary contractors is their belief in standard contract forms. Often, long double-sided pages of small print intimidate these contractors, leading them to accept any such form as 'standard'; and, so long as they are standard, the reasoning goes, it is okay to sign—so they do.

Word processors, laser printers, and fancy-bordered colored paper can produce the most standard-looking contracts money can buy.

To free yourselves from this intimidation, scan and dissect the contract by first highlighting the titles of those clauses that concern you most; then, review their content and underline your objections. When you are done, analyze your objections and decide whether you want to renegotiate or just walk away.

Never underestimate the responsibility and the risk you are taking when signing a contract. A clause that appears trivial or misplaced has no meaning until someone invokes it. Communicate with your super, estimator, secretary or anyone else involved in the outcome of the contract. A thought or suggestion from the unlikeliest people can change things for the better. If you have doubts, try to have such clauses crossed out, or at least take legal advice before you sign such an agreement.

The purpose of this chapter is not to paralyze you from signing contracts. On the contrary, it should encourage you to take jobs that you would otherwise walk away from due to misunderstanding the contract.

The intention is to give you the ammunition to negotiate sound and fair contracts.

In contracting, the number of good customers far outweighs the bad ones. It just happens that the bad ones are easier to reach for they are always on the lookout for new contractors, thus they appear to be greater in number. Our challenge is to find those good ones that are held tightly captive by the competition.

Chapter 16

NEGOTIATIONS

MEETING THE PROSPECTIVE CUSTOMER

We all long for the day to meet, negotiate, and sign the job up. However, negotiating the job goes beyond the legal aspects of the contract. The next step involves translating offers and acceptances into a fair and equitable agreement.

In life, we constantly have to negotiate for what we want. 'I'll give you this for that.' Most often, though, what we want comes with strings attached; that is, we must exchange things we already have for those things we want.

In contracting, we must sharpen our skills and know the relative value of what we want compared to what we are willing to pay or give up to receive it.

Before we enumerate the most common items a contractor should bargain for in negotiating a contract, let us analyze the reason why we are meeting with the customer first.

The most obvious reason is that both of us think we can deal with the other. In other words, that there will be a meeting of the minds on two of the three basics of contract: solicitation, offer, and acceptance.

The solicitation—invitation to bid—has been accepted by us. The offer—our bid price—is acceptable to the customer. The acceptance of the terms and conditions under which the work is to be carried out is open for negotiation—that's why we're meeting. To close the deal, each will have to give and take a few points.

Going to such a meeting unprepared is counterproductive, to say the least. To no one's surprise, what the customer wants most is a lower price and legal protection. In return, the customer is willing to compromise on the scope of work as well as on the terms and conditions.

This is an opportunity that comes only once in the life of the contract, and that time is before we sign it. Future modifications must be made through change orders, and with heavier price tags.

As astute contractors, we must stand ready to negotiate contracts without rehearsal. We master this skill by developing two mental lists: one for general conditions and one for the scope of work (detailed later in this chapter).

Each list should deal with items we are willing to trade off for a fair compensation and that the customer will most likely accept.

Assign a dollar value to each item and use it as a bargaining chip either to get what we want or to offset any cut in price. The value of each item determines its priority.

However, before we proceed with this concept, we need to ascertain that our price includes every item we are putting on the table or we'll be giving away moneys not allocated in the bid.

With some practice, you will be in control of all your bargaining chips and get something in return for every dollar you shave off. For more bargaining power, supplement the two lists that follow with the 'Estimate Pre-takeoff Checklist' of the job (see Chapter 10), which contains major bargaining chips.

General Conditions

We list these items because, generally, they favor the writer of the contract document—the customer—whose 'standard' contract form is designed to protect him against an array of circumstances. Unless we point out its lopsidedness, it will stay as written.

Staying within the spirit of negotiation, negotiate those items you feel will benefit you most toward your corner or at least toward center. You will be surprised how many items will fall into your corner just because you have made the request.

Method of Payment

Whatever payment schedule you work out is fine, as long as you don't burden your cash flow and as long as the balance due upon physical completion does not exceed 10% of the contract price.

Down Payment

Use your judgment and don't be bashful to ask for it, especially if you think the job warrants such a payment.

Retainer Reduction

Most contracts allow the 10% retainer to be reduced to 5% or less after the job is 50% complete. Have that stipulated in the contract.

Substitutions

There is no better time to have specified material or equipment substituted than at the negotiating table. Because such items can be high-priced, know the facts beforehand.

Special Equipment

A well thought-out presentation can pay large dividends here. Review Chapter 1 - Pitfalls of Contracting.

Limit the Change Order Amount

There are times when large change orders can adversely affect the job. For example, say you've signed a $40,000 contract to wire a commercial shell that you now wish you had not signed. The customer, in accordance with the terms of the contract, issues a change order to wire a tenant space on a time and material basis, which is worth $90,000 but you don't want to do it. The customer can hold you liable for breach of contract, thus jeopardizing the base contract.

To prevent this situation, especially in jobs where large change orders are probable, evaluate all possibilities and then, if necessary, have a clause added to the contract requiring change order amounts not to exceed say, 30% of the contract amount, giving you the right to refuse if they do.

No Back Charges without Notice

The practice of customers back charging contractors at the end of the job is both common and difficult to defend against, especially when legal fees larger than the amount due overshadow the prospect of collecting the final payment.

A fair safeguard is to add a clause similar to this: 'The customer shall notify the contractor of any impending Back Charges when they arise. Back Charges shall be treated as Change Orders.'

Completion Date

The electrician, in most jobs, is the first one in and the last one out. Mostly, our completion is dependent on others. If you can, stay away from fixed dates. They breed liquidating damages.

Premium Time

This is a very costly item if not clearly defined. In many cases, it can get out of control easily.

Surplus Material

In alteration work, it is good to know who owns surplus material. State it clearly; it is worthless until a salvage company makes an offer to your customer.

Scope of Work

Before the negotiations, know the cost of each of the following items, when applicable:

- Survey work: benchmarks and coordinates
- Concrete cutting and core boring
- Trenching, back-filling, and compacting
- Cutting and patching
- Garbage removal
- Fixture supports
- Lamp installation

- Fireproofing

- Hoisting and warehousing

- Maintenance of temporary light and power

Negotiating fair contracts is a challenge. People always respect a good negotiator, especially when he delivers on his promises. It is the basis for long-lasting relationships.

Chapter 17

PROTECTING THE JOB

SETTING THE STAGE

Because unscrupulous contracting is as detrimental to business as cancer is to society, we have to deal with it effectively. While we are most concerned with unscrupulous contracting, disputes can arise out of most business relationships.

We protect our interests better if we record pertinent events in a relationship in a chronological order right from the start. Attempting to trace events back when the relationship blows up into a dispute and everyone has gone home is almost impossible.

The ultimate resolution to a dispute takes place in a court of law. However, the most practical and most profitable course of action is to prevent it in the first place—that is the subject of this chapter.

We should always seek to avoid legal maneuvers or starting a war with our customers. When we adhere to good practices, we select and preserve items of contractual importance for our files. Should the need arise, we will have the one ounce of cure that can often settle disputes out of court.

DOCUMENTATION

To document the most pertinent information besides drawings, use a:

- Job Folder
- Diary
- Intelligence File

Job Folder

An efficient job folder is of six-section legal size, similar to the one for Estimating, with each section labeled as follows:

- Section 1 – Estimate/ Contract / Permits / Correspondence
- Section 2 – Contract Breakdown / Billing
- Section 3 – Pending Change Orders
- Section 4 – Approved Change Orders
- Section 5 – Pending Submittal – Letter of Transmittal only
  (Shop drawings and the like are filed as drawings)
- Section 6 – Approved Submittal – Letter of Transmittal only
  (Shop drawings and the like are filed as drawings)

Diary

An accurate diary constitutes the backbone of this procedure. On jobs with field offices, maintain the diary there.

In jobs where your labor force presence is periodic, maintain the diary in the main office and have the lead-persons report all events at the end of each working day.

Understand that field people tend to procrastinate on paperwork, and tomorrow, not to mention the day or week after, their recollection is not as sharp as it is today.

Standardize the diary to basic entries so the person reporting and the person taking the report have a consistent guideline to follow each day that is typical for all jobs.

Aside from its advantages for recordkeeping, a diary enables you to follow the progress of the job and recount each event with accuracy. It is an influential record in a court of law.

The most credible diaries are those maintained in inexpensive spiral-bound notebooks. Provide the report taker and the reporter with the following checklist, making all entries uniform for every day recorded. Another benefit is that the report taker can prompt the reporter's recollection by asking for answers under each topic.

- Date and day of the week

- Weather, including the day's temperature

- Workers' names and hours worked

- Items worked on

- Change orders and directives issued or received, if any

- Material received

- Inspections

- Visitors' names and times

- Rental equipment received or returned

Intelligence File

Most newcomers to this concept may frown at the thought of setting up an intelligence file, especially on business associates. However, many contractors wish they had done so long before they got hurt.

This legal size folder contains confidential information about the customer. The most common information is:

- Postal stamped envelopes in case there is a discrepancy between the date received and the date claimed in the contents of the envelope. Faxes and emails fall into this category.

- The invitation-to-bid transmittal along with the list of drawings they sent you. This is essential evidence in case they ask you to do work shown on drawings you didn't know existed.

- Photocopy of the customer's check. Suing deadbeats for your money is something you will eventually face. Having the customer's banking record handy facilitates that process.
  At times, getting a judgment is easier than getting a bank account number. Keep an eye on all the checks you receive; they can reveal information about the customer and what he is doing. For example, payer and bank name changes can signal a deceptive transition to an entity that has no legal ties to your

contract.

Checks that you receive from other parties on behalf of the customer can have a special legal significance or ramification.

Save copies of the different bank drafts you receive. Once you deposit them you lose possession of their valuable information.

- Credit reports, if any
- Customer personal data—home address, phone, etc. The customer or general contractor's superintendent's name, home address, phone number or at least his vehicle license plate number and model.

At times, honorable job superintendents are fired in the middle of the job, leaving behind an array of commitments the customer will rarely honor. When this occurs, such a superintendent would welcome the opportunity to defend his integrity, if only he were asked. However, industry practices and contractual obligations to his former employer may prevent him from freely coming forth on your behalf.

Having his address and phone number allows you to get in touch with him promptly, rather than tracking him down through costly and time-consuming legal procedures.

Keep a record of:

- Auto and truck license plate numbers

- S.S. and driver's license numbers

- Occupational and construction license numbers

- Other subcontractors' data

- Recording other subcontractors' names and phone numbers in this file helps you communicate with those who may be experiencing the same problems as you. Collectively, you may be able to help each other.

Many of these items may seem hard to get, but as you sharpen your skills and get more in tune with the industry, you will notice that most of this information at one time or another flows right through your office. Things such as permit applications, notices of commencement, occupational licenses and the like are abundant sources that you can access easily.

FILING NOTICES

As to Mechanic's Liens law, each locality has its own set of rules.

If you comply with their rules and file the appropriate notices in a timely fashion, you will retain valuable rights that can help you protect your investment and collect your money.

Therefore, it is advantageous to learn your local rules and follow their procedures to the letter. In most areas, this information is available from the local building and zoning department.

Usually, the procedure entails the filing of a Notice to Owner within a specific numbers of days from the day you started working. Then, if you are not paid, the filing of a subsequent Mechanic's Lien within a specific number of days from the last day you worked on the job.

In many areas, there are specialized companies that perform this kind of service for a nominal fee. This is the best option for most contractors (See Chapter 23 - Mechanic's Lien).

However, no matter who does the legwork, it is imperative that you file all notices on time. For those of you who feel you may be offending your customers, The 'Notice to Owner' procedure is not offensive to those customers who intend to pay; in fact, it is accepted for what it is—notice of your intentions to protect your interests under law.

OTHER FORMS OF PREVENTION

Unscrupulous customers, like predators, crave wounded prey. Anyone who is or appears wounded becomes fair game. This is why the ploy of claiming poverty often backfires.

The moral here is not to resort to unnecessary claims when demanding what is rightfully yours. In fact, under no circumstances should you invoke extraordinary claims. When asking for moneys due you, there are two fundamental things you should never say or do. The first is to never explain 'why' you need the money and the second is never to say, 'I will sue you' or use similar phrases.

Avoid deadlines; the customer is well aware of your rights. You can do as you please anytime. Saying, 'I will sue you' is music to the ears of some customers.

Telling the customers your financial problems does more harm than good, even when it appears to have been received well.

No matter how you look at it, when you claim hurt you are wounded prey. If the customer is unscrupulous, you just walked into his den, and if he's not, this may be the last job you do for him. Being wounded—or just playing the part—is a losing proposition either way.

A good safeguard is being financially healthy, even if it only appears that way to the customer. If the customer senses that you have the financial strength to wait it out, your chances of collecting are greater than by using any other ploy.

SECTION VII

CONTRACT ADMINISTRATION

Chapter 18 Contract Management

Job Compliance

Chapter 19 Requisition for Payment

The Requisition

Chapter 18

CONTRACT MANAGEMENT

JOB COMPLIANCE

If we use sound managerial procedures from the acceptance of a sales lead to the signing of a contract, then all subsequent tasks such as contract management and payment requisitions will be straightforward, for they are simply a continuation of the original paperwork. Otherwise, these managerial tasks can be complex and inefficient.

For example, if we set up an estimating folder with data from our sales lead and compile the bid data from the estimating folder, we then have the basis for an efficient job folder that is ready and easy to manage, like the one described in Chapter 17.

This method, besides using information that is otherwise wasted, allows us to begin the contract administration promptly and mobilize the job smoothly. At this stage in the job, any procrastination breeds only unwanted and costly delays.

The following guidelines cover the most common items of work. For specifics, read the contract documents, paying special attention to deadlines and format requisites. Some customers accept payment requisitions and releases of lien only on specific forms.

Things to Do

Permit Applications

Comply with the local Building and Zoning requirements by completing all necessary applications for electrical permit(s) in good time.

Insurance Certificates

Have your insurance agent send certificates of workmen's compensation and general liability to the customer. Ascertain they comply with the specified limits covering the correct party. Also, check for other insurance requirements such as automobile and other special coverage.

Notice to Owner

Protect your Mechanic's Lien rights. Whenever applicable, comply with the state requirements. Don't overlook this important procedure.

Utility Companies

Notify or apply to those utility companies such as electric, telephone, cable, security, and the like that provide services for the contracted work.

Submittals

Shop Drawings and Samples

Follow the chain of command and submit, within the specified number of days, the correct number of copies to the architect. Do not release materials that are subject to the architect's approval until you have obtained such approval.

When you receive the approval, pay close attention to the 'Stamp of Approval.' Some shop drawings are 'Approved as Noted,' which means their approval is conditional on the architect's notations.

Once you are satisfied, transmit a copy to your vendor and release the material subject to his compliance with the architect's 'Stamp of approval."

Substitutions

Whenever a vendor wants to substitute a specified item and you are willing to accept the substitution, make these submissions early—preferably before you start the job— for the processing time can be extensive.

Payment Schedules

When required, submit the contract breakdown soon after you sign the contract (see Chapter 19).

Special Documentation

Due to various federal acts, similar jobs may be subject to different rules, especially when built in different localities. Whenever you are involved with such jobs, be sure to maintain and file the necessary reports promptly. These include Weekly Payroll Reports, OSHA, Environmental, Affirmative Action Reports, and the like. Your failure to comply can give rise to a breach of contract.

Change Orders

Your skills in detecting, writing, and reporting changes can affect the job profit. To validate changes effectively, apply guidelines similar to those accompanying the change order form shown in Chapter 5 as well as considering the following:

How Many Change Orders?

To expedite approval, completion, and collection, we write as many change orders as it takes, i.e. one change order per event.

Typically, customers and designers are reluctant to accept change orders, especially those that add costs to the job. Therefore, in an attempt to prevent or minimize the cost of change orders, special terms and conditions restricting markups, accounting methods, and the like are constantly updated, making the process more complex.

Writing a change order for each event and keeping unrelated subjects separate is fundamental. Besides facilitating better recordkeeping and expediting the overall process, it aids the customer-contractor relationship.

Conversely, when we compile several change orders into one, often well after their completion and with weak or non-existent backup documentation, the customer (as well as the contractor) loses perspective on the work, creating unnecessary and costly disputes.

Successful contracting depends upon understanding the business we are in and the position we hold as subcontractors in relation to the general contractor, the owner, the architect, and anyone else who has anything to say or do with the approval and collection of our money.

Prevent situations that may hinder the smooth completion of the job, the collection of your money, and the preservation of your name.

The following is a list of items that most often fuel such disputes. The comments point out some preventive measures that might help you in that endeavor:

Pricing

Most customers resent unexpected price increases. This resentment worsens with each added dollar and each passing day that we fail to report the change. Understanding and dealing with this psychological effect is essential to contracting.

Submit a lump sum $10,000 change order at the tail end of a $30,000 contract and you will jeopardize collection by turning a good customer into an instant enemy.

However, submit ten $999 change orders promptly, perform the work only after the customer approves each change order, and you will be paid cheerfully.

Clarity

Writing a change order for each item of work allows us to describe the scope of work clearly as well as other specifics that might otherwise be confusing and misleading.

When describing a change, never confuse clarity with brevity. At times you may have to write a lengthy explanation to give the reader a clear perspective of the work involved and to justify the cost.

For example:

> Furnish and install 2-250 A circuit breaker enclosures in meter room.

While brief, the description is very different from the following:

> Scope of Work - Rework the meter room as directed by the electrical inspector and as laid out by the architect to protect two existing feeders, each serving power panels A and B.
> Remove two existing 2-½" RGC each with 4-#3/0 cu from the existing 400 A 3 phase main disconnect.

Install one new 8" x 8" x 36" wire-way inclusive of wire and splicing kits.
Install two new 400A frame enclosures each with 250 A three-pole circuit breakers.
Rework and connect the 2-½" conduits into new disconnects.

The above example is an abstract of a true dispute where the second explanation caused the architect to change his position and approve the change order as originally priced.

Paper Trail

Individual change orders make it easy to track down specifics such as who ordered and approved a specific piece of work or who worked on it and for how long.

Authorized Signature

Usually, authorized field personnel can sign and approve change orders up to a certain amount. When you submit a change order in excess of that amount, you will introduce into the process people remote from the field, thus delaying what otherwise would be a routine procedure.

Getting the Change Order Approved

When a change order is a composite of different changes, the entire change order can become disputed if only one element is disputed. It can be held back until that one item is settled.

Keep each change order independent from the other so they can be approved on their own merit and quickly.

Change Orders Profit

Smaller change orders offer better profit opportunities.

Record the Change Order onto As-built Drawings

Record all changes to the scope of the work in the as-built drawings set. Individual change orders facilitate this task. For easy reference, you can label each change on the as-build drawings with its change order number.

A Final Note on Change Orders

When a change to the scope of work arises, adopt the individual change order method described above. Saving a few pennies worth of paper and a few minutes of writing is not worth the consequences. To have a smooth relationship with the customer, write as many change orders as necessary—and write them with clarity.

Back Charges

Back charges should be treated as change orders and should be subjected to the same procedure.

Chapter 19

REQUISITIONS FOR PAYMENT

THE REQUISITION

In contrast to change orders and contract basics, compiling requisitions for payment should be fun. We see and feel the return on our investment firsthand, giving a sense of accomplishment similar to that of a farmer harvesting his fields. All that we have planted is now coming to fruition. How much it will yield, however, is dependent on how well we have worked our fields (see Chapter 20).

To compile an effective requisition requires five basic elements:

- Schedule of Values (Contract breakdown)

- Change Orders Schedule of Values

- Percentages of Work Completed

- Statement of Account

- Invoice

Schedule of Values

A schedule of value is the contract amount broken down into as many pay items as you find necessary to facilitate accounting and alleviate cash flow concerns. Once you complete this task, you get the customer to approve it with the signing of the contract or before submitting the first requisition. The most effective way of generating a schedule of values is to do it while you estimate the job (see Chapter 10 - Estimate Recap Sheet).

The sample form that follows is based on the sample job used in this book. We choose Requisition No. 2 for it reflects previous, present, and total to date accounting for the basic contract as well as for the change orders.

Figure 40, Contract Schedule of Values; Figure 41, Change Order Schedule of Values; and Figure 42, Statement of Account collectively entail the makeup of a periodic requisition for payment.

John Doe Electric Requisition No. 2 Page 1 of 3

SCHEDULE OF VALUES

Job Name: Sample job 1, Warehouse **Job #**02-1231

Requisition Period: (x) Monthly () Weekly () Other: Date: 02/28/20--

Prepared by: MS Submitted to: Owner Period Ending: 02/28/20--

	Items of Work	Base Contract Amount	Last Period %	Amount	This Period %	Amount	Total To Date %	Amount
1	Mobilization/DJE	2,077.00	30	623.10	20	415.40	50	1,038.50
9	Service	4,579.00	20	915.80	60	2,747.40	80	3,663.20
10	Secondary feeder	5,296.00	30	1,588.80	50	2,648.00	80	4,236.80
11a	Switching gear on site	4,044.00	60	2,426.40	20	808.80	80	3,235.20
11b	Sw-gear back boxes installed	300.00			80	240.00	80	240.00
11c	Switching gear final	278.00						
12a	Branch circuit conduits	2,094.00	20	418.80	40	837.60	60	1,256.40
12b	Branch circuits wire	1,500.00			30	450.00	30	450.00
13a	Lighting fixtures on site	4,520.00						
13b	Lighting fixtures installed	960.00						
14	Wiring devices	598.00						
15	Equipment connections	649.00			20	129.80	20	129.80
20	Fire alarm	3,876.00						

(This and other forms may be downloaded online at www.theestimatingroom.com)

Base Contract Total	30,771.00		5,972.90		8,277.00	46	14,249.40
(From other side) Change Orders Total	985.00		125.00		465.00	60	590.00
Revised Contract Amount	31,756.00		6,097.90		8,742.00	47	14,839.40

Note: Unit prices shown on this form are for billing purposes only. They don't represent the actual cost of the item and as such, they should not be used as base-cost for adding or deleting work from the contract.

Form EA-201-1-rev05 ©2005 The Estimating Room™ Inc.

Figure 40: Schedule of Values

John Doe Electric

Requisition No. 2   Page 2 of 3

CHANGE ORDERS SCHEDULE OF VALUES

Job Name: Sample job 1, Warehouse   Job #02-1231

Requisition Period: (x) Monthly   ( ) Weekly   ( ) Other: Date: 2/28/20__

Prepared by: MS   Submitted to: Owner   Period Ending: 2/28/20__

	Change Orders Status					Percentage and Value of Work Earned					
	Contractor's Data		GC	Add/Deduct		Last Period		This Period		To Date	
#	Title	Date	Approval	Days	Amount	%	Amount	%	Amount	%	Amount
1	Add interior lights	1/8/__	1/12__	0.50	450.00			40	180.00	40	180.00
2	Wire irrigation pump	1/16/__	verbal	0.75	625.00	20	125.00	60	375.00	80	500.00
3	Relocate power devices	1/22/__	pending	0.50	(350.00)						
4	Delete 2 outlets (Credit)	1/23/__	1/23/__		-90.00			100	-90.00	100	-90.00
5											
6											
7											
8											
9											
10											
11											
12											
13											
14											
15											
16											
17											
18											
19											
20											
	Total (Post to Requisition Form)			1.25	985.00		125.00		465.00	60	590.00

Form EA-201-2-rev05 ©2005 The Estimating Room™ Inc.

Figure 41: Change Orders Schedule of Values

John Doe Electric Co.
Licensed Electrical Contractor E-12345

123 Main St, Our City, USA, 12345,   Fax (123) 456-7890

(123) 555-6400

Requisition No. 2   Page 3 of 3

Date: 2/28/20__

Period Ending: 2/28/20__

Customer

Contact: John Smith

Name: XYZ Development

Add: 3456 Washington Street

City/St/Zip: Any City   USA   12345

Phones: Hm: Wk:

Beeper: Fax:

Job

Job Name: Sample job 1, Warehouse

Contract No. 02-1231   Dated: 10/15/__

Add:

Owner: XYZ Development

Job Phone:

Documentation

Attached   (X)   Number of sheets including this sheet: 3   Not applicable ( )   Will Follow No Later Than   / /

Contract Recap

Basic Contract Amount	$ 30,771.00	Prepared by: MS
Approved Change Orders	$ 985.00	Approved by: LS
Back Charges	$	Date Faxed: 2/28/____
Other (+/-)	$	Invoice No: 00234
Revised Contract Amount	$ 31,756.00	Payment Due Date: 3/10/____

Requisitions Recap

	Last Period	This Period	Total To Date
Amount Earned	$ 6,097.90	$ 8,742.00	$ 14,839.90
Less 10% Retainer	$ 609.79	$ 874.20	$ 1,483.99
Net Amount Earned	$ 5,488.11	$ 7,867.80	$ 13,355.91
Less Payments Received	$ 5,000.00	$	$ 5,000.00
Other	$	$	$
Amount Due	$ 488.11	$ 7,867.80	$ 8,355.91

Submitted by: _____

Signature: _____Title_____

Form EA-220-Rev05 ©1994 The Estimating Room™ Inc.

Figure 42: Statement of Account

Note to Requisition

When you submit the Schedule of Values for approval, insert the word "Initial" right after the checkbox '( )Others,' and mark it off. This one-time submittal reflects your contract breakdown. You should not submit requisitions for payment until the owner/customer first approves 'your' schedule of values.

Notes to Contract Schedule of Values

Items of Work

In this column, you break down the scope of work into as many items as necessary—one per line, each referred as system.

For example, you may choose a short list such as rough, trim, and final, or a detailed list such as service, feeders, branch circuits, lighting fixtures, low voltage and other systems as shown in the sample form.

In preparing a requisition for payment, the objective is to minimize cash outlay and to facilitate collection. To achieve this goal, bill special equipment independently from its installation. In some jobs, you may bill conduits installation independently from wires. In the example, switching-gear is subdivided into three pay-line items— 11a, 11b, and 11c.

In larger jobs, you can further subdivide pay-line items to allow, for instance, for final testing or any other specialty the job calls for.

System 11a, 'Switching gear on site,' allows you to request payment when the switching gear is on site—i.e. no installation necessary. In the schedule of values, 'Last Period' is reported at 60%; 'This Period' at 20%; and

'Total to Date' at 80%. You can bill the remaining 20% when the shipment is complete.

Pay-line items 11b and 11c allow you to bill for the installation independently of the material on site.

Another example of how subdivided systems help you to collect the money you have earned is Pay-line item 12, 'Branch Circuits.'

If you set up branch circuits—conduit and wire—all under one system, if not all the wires are pulled, because of the empty conduits and undone splices, then at walkthrough time the percentage requested becomes a disputable item—and not in your favor.

However, if you subdivide the pay-line item 12 into 12a and 12b as shown, the conduit installation becomes indisputably 100% complete. The value of the wire pulled, independent from the conduit, becomes much easier to assess—and with less effect on your cash flow.

Whenever you set up a schedule of values without subdividing easy-to-dispute items, you risk losing control over cash flow and leaving it to the discretion of the customer.

The more you single out an item of work, the easier it is to assess its progress and value earned. When an item is completed and not paid in full when due, then you can prove the owner in a breach of contract dispute thanks to the clarity of your contract breakdown.

Contract Amount

The total dollar value of all the pay-lines in a lump-sum contract is equal to its prime cost plus a percentage for profit and overhead. For our sample job (see the Bid Recap Sheet Chapter 11, Figure 33), that percentage is averaged as follows:

Sale Price ($30,771) − Prime Cost ($22,528) ÷Prime
Cost ($22,528) x 100 =36.59%

When compiling a schedule of values, use this equation to
convert systems prime cost into a contract pay-lines
amount.

In the example, to compute schedule of values add
36.59% to each system's Prime Cost in Column (g) of the
Estimate Recap Sheet.

Then, adjust the pay-line amount in the 'Contract
Amount' column to jibe its total with the contracted
amount of $30,771.

To facilitate this task, we added the difference between
the two totals to Mobilization (DJE), which is not part of
the Estimate Recap Sheet markups, and is adjusted from
$1,675 to $2,077.

Getting your schedule of values laid out and approved
before you start working is essential for a good cash flow.

Change Orders Schedule of Values

The form shown in Figure 41 is vital to the requisition set.
With each submission, it provides the customer with a
status report of pending and approved change orders and
an efficient system of recordkeeping that supports most
systems—manual or computerized.

Change Orders Status

The change orders 'Status' section deals with yours and
the customer's data. It shows each change order number,
the date originated, and the extensions of time and
amount.

The section 'Values Earned,' shows percentages and amounts earned for each change order.

Approvals

Most likely, your contract states that no extra work shall be done unless first approved in writing. This means get your change orders signed, sealed, and delivered—including dollar amount, extension of time (when applicable), method of payment, and a clear scope of work, before you do extra work, or you may not be paid—no exceptions.

Short of that, unless you have established a different procedure, working on pending or verbal change orders give rise to breach of contract situations, not to mention financial exposure.

In dealing with change orders, pay special attention to the word 'order.' A change has to be ordered and it is not official until the customer signs and issues such an order.

Statement of Account

The requisition cover sheet or Statement of Account is a recapitulation of the contract.

The Statement of Account shown in Figure 42, thanks to its 'Requisitions Recap' section, is your best insurance against oversights and accounting errors.

Assuming a pay line item has been omitted, under- or over-billed, or that a previous requisition has been underpaid, the error will sooner or later show up here, making it impossible for it to balance.

In computing this section, it is good practice to crosscheck your calculations. For example, each line's 'Last Period' plus 'This Period' has to equal the 'Total to Date' amount. If any one line doesn't add up, an error exists in the requisition. Crosscheck each line and column. If need be, also crosscheck the contract and change orders schedules until you find the error and the recap sheet balances as it should.

Invoicing the Requisition

The next step is to write an invoice for the amount due 'This Period.' The description can be a simple line, 'Partial Billing, Requisition No. 2. Amount due this requisition $7,867.80.' If there are other balances due, don't include them in the invoice. If need be, attach copies of previous open invoices or a statement reflecting all monies due.

The amount invoiced with each requisition is the Amount shown in the 'This Period' column and not the 'Total to Date' or 'Last Period.'

The amount due shown in the 'Last Period' column is the sum of any unpaid balances on any previous requisitions. The amount due shown in the 'Total to Date' column is the sum of any balances due plus the present requisition.

Standard Requisition Forms

In preparing requisitions, it is important to consider your familiarity with the forms you are using. The more frequently a system is used, the more efficient people become, thus minimizing errors. This is the very reason many owners impose their own forms. While this rule makes the customer's life easier, it leaves you with different paperwork for different customers, which increases your workload and can often reduce your paperwork to a shambles.

To prepare efficient requisitions, standardize your own forms for compiling Schedule of Values, Change Orders Status, Requisitions, and Statement of Accounts and use them as the official paperwork for supporting or filling out the customer's requisition forms when required.

SECTION VIII

DOING THE JOB

Chapter 20

MOBILIZING THE JOB

IMPLEMENTATION

In the Schedule of Values, mobilization represents Direct Job Expenses. However, in this chapter, it represents elements that can make the difference between profit and loss.

We start the job by implementing the paperwork (see Chapter 18 - Contract Management), followed by the physical mobilization of tools, equipment, and workforce. Any slip-up in this process sets a weak foundation on which to build a profitable job.

Before we proceed with mobilization, it is important to note that in contracting, the job is our main source of income. Therefore, to make the most profit out of each job we must use proven methods while paying special attention to their implementation.

For example, if we take two contractors with opposite approaches to mobilization and we ask each to do the same job, in the end one will lose out and one will profit.

This section—Doing the Job—deals with the details of profit making. The implementation of the following elements, as described in this chapter, forms the cornerstone of contracting:

- Job Layout

- Labor

- Material

- Tools

Job Layout

The drawing board is where you set the stage for delivering profitable jobs. Here is where your skills, experience, and knowledge of the various building codes will serve you well.

The drawing board is the place to dissect the scope of work to fit your scope of operation, as you decide what crew will be most productive for each segment of the job.

On the drawing board you also aim to discover and correct errors and oversights before they cost you money. You are entitled to compensation for errors committed by others, but if errors are due to unread or ambiguous notes and you fail to uncover those errors, then the outcome can be costly.

To prevent this, scrutinize the contract documents and your estimate before the work starts. Lay them out and tear them apart, if need be, for in the end you will optimize your profit.

Limitations of Contracted Items

To lay out a job, first define the contracted work clearly and then reflect your interpretation on an easy-to-follow form called 'Limitations of Contract.' By doing this, you:

- Formally communicate to the field the latest revisions in a concise format, rather than revealing copies of your contract or other confidential documents

- Prevent costly errors by pointing out special materials and pay-line items

- Reduce the number of productive labor-hours spent in the field interpreting plans and specifications, often resulting in interpretations that are more costly then yours.

- Increase productivity

This method, besides closing an expensive communication gap between administration and production, supplies the lead-person with a worthwhile tool to help him expedite work decisively and effectively.

In the form that follows, in the 'Work Description' column, use the standard systems list as shown or describe items of concern freely.

This form is used for an entire job or part thereof; a change order, a work order, or day-work. Its clear and concise directives do away with guesswork in the field.

LIMITATIONS OF CONTRACT

Project: Sample job 1, Warehouse		Job No: 02-1231	
Prepared by: **MS**	Date:	Sheet # 1 of 1	
(x) Full Contract	( ) Partial: Syst. # _____ Title _____	C.O. #____	

Code: R = Remove   F = Furnish   I = Install   C = Connect

System No.	Work Description — When applicable, note the type and size of material	Electrical Contractor				Others			
		R	F	I	C	R	F	I	C
9	Service: Trench and back-fill for lateral 36" deep						X		
10	Secondary Feeders: Substitute EMT conduit with PVC schedule 40. Use straps and back-straps every 36". Add #6 green wire		X	X	X	X			
12	Branch Circuits: EMT conduit Use compression fittings in warehouse and die cast setscrew in office area. Pull #12 a green wire in all conduits. Mud-rings 5/8" deep		X	X					
13	Lighting Fixture and Lamps		X				X		
14	Devices: Toggle switches and convenient outlets 20A 125V Plates: in office area ivory and in warehouse area brown		X	X					
15	Equipment Connections: Cords and caps for plug-in Hard-wired connections Motor starters and disconnects		X		X		X X X	X X	
17	Telephone: Complete system including electrical permit					X	X	X	X
20	Fire Alarm: Empty conduits and boxes Equipment, wiring, and testing Manuals, certifications, training		X	X			X X	X	X
	(This form and others maybe downloaded online at www.theestimatingroom.com)								

Form EF-501-rev05 ©2005 The Estimating Room™ Inc.

Figure 43: Limitations of Contract

Redesigning the Work

To begin, consider the project-to-be as an abstract. At this stage, you have the opportunity to rearrange an array of randomly drawn lines and differently shaped symbols called electrical work in a way that can earn you substantial savings.

While most contractors brag about the insights this opportunity offers, only few take proper advantage of it. Either from lack of confidence in their redesigning skills or due to lack of time, they tend to rely more on their field personnel's foresight. The result, quite often, is on the fly changes that bruise the bottom line.

A good redesign saves money without affecting the scope of work or violating electrical codes. Because you are carrying out the work as per the agreement, the redesign will generate savings of which you are the only beneficiary. This rule is supported by the familiar clause found in most contract documents: 'The job shall be constructed in a workmanlike manner, and all conduit-runs shall be installed parallel and perpendicular to the building lines and not as shown on the drawings.'

Before we address this subject further, consider the following:

- The only time you can save substantially on something is when that something exists to the fullest. In your case, that something is the total labor and material that you will spend doing the job. Be decisive. The sooner you start, the more there is to save on. To start the process at the tail end of a job is futile, for what is left is not enough to make a difference. Redesigning is a well of opportunities—dip in while it is full.

- Don't rely on others to do the saving for you. Delegating this task to others is no different from relying on others to guide you through a dark alley. If time is your concern, make a distinction between designing and drawing. You can quickly draw ideas on a brown paper bag if you have to, then later have it drafted neatly.

Who is best suited for laying and redesigning a job—the office or the field? We can settle this question simply. It's both.

There is no better time for a team to pull together than in the redesigning stages of a job. Each member can contribute his or her expertise to the common cause of the company.

Since the field determines the actual scope of work, it will always be scrutinizing the office. However, the office is where it all starts and ultimately ends.

In redesigning a job, the most common items to consider are:

- Bench marks and survey
- Exposed or slab work
- Trenching and back-filling
- Concrete cutting and core boring
- Feeder layout and conduit fill
- Circuit layout and conduit fill
- Conduit routing and fastening methods
- Device locations and heights
- Lighting fixture pre-assembling

- Lighting fixture support methods

- Control wiring and diagrams

Due to the remote and, most often, liberal design criteria, these items are fountains of opportunity for the electrical contractor. Take advantage of your skills and the National Electrical Code's rules and rework all you can in your favor. Simple research of a code rule or a pay-line definition can help you boost your profit considerably.

To boost that profit further, nothing stimulates your field into a higher productive mode than your genuine concern and support for detail work.

This support, when given with authority through job layouts and the like, prevents confusion and unnecessary downtime. It also spreads a feeling of confidence throughout the organization. Along with your field directives, a sketch or detailed drawing of how the work should be done will be time very well spent.

Every minute spent on the drawing board increases the job productivity many times over. Set the groundwork to hold on to your anticipated profits. Apply all the skills you can muster and lay out each item of work in the office, for in them you may find your only profit.

Labor

In an attempt to make greater profits, some contractors attempt to make a $14-per-hour worker produce like a $24-per-hour electrician. However, if they would assemble trained workers into specialized crews and pay them at the same $24 dollars per hour or less and if a qualified person leads each crew, the increased productivity will far exceed the increased labor cost.

To keep estimated and actual labor cost in balance, it is necessary to keep the estimated labor rate in the proper prospective, for that is what got you the job in the first place.

In other words, you cannot estimate a job at an average labor-rate of $17 per hour, pay $20 and expect to make a profit. Nor will the job be profitable if the productivity is lower than estimated.

Labor cost is the product of labor-rate times labor-hours. The only way you can maintain or increase profit is to maintain or reduce labor costs. This is done by maintaining or decreasing labor-rate or labor-hours or both. Because job profit is bound to this equation and to your expertise, it is up to you to police it.

A sure way to kill productivity is to send a disorganized crew to a job for a couple of hours at a time just for show—a practice some shops are afflicted with when they are overwhelmed with cheap work.

In accepting a job, you have undertaken the responsibility of completing it on time and in a businesslike manner. As a responsible contractor, you must monitor the job's progress and schedule your workforce and materials in ways that suit you best.

The following two lists outline the advantages and disadvantages of this:

Advantages

- On schedule with job progress

- Control over the makeup of productive crews

- Confident workforce

- High productivity

- Use workforce from other jobs

- No overtime

- Good business relationship

Disadvantages
- Behind schedule

- Disorganized workforce

- Low morale and confused workforce

- Low productivity

- Forced into overtime without compensation

- Poor business relationship

- Responsible for liquidated damages

If your shop is 'slow,' your best hedge against falling into a vulnerable position on a new job is to stay ahead of schedule by doing all that can be done at the start of the job. However, if your shop is busy making money on other jobs, then your best bet is to blitz the job as soon as possible, even if it means hiring extra help.

Procrastination will lead you into disruption—not only of the new job, but of other jobs as well. Ultimately, the best policy is not to take more work than you can handle in the first place.

Labor comes with moods, time clocks, and a variety of personal problems that we have to learn to respect and to deal with. Because labor responds to moods and attitudes, it is easy to control. However, when you disregard a worker's need for acceptance and recognition, you lay the groundwork for an explosive situation.

In addition to coordinating work experience and expertise when making up crews, you must also consider the human factor. Put two veteran electricians—for that matter, any two workers—who don't get along in the same crew, and no matter how hard they try, no experience and expertise will prevent them from disrupting that crew. On the other hand, place the same two fellows in different crews and each will increase his crew's productivity.

The workforce is most productive when the relationships are simple and workers are part of the team. Telling a worker he did a good job when he did not just to make him feel part of the team or not to hurt his feelings is deceptive not only to the team but to the worker as well.

However, taking the worker aside and telling him what is expected of him and assisting him through the reasoning process is a productive approach that is good for all parties concerned.

When you least expect it, a bombshell can explode, putting you back to square one and looking for 'good' key workers. The best way to prevent this kind of explosion is not to lay the groundwork for it in the first place. Talk straight and never promise what you are unable or unwilling to deliver. For more on this subject and on job control, see Chapter 21.

Material

The third item on our list is perhaps the simplest to deal with—material. However, when quantities bought are greater than quantities installed, the subject becomes just as significant as the others.

The materials with which you should be most concerned are the basic conduit and wire and related fittings, fasteners, boxes, plates and terminating devices that generally abound in flea markets and garage sales.

To minimize surpluses, you need to understand the purpose of estimated and field takeoff quantities and the differences between them.

In estimating, we compile quantities to generate an estimated bill of material that is in keeping with takeoff practices and bidding documents. These quantities are not necessarily the quantities the job will require. The difference between the two quantities does not only include the cost of material but its relative labor-hours as well, also a factor for accurate labor cost control.

Therefore, it is unwise for the office to order materials using the estimate takeoff sheets without the field or installers' input. In fact, we should keep these takeoff sheets off limits to the buyer. Quantities should be revised at the redesigning stage and obtained from the field.

Buying more material than is needed is a poor investment, as a surplus rarely pays back more than 20 cents on the dollar. Moreover, it invites theft.

Buying excessive quantities for the sake of saving a few points is, in most cases, not as economical as it seems. Buying a box of 12 or a box of 100 of a special item when we only need a few just because the counterman says it is cheaper is like listening to an ordinary worker telling us what stock to buy on Wall Street. When a good opportunity comes along, be sure to include handling and warehousing costs plus pilferage in your savings computation.

Another item to consider along with material is cash flow. To keep your cash flow fluid, feed a job periodically and only purchase the materials needed for that period. When possible, synchronize material releases, including special equipment, with payment schedules and suppliers' billing cycles.

For example, receiving material on the 28th of the month when your requisitions cut-off date is the 25th delays payment for that material for 60 days. However, if you arrange its delivery three days earlier, you will be paid within 30 days and meet your suppliers' due date.

Good material management is essential for keeping job costs down, progress smooth, and cash flow fluid.

Tools

'Give me a point of leverage and I'll raise the world,' was said long ago. Tools have been on man's mind since the beginning of time. Those who acquire them will prosper, for they can accomplish otherwise impossible tasks in record time.

As much as we long for high productivity, safety has to take priority. A safety policy for distributing power tools to workers who are qualified to operate them safely will achieve a suitably high level of productivity.

With that commitment to safety, you can explore the benefits of tooling up a job properly.

Wire pullers, pipe benders, rolling scaffolds, hydraulic lifters, trenchers, electric saws, crimping tools, knock out, stud punches, cable cutters, circuit tracers, amp meters, ladders, and the like are the arsenal of your workers. The role these tools play in doing the job you will most often take for granted until one tool breaks down or goes missing from the toolbox.

The tools to do a job, like labor and materials, need to be laid out in advance. Is it more economical to buy or rent? To wait until the last second to repair the electric drill that broke down a few months ago can prove costly today. Often, all the willingness and momentum gained by your work force can be lost because of a wrong-sized tool or a dull drill bit. Now the tool no longer aids but hinders, for it frustrates rather than helps workers.

To emphasize further the importance of tools, remember that estimated labor rates, including those we've developed, are based on readily available materials and tools at the job site and not at a supply house or a rental place. The very job you are doing is based on that principle also.

Your job profit is dependent on your ability to supply and coordinate labor, material, and tools in such a manner that each enhances the performance of the others, thus reducing, or at least maintaining, anticipated costs.

Properly mobilizing a job is essential to its outcome. The material covered in this chapter is applicable to most jobs, large and small alike. Failing to apply these principles will eventually bruise your profit.

Chapter 21

CONTROLLING THE JOB

CONTROL DEFINED

By controlling, we don't mean dominating but managing the budget of the job. This chapter deals with measures an electrical contractor should take to protect the cost of estimated labor and material.

To achieve this feat we rely on three systems:

- Labor Cost Control

- Material Cost Control

- Job Environment Control

Labor Cost

Labor is the most difficult cost to control. However, when managed properly, it is the only element that can be motivated into a higher productive mode. Therefore, you should employ methods that help that endeavor.

For labor to produce to your expectations, you must let labor know what those expectations are. Provide the lead-persons with tools that help unleash their knowledge and desire to produce. Given the opportunity, people will always strive to excel.

One way of doing this is to set out a roadmap so the lead-persons know where you are coming from and where you want to go. Clearly delegate to them the responsibility for getting you all to your destination safely. In this equation, 'where you are coming from' is your estimated labor-hours. 'Where you intend to go' is the allocated labor-hours, with 'your destination' being the actual labor-hours spent getting there.

The simplest method of conveying estimated, allocated, and actual costs to a lead-person is in labor-hours for labor and quantities for materials. To expect the lead-person to work with an array of computed ledger sheets reflecting extended labor and material costs is an imposition that overburdens him with paperwork unnecessarily.

Providing the lead-persons with a concise and tangible method for tracking estimated and allocated labor-hours versus actual labor-hours spent communicates your expectations in a clear-cut manner.

Most lead-persons welcome this kind of roadmap for managing the job. In doing this, you show positive leadership which spreads throughout the workforce—a domino effect, if you will. You instill pride and responsibility in everyone involved. In giving the lead-persons that roadmap, you are giving them a sense of purpose and direction that stays with them 24 hours a day, 7 days a week.

Set up this roadmap openly and jointly with the lead-person, for it establishes good foundations for a productive relationship. For example, the 'Labor Master Control Sheet' below shows the breakdown of the estimated hours. For the first time, you and the lead-person should jointly evaluate and lay out crew types and agree on the number of hours needed to do the work. Then, insert the agreed crew types and hours in the 'Allocated Hours' column.

To overlook this process is to lose the only opportunity you have to set a realistic labor goal endorsed by the lead-person before you start the job. Most lead-persons take pride in their commitments.

A control system, when laid out as shown below, also assists the lead-person in pinpointing the production rate of his crews, thus averting setbacks.

For example, to monitor the installation of a 1000 ft. 4" EMT run for which you have allocated 100 labor-hours and a two-member crew, the lead-person can compare the production output to the expected rate at any time during the installation—in this case two lengths per crew-hour. If at the end of the second day he does not see 320 ft. of conduit in place, he knows that his production is off-target.

You can set similar production references for any item of work listed in the job breakdown. Anyone can monitor it, including the installation crewmembers.

Labor Incentive

If you wish to set up an incentive program for the lead-persons or for the entire work force, this method is realistic and motivating. It's realistic because it deals with tangible numbers that everyone can relate to and rewards a lead-person for what he was hired to do—manage labor. It is motivating because the outcome is independent of the company's overall performance. In other words, regardless of bottom line, the lead-person is assured a flat rate bonus for every hour he saves.

To keep the flame burning, you can allow the lead-person to draw a monthly percentage of his anticipated bonus using the overall job production rate as a guideline. To avoid misunderstandings, agree to a per-hour rate before you implement the incentive program.

The hourly rate for computing bonuses is not to be confused with the average labor rate used to estimate the job. The objective is to simplify bookkeeping by establishing a dollar rate you will pay for each hour saved. For example, you may agree to pay an arbitrary rate between $3 and $14 per hour or you many base it on a percentage such as 25%, 50% or more of the job's average labor rate. Whichever method you use, keep in mind that the program is based on labor-hours saved and not on percentage of profit.

To compute the bonus earned, neither the lead-person nor you have to examine unrelated and confidential documents, nor has the lead-person to wonder whether he will be credited the full amount earned, for he will be doing the recording.

Labor Control Design

Besides enhancing productivity, a labor control system gives the lead-person an indispensable tool to manage and report field-generated information.

Chief among these reports are percentages of items of work or change orders completed in one concise report— the 'Weekly Labor Report Sheet.'

This form, along with the 'Daily Assignment & Time Card Sheet,' provides detailed information for weekly payroll, payment requisitions, labor productivity, job cost analyses, or any other report the data can support.

The Labor Control System consists of:

- Labor – Master Control Sheet

- Daily Assignment & Time Card

- Weekly Labor Progress Report

Before you read the explanatory notes to these forms (Figures 44, 45, and 46), you should photocopy them for quick reference.

LABOR MASTER CONTROL SHEET

Base Contract

Job Name: Sample job 1, Warehouse   Job #02-1231   Ending Period: 2/28/__

Lead-Person: Allan Smith | Incentive Rate: $7.50   Per Hour | Approved by: LS | Date: 2/28/__

(1)	(2)	(3)		(4)		(5)		(6)	(7)	(8)	(9)
		Estimate		Production					Incentive		
		Estimate		Allocated		Actual Used		% of work done	Earned hours	Paid hours	Balance hours
No	Item of Work	Crew type	Hours	Crew type	Hours	Hours	%				
1	Mobilization (DJE)										
9	Service	II	49.30	II	36.00	28.00	57	80			
10	Secondary Feeders	II	68.68	II	54.00	40.00	58	80			
11a	Switch-gear on site	II	2.00	IV	1.00	1.00	50	80			
11b	Switch-gear install rough	II	11.35	II	16.00	13.00	81	80			
11c	Switch-gear install final	II	4.00	II	2.00						
12a	Branch circuits conduit	II	59.82	II	48.00	28.00	47	60			
12b	Branch circuits wire	II	25.92	II	16.00	5.00	19	30			
13a	Lighting fixtures on site	IV	6.00	IV	3.00						
13b	Lighting fixture installation	IV	48.50	IV	42.00						
14	Wiring devices	IV	14.03	IV	16.00						
!5	Equipment connections	II	4.87	II	6.00	2.00	33	20			
20	Fire alarm	II	57.44	II	40.00						

(This and other forms may be downloaded online at www.theestimatingroom.com)

Base Contract Total		351.91		280.00		123.00	35	46			
(From Other Side) C.O. Total		11.00		11.00		6.00	54	60			
Revised Contract Total		362.91		291.00		129.00	36	47			

Form EC-401-rev05 ©2005 The Estimating Room™ Inc.

Figure 44: Labor Master Control Sheet - Base Contract

LABOR MASTER CONTROL SHEET

Change Orders

Sheet #   1 of _____

Job Name: Sample job 1, Warehouse   Job #*02-1231*   Ending Period: *2/28/__*

Lead-Person: Allan Smith | Incentive Rate: *$7.50* Per Hour | Approved by: LS | Date: 2/28/20___

		Estimate		Production				Incentive		
(1)	(2)	(3)		(4)	(5)		(6)	(7)	(8)	(9)
		C.O. Status		Allocated	Actual Used		% of			
No	Change Orders	Pending	Approved	Crew type	Hours	Hours	%	work done	Earned hours	Paid hours	Balance hours
1	Add interior lights		3.00	IV	3.00	1.00	33	40			
2	Wire irrigation pump		10.00	IV	10.00	7.00	70	80			
3	Relocate power devices	6.00									
4	Delete 2 outlets		-2.00	IV	-2.00	-2.00	100	100			

(Full size template of this form   may be downloaded online at www.theestimatingroom.com)

	Total this sheet (No. 1)	6.00	11.00		11.00	6.00	54	60			
	Total from sheet No. 2										
	(Transfer to other side) Grand Total	6.00	11.00		11.00	6.00	54	60			

Form EC-401-rev05 © 2005 The Estimating Room™ Inc.

Figure 45: Labor Master Control Sheet - Change Orders

Notes to Labor Master Control Sheet

These two forms will allow you to compile data pertinent to the production of a job and its incentive program.

To save time and avert errors, create a template for the job you intend to control. Each template should carry constant data such as the information for the top three lines, exclusive of the date, and Columns 1, 2, 3, and 4.

Any time information becomes constant, modify the template accordingly and make new worksheets. Constant information is an item that is 100% complete.

The form has two sides: Base Contract and Change Orders. Both sides are divided into three sections: Estimate, Production, and Incentive.

Estimate Section - Base Contract

- Columns 1 & 2 – No. and Item of Work
  Item of work and system numbers should be consistent throughout the paperwork. The example shows data taken from our 'Sample Job 1, Warehouse Requisition No. 2.' See the Estimate Recap Sheet in Chapter 11.

- Column No. 3 – Estimate Crew - Hours
  This column reflects the crew types and the estimated hours taken for the job.

Estimate Section - Change Orders

- Sheet No. __ of __
  If the number of change orders exceeds the number of lines, attach another sheet to the Master Control Sheet, identify it as Sheet No. 2, then follow the instructions at the bottom of Sheet No. 1.

- Column No. 1
  Insert change orders number here, regardless

whether it is pending or approved.

- Column No. 2
  Change orders title or a brief description.

- Column No. 3
  This column keeps the change orders status up to date. If a change order is canceled, do not delete it from this list; instead, insert a code letter such as "R" for Rejected or "H" for Hold in the Pending column.
  A change order submission, especially the one generated here, is a report and a notice to the customer on how you will change things, why, and how much it will cost. This method assigns a sequential number to each change order.

- Pending and Approved Columns
  Insert the labor-hours of a pending or approved change order in its respective column.

Production Section
- Column No. 4 - Allocated Crew – Hours
  Insert the allocated labor-hours and crew type in this column.

  Insert in this column the labor-hours that the lead-person and you agreed for completing each item of work.

  If the allocated hours for a specific item turn out higher than the estimate, remember that the lead-person did not estimate the job. Any suggestion to the contrary is counter-productive. At this stage, the best you can do is to analyze all possibilities and agree to the number of hours that the lead-person needs to complete that item of work, and hope the total will average into a safe number.

- Column No. 5 - Actual Used Hours - %
Insert in this column the hours shown in Column No. 8 of the Weekly Labor Progress Report (see Figure 47). You need not update the Master Control Sheet. You may update it at requisition time or any other time by inserting data from the latest Weekly Progress Report.

  To compute the % for this column, divide the Actual-hours Used by the Allocated-hours times 100.

- Column No. 6 - Work Done - %
Insert in this column the lead-person reported hours in Column No. 10 of the Weekly Labor Progress Report.
Because these percentages are the basis for payment requisition, the incentive program, and monitoring job productivity, they should be field-verified.

Incentive Section
- Column No. 7 - Earned Hours
Earned hours are the number of hours the lead-person or crew has earned under the incentive program. These hours are the difference between allocated and actual hours. They become fixed when the item is 100% complete.

- Columns 8 & 9 - Paid & Balance Hours
These columns track hours paid as bonuses and balances.

Red Flags

Figures 44 and 45 show shaded lines. These are red flags indicating that the allocated hours for items 11b and 14 are greater than the estimated hours. Use a highlighter to monitor those items out of danger until they are 100% complete.

Analysis – The interpretation of the bottom line has a lot to do with perception of the Labor Control System. Inserting and tracking hours just for the sake of knowing has a certain value; however, being able to see red flags in time and recover while you still have the chance makes the system invaluable.

Using and understanding these numbers is the key to successful contracting, for they are the foundations for your next estimate.

Weekly Labor Progress Report

The Basic Contract and Change Orders reports are printed on both sides of a sheet. The data is generated from the Daily Assignment sheet (Figure 48). The totals are transferred to the Master Control Sheets.

WEEKLY LABOR-PROGRESS REPORT

Base Contract

Job Name: | Job # | Week-ending:

Lead-person | Checked and Posted by: | Date:

(1)	(2) Items of work	(3) Crew	(4) Allocated hours	(5) As of last report	(6) This report							(7) Total hours	(8) To date (5 + 7)	(9) Hours to complete (4 - 8)	(10) % Work completed to date
					S	M	T	W	T	F	S				
	(This and other forms may be downloaded online at www.theestimatingroom.com)														
	Base contract total														
	(From Other Side)	C.O. total													
	Revised contract total														

Form EC-405-rev05 ©2005 The Estimating Room™ Inc.

Figure 46: Weekly Labor-Progress Report - Base Contract

WEEKLY LABOR-PROGRESS REPORT																
Approved Change Orders														Sheet #		of
Job Name:						Job #						Week-ending:				
Lead-person					Checked and Posted by:							Date:				

				Actual Hours Used										Balances		
(1)	(2)	(3)	(4)	(5)	(6)								(7)	(8)	(9)	(10)
				As of	This report										Hours to	% Work
			Allocated	last	S	M	T	W	T	F	S	Total		To date	complete	complete d
	Items of work	Crew	hours	report								hours	(5 + 7)	(4 - 8)	to date
	(Full size form may be downloaded online at www.theestimatingroom com)															
Total this sheet (No. 1)																
Total from sheet No. 2																
(Transfer to other side) G total																

Form EC-405-rev05 ©2005 The Estimating Room™ Inc.

Figure 47: Weekly Labor-Progress Report - Change Orders

- Columns 1, 2, 3 & 4 - Items of Work
  Synchronize this information with the Master
  Control sheets. Once the information is inserted on
  both sides of the sheet, use it as a template to
  generate subsequent worksheets.

- Column No. 5 - As Of Last Report

In the first report, the value of this column is zero. In all subsequent reports, its value is that of Column No. 8 of the previous report.

- Column No. 6 - This Report
  The information for this column is generated from your Daily Assignment Sheets—one for every day worked on that job. For better recordkeeping, insert the day's date in the blank spaces below the weekday.

- Column No. 10 - % Work Completed
  This is the lead-person's estimate of the percentage of the work completed, up to and including this report. These percentages are essential to complete the payment requisitions and to monitor the incentive program. Verify them at least once per billing period.

Change Orders Side

As with all forms presented in this book, the change orders side of these forms can be extended into as many sheets as needed.

Daily Assignment & Labor Report

This form, besides helping the lead-person assign work every day, is the basis for the labor control system and an integral part of the diary, for it offers detailed information on who worked where and when. In essence, it supports both systems—Labor Control and Diary.

The Change Orders side of this form is not shown because it works on the same principles as for all other forms.

Template

Once you insert the constant data as listed below, keep the original as a template to generate all subsequent worksheets.

- Crew I.D.

- The crew type used in the Master Control and Weekly Progress Reports should jibe to this line. That is what you and the lead-person planned and agreed to at the start of the job. Any deviation can disrupt that plan.

- Shop, Job, Single System
  The third line down from the top gives three choices:

- Shop - Use this as a daily schedule for your entire shop, in which case the items of work are the jobs or work orders and the crew I.D. may be the truck number.

- Job - Indicates that the form is used in conjunction with the Labor Control System, listing the original contract breakdown as items of work as laid out in the Master Control Sheets (see Figure 44).

- Single System - In large projects, it is advantageous to subdivide individual systems. In such a case, use a sheet for each system, or a sheet for each crew.

The function of this sheet is to track the hours spent completing an item of work or an entire job.

DAILY ASSIGNMENT SHEET–BASE CONTRACT

Job Name:	Job #	Lead-person:
( )Shop ( )Job ( )Single System:	Day of Week:	Date:

Base Contract		Daily Production Schedule	Hours total
Items of work	Crew Type→	Worker's Name or I.D. #	
(This and other forms may be downloaded online at www.theestimatingroom.com)			
This sheet total			
(From other side) C.O. Total			
Today's grand total			

Form EC-401-1-rev05 © 2005 The Estimating Room™ Inc.

Figure 48: Daily Assignment & Labor Report

Material Cost

As with other costs, it is necessary to manage material or it can overrun our budget. A common mistake is delegating the entire management responsibility to the job lead-person. While he can and should control quantities ordered and installed, the buyer is responsible for controlling the costs.

Buying power is a direct function of your relationship with your vendors. If you discount the bills, you not only get few extra points off their face value but also the preferred customer's discount, not to mention the extra consideration with special equipment quotes at bid time.

Here, we present a material cost control that, like the one for labor, keeps the job running smoothly and profitably.

The first managerial objective is to open the channels of communication between your buyer and your field lead-person, for their interaction is essential to the success of the job. For example, the lead-person makes up a bill of material for a specific phase of work and the buyer, after the acquisition, tells the lead-person what was bought from whom and when to expect it.

The Bill of Material shown in Figure 49 is used for that purpose. It allows the user to submit a list of materials and tools for acquisition and the buyer to place orders with the various suppliers. As the buyer places the orders, he records the supplier's name, purchase order number, delivery date and price and returns a copy to the field for follow-up.

BILL OF MATERIAL

Job Name: Sample job 1, Warehouse   Job #02-1231

(x)Job   ( )Single System: Prepared by: MS   Date: 1/20/20__

Purchase Order #	Ordered By	Source Code	Vendor	Contact Person	Contact Person Phone #
2345-021231	John	A	All Star Electric Supply	Mark	(123) 444-5555
2355-021231	John	B	Sunset Electric	Adams	(123) 356-4545
2358-021231	Joe	C	ABC Rental	Jim	(123) 345-2234
		D			

Codes: **A** through**D** = Suppliers—Alternate sources **S** = Shop **J**= Job Site **O**= Other job sites **X**= Purchase order

	Quantities			Source Code	Materials/Tools	Delivery Date	Quoted	
	Ordered	Recv'd	Bk-order				Price	Per
1	1200			A	½" EMT	1/24	14.75	C
2	380			A	¾" EMT	1/24	24.10	C
3	100			S	½" EMT Couplings DC SS			
4	36			S	¾" EMT Couplings DC SS			
5	8			A	1" EMT Couplings DC SS	1/24	0.74	E
6	128			S	½" EMT Connectors DC SS			
7	6			S	¾" EMT Connectors DC SS			
8	2			A	1" EMT Connectors DC SS	1/24	0.68	E
9	125			S	½" EMT Straps			
10	250			B	½" Caddy Clips	1/28	0.40	E
11	250			B	¾" Caddy Clips	1/28	0.41	E
12	18			B	¾" EMT Beam Camps	1/28	0.41	E
13	2			A	½" to ¾" J.B. Combo	1/24	1.45	E
14	10			B	4" Square Box w/cover	1/28	1.60	E
15	34			B	4" Round Box w/cover	1/28	1.10	E
16	1			O	2 Section -6ft Rolling scaffold	Pick-up		
17	1			C	Rotating Hammer	1/26	16.00	Day
18	2			X	Back boxes for Panels A & B	1/26/	Fixed	
19								
20								

Form EC-430-rev05 ©2005 The Estimating Room™ Inc.

Figure 49: Bill of Material

Material Control System

Material control, like labor, offers its own managerial challenges. The best approach for averting the inevitable overbuying of standard material is to scrutinize the invoices as they come in from the vendor. If necessary, insist on daily billing.

The second best approach is to discard the estimated quantities used for the bid and generate a bill of materials that reflects actual job conditions and the latest revisions. As discussed earlier in Re-designing the Work, using these estimated quantities to buy material defies cost control.

The following form is part of the Cost Control System. It facilitates tracking of estimated versus used material.

MATERIAL COST CONTROL

Job Name: _____ Job # _____ Prepared by: _____ Date: _____ Period Ending / /

Items of Work	ESTIMATED COST — MATERIAL			AS OF LAST REPORT			ACTUAL PRIME COST — THIS REPORT			TOTAL TO DATE		
	Standard	Quote	Total	Standard	Quote	Total	Standard	Quote	Total	Standard	Quote	Total
Base Contract Total Material Cost:												
(From Other Side) C.O. Material Cost:												
Grand Total Material Cost:												

(This and other forms may be downloaded online at www.theestimatingroom.com)

Form EC-440-1-rev05 ©2005 The Estimating Room™ Inc.

Figure 50: Material Cost Control

Job Environment Control

Whether using a computerized system or a manual system similar to the one presented here, you must begin the process at the start of the job if you want to control the cost of the job effectively. To re-emphasize this point, this passage from Redesigning the Work (Chapter 20):

> The only time you can save substantially on something is when that something exists to the fullest. In your case, that something is the total labor and materials that you will spend doing the job. Be decisive. The sooner you start, the more there is to save on. To start the process at the tail end of a job is futile, for what is left is not enough to make a difference. Redesigning is a well of opportunities—dip in while it is full.

The job cost control system—in fact, all cost control systems presented in this book—can be converted into electronic spreadsheets. If you are versed in electronic spreadsheets, take full advantage of these systems presented here and convert them into your favored computer program. The following form (Figure 51) is a prime candidate for such a conversion.

| | JOB COST CONTROL | | | | | | | | | | | | |

Figure 51: Job Cost Control

Jobs Cost Control Form

The form is divided into two sections, 'Estimated' and 'Actual Cost.' The front side reflects the Basic Contract and the back Change Orders.

Labor is reported in dollar amounts rather than in hours, and material includes DJE. Mark-ups and anticipated profits are not posted here. This sheet deals in prime costs only.

- ( ) A Job ( ) All Jobs
  If using this form for a single job, list the standard 'Items of Work.' If using it for several jobs, then list one job per line.
  When using this form for all jobs, summarize each job on its own form before listing it here. The 'All Jobs' sheet gives us an overview of the overall performance of the company, for it reflects all active jobs.

- Estimate Cost
  These are your estimated costs from the 'Estimate Recap Sheet.'

- Actual Prime Cost
  The labor cost reported here is your gross payroll cost plus labor burden. You may choose to multiply used labor-hours times by your labor rate.

Conclusion to Job Cost Controls

The most effective cost controls are those that are well maintained by the principal parties. When implementing a new system, remember that all participants are people, and like most people they will oppose anything that threatens the way they are accustomed to doing things.

The cost control system outlined in this chapter is designed to enroll many participants, thus enhancing each person's contribution. For example, the lead-person manages labor, the buyer manages material, accounting converts both reports into the job cost control sheets, and you, with all the facts in hand, make periodic field inspections to verify the progress of the job and the company overall performance.

In other words, while everyone is contributing something of value, the system provides you with a reliable check and balance method.

If you choose to adopt a control system, you must educate your people and police them until they become dependent on that system. As stated earlier, any new system is bound to face opposition, with people citing all sorts of reasons for abandoning or simplifying it.

Job Environment Tips

Job Environment Control—as opposed to Job Cost Control, which is based on hard figures—offers another way of controlling the outcome of a job. It is based on what experience teaches you.

- Alteration Work
  Never allow others to do work under your permit; for example, the property owner who wants his handyman to install a couple of exits and emergency lights down the hall. Besides being legally responsible for the work, you are giving up work that belongs to you or some other licensed contractor.

- Time and Material Work
  Don't allow the customer's workforce to assist you. Aside from the issues of legality and responsibility,

in T&M work, the use of outside workers cuts into your profit (unless they go through your payroll and billing system).

- Field Wiring of Equipment and Machinery.
  Before you start field wiring equipment or machinery, make sure the customer supplies you with workable and complete electrical diagrams. Analyze them well and keep copies for your files.

  Your work is to wire electrical apparatus according to sets of workable drawings and not to lay out and design logistic diagrams.

  Too many contractors cross their line of responsibility by misunderstanding this relationship. What begins as goodwill usually ends up in disputes and disappointments.

- When to Start the Job
  Don't depend on others to tell you when the job is ready. You are the electrical contractor, not the customer. Relying on his judgment as to when you should start a certain phase of work is no different from listening to him when he arbitrarily calls for more workers.

  From beginning to end and in between job phases, always visit the job and look for opportunities to advance the work in the most economical way. For example, calling you to rough in a bunch of home runs under a slab that was to remain and is now removed will be the last thing on your customer's mind.

- Shop Drawings
Never install material that is not approved for that use. Before you install any material, make sure the shop drawings have been approved for the intended use and jibe with your scope of work.

Shop drawings that are 'Approved as Noted' often have subtle changes that escape many reviewers. For example, a stamped blue arrow pointing to a specific detail may be lost in a color background or washed out in duplications.

One of the most frequent blunders is voltage change in lighting fixtures and equipment, making a shambles of an entire installation, especially when you have combined power and lighting circuits in the same raceways.

- Photographing the Work
Most contractors fail to take full advantage of photographs. Make it a special task.

Recording your work before walls or ceilings are closed may be the only witness to what was there before someone damaged, covered, or relocated your work. It also determines the amount of work completed at a given time and may substantiate or defend future claims or could be used as promotional material for your company.

An example of photographs saving a contractor a bundle occurred when a customer wanted to back charge the electrical contractor for redoing a hard ceiling. When the ceiling was completed it became apparent that most of the 400 hi-hats were misaligned. However, photographs taken of the hi-hats in place before the ceiling was installed clearly showed each row in perfect alignment. Apparently, the mechanical contractor who had accessed the ceiling in several areas to rework ductwork and equipment was the culprit. Thanks to photographs, the electrical contractor proved his case and charged the customer for the extra work.

- Diary
  A diary is like a photograph of the day's events documented in words. Like photographs, a good diary can prove invaluable in a dispute.

- Pay-line
  That fine line between getting paid and not getting paid for the work you do is called pay-line. Don't forget that all you are paid for is what you do. Doing work that is not part of your contract is a loss. Pay special attention and maintain a contract overview of the scope of work.

- Extra Work
  Anything beyond your pay-line is extra work for which you must get paid. Confirm the proper documentation and payment method before commencing any extra work. The emphasis here is on sticking to the terms of your contract.

- Change Orders
  Proceeding with an unauthorized change can make you liable for the change itself. Only written directives called 'Change Orders,' which are issued by the customer, can modify the scope of work.

Doing the job can be fun; in fact, if you apply good working principles and use qualified labor, it is not only fun but also profitable. Moreover, profit is the reason you are in business.

Chapter 22

INSPECTION

THE ELECTRICAL INSPECTOR

The electrical inspector represents the people in his community. His job is to ensure that the work he inspects is done in accordance with applicable codes and ordinances. He also checks for hazardous conditions that can affect the present or future occupants of the premises.

More than ever, municipalities are targeted for accountability regarding faulty installations under the permits they grant. Therefore, they are demanding very thorough inspections from their inspectors that at times may appear intimidating and unwarranted.

Municipalities are mandated to protect themselves against inevitable lawsuits, and in doing so, they set up extraordinary procedures. However, the frustration that some contractors experience in dealing with municipalities most often stems from non-compliance with local ordinances or lack of recordkeeping and follow-up. This is not to say that some municipal employees don't take their mandate to extremes at times.

Conventionally, contractors use a filing method where permit applications and related documents are scattered in job and general folders. To stay in touch with the ever-increasing regulations and demand for recordkeeping from the various municipalities, the contractor who seeks relief can no longer afford this method.

To cope with this trend we must offset the disparity between ourselves and City Hall. When we need accurate information, we don't want to have to spend days searching completed job folders hoping to find what we need.

Most often, a well-kept 'Municipal Folder' and an 'Inspection Log Book' similar to those shown below will do the job.

Municipal Folder

Use a six-section legal-size folder for each municipality. It is worth the investment. When dealing with several municipalities, allocate an entire filing drawer and label it 'Inspections.'

Label each section of each folder as follows:

- Section 1 – Copies of all applicable licenses required to register and to pull permits.

- Section 2 – Copies of insurance certificates sent.

- Section 3 – Active permits issued by that municipality. If needed, make a copy for your job file.

- Section 4 – Inspection reports such as rejections and approvals. If needed, make a copy for your job file.

- Section 5 – General correspondence and yearly

renewal applications.

- Section 6 – Blank permit applications.

Inspection Log Book

An important part of contracting is to keep a record of all inspections. The following 'Inspections Log Sheet' is set up for a three-ring binder to form an inspection logbook.

Read the explanatory notes following the form.

INSPECTIONS LOG SHEET

Code for P/F Column: P = Passed; F = Failed
(Write with erasable material)

Job Info	Municipal Info	Cell #	Temp Date	P/F	Slab Date	P/F	Walls Date	P/F	Ceilings Date	P/F	Service Date	P/F	Final Date	P/F
Job #	Permit #	1												
Name:	Inspector:	2												
Addr	City:	3												
Phone:	Phone.	4												
Job #	Permit #	1												
Name:	Inspector:	2												
Addr:	City:	3												
Phone:	Phone:	4												
Job #	Permit #	1												
Name:	Inspector:	2												
Addr:	City:	3												
Phone:	Phone:	4												
Job #	Permit #	1												
Name:	Inspector:	2												
Addr:	City:	3												
Phone:	Phone	4												

(This and other forms may be downloaded on line at www.theestimatingroom.com)

Job Records in this sheet are from Job # _____ to Job # _____

Check this box when all the jobs in this sheet are completed ( )   Sheet No. _____

Form EG-150-rev05   ©2005 The Estimating Room™ Inc

Figure 53: Inspections Log Sheet

Notes to Inspections Log Sheet

- Erasable Writing
  Because the information is bound to change often, you should use a pencil or something else erasable.

- Job Info & Municipal Info
  These fields provide the basic information needed to call in an inspection.

- Types of Inspections
  The description for each type of inspection—Temp, Slab, Walls, Ceilings, Service, and Final—can be expanded or modified to fit our needs.

- Call #
  Each type of inspection can be called in four different times.

- P/F
  P = Passed inspection; F = Failed inspection.

Job Inspection

Visual impact, as discussed in the Marketing section, goes a long way. Presenting a job for inspection means marketing your mechanical skills to those who are in a position to pass or fail your work.

The visual impact your work creates tells the trained eye—and most often the layperson—the type of work you do.

For example, if you install a horizontal ½" PVC conduit to a pool's time-clock with sufficient straps and back straps to keep it from sagging and to allow the rainwater and the dirt to seep through between the wall and the conduit, and ½" liquid-tight to the pump with two mineral-lack straps instead of one, the visual impact we create builds the inspector's confidence in your work and in you as a conscientious mechanic.

On the other hand, if you present the same job with straps at three foot intervals with no back straps and one mineral-lack strap, even though you may pass the electrical code, you may not pass the unwritten workmanlike-manner code. The work sends the message of a marginal installation at best, prompting an inspector to scrutinize all other work in detail.

The visual impact referred to here can only be created by mechanics who are capable of installing quality work and who are dedicated to serving the industry well and want to excel.

Therefore, when an inspector encounters this kind of work and passes over it with light scrutiny, you can be assured that his decision did not result from any deception, but from good judgment.

When you lay out a job, keep those thoughts in mind and make that extra effort that makes the difference between passing and failing.

SECTION IX

COLLECTING YOUR MONEY

Chapter 23 Collecting Your Money
Prevention
Protection

Chapter 23

COLLECTING YOUR MONEY

PREVENTION

One of the most talked about subjects among contractors is collection. Prudent contractors make provision for collecting their money before they take the job, which is extending credit. They also never attempt to collect the full contract amount in a lump-sum payment at the completion of the job. They break down the contract amount into installments, each triggered by a due date. Each installment is set according to the completion of certain items of work or a periodic cutoff date. Their contract will also have a specific provision for payment and for work stoppage.

An important factor that will aid collection is your right to stop work when not paid on time. You cannot stop working on a job because of late payment and shift the liability to the customer, unless your contract stipulates this and under what conditions.

Typically, most contractors treat this matter lightly and go on signing lopsided contracts, subjecting themselves to undue frustrations and losses. An example of a lopsided provision is the contractor agreeing to be paid when the owner pays the general contractor, with no specific due date or right to stop work if payment is not made as scheduled.

To prevent this, you must read the contract carefully (see Chapter 15) and ensure that a right-to-stop-work clause exists.

The clause need not be complex. In fact, clauses are also effective when handwritten on the contract form at the time we negotiate the contract. Such an insertion may read:

> If the customer fails to make a payment within seven days from its due date, then the contractor has the right to stop work until all moneys due are paid in full.

Then, if the customer breaks his promise, we can stop work without liability.

Negotiate this element of the contract, for no reasonable customer will refuse to negotiate. In fact, many expect objections. If we don't, they may grow suspicious, for they know that most other contractors have asked for the same changes you should ask for.

PROTECTION

Credit Check

The best protection is prevention. Check all prospective customers for credit references before you extend credit.

Mechanic's Lien

While a Mechanic's Lien is a good legal instrument, if you don't follow proper procedures and adhere to filing deadlines that guarantee enforcement, a Mechanic's Lien can be as worthless as a bad check.

The laws that govern Mechanic's Lien vary from state to state. The suggestions that follow are general and solely presented to acquaint you with the subject. Learn the specific procedures required by the laws that govern Mechanic's Liens in your state and, whenever possible, use the expert services of a lawyer or that of a local filing firm that specializes in this field.

You must make a distinction between public and private properties. Mechanic's Liens are mostly applicable to private properties where the performance of and payment for the work is most often not guaranteed by Surety Bonds.

An owner is a legal entity that can be natural, corporate, or a partnership. Statutory Bonds are not for subcontractors and should not be confused with Surety Bonds.

The Spirit of the Law

The spirit of the law should protect those who supply labor and material for the improvement of others' properties and prevent the owner from paying twice for the work done. The general concept is that the general contractor files a notice of commencement and the subcontractors or suppliers notify the owner that they have been hired by the general contractor to improve the property. Obviously, if our contract is with the owner, the Notice to Owner is not necessary.

The timely filing of a Notice to Owner gives you the right to file a Mechanic's Lien on the property for money due and to subsequently foreclose on it.

Filing

As stated earlier, filing deadlines may vary from state to state; however, taking the State of Florida as an example, as of this writing the following documents are mandatory and must be filed within their designated deadlines.

- Notice to Owner
  This must be filed by a certified service with the owner and with other parties having an interest in the property (such as financial institutions) within 45 days from the day work commences or any material is ordered or any direct expenses are incurred for the job.

- Mechanic's Liens
  A claim of lien must be filed with the office of the clerk of the circuit court of the county in which the property is located within 90 days from the last time you worked on the job.

- Lawsuit
  A lawsuit to collect on the Mechanic's Lien must be filed within one year from the Lien's filing date.

Releases of Lien

Releases of Lien can be conditional and non-conditional, partial or full, each reflecting a specific amount and an effective period-ending date. If you don't want to give up your rights to what is rightfully yours, you must pay attention to the type of instrument you are signing. For example, if you are to be paid by check, sign a release that is conditional upon the bank clearing the check.

Period-ending Date

Regardless of the type of release you are signing, it will show an amount and, most significantly, a period-ending date. Of the two, the period-ending date is the most important to consider. This establishes a date beyond which you cannot make additional claims for monies due.

In other words, you state that you have been paid in full up to and including that date. The amount shown on the release of lien, unless specifically provided for, has no bearing on the release of lien for that period. In fact, many releases, although they are for thousands of dollars, are issued for $10 and other considerations but with a specific period-ending date.

When we are most concerned with collecting our money, we may inadvertently sign a release showing the amount due as of the 25th of the previous month, with a period-ending listed as the 30th of that month, and at times the 25th or the 30th of another month.

In such a case, you have released any work you have done or will do between the 26th of the previous month and the 30th of whatever that month is, even though you were not paid for it.

When signing a release of lien, check the period-ending date as well as the amount shown.

Releases of lien come in many shapes and forms; however, the fundamental thrust of the instrument remains the same. You release your claim of lien by the amount of money or other compensations for work done on a property.

For every partial payment you receive toward a contract, you are expected to execute a partial release. When you receive the final payment, then and only then do you execute a waiver or a final release of lien.

There will be times when the customer will expect you to execute a partial release of lien even though he is paying you with a post-dated check. Even though it is a risky business, the least you can do if you decide to go along with the deal is to execute a conditional release of lien— your release is valid only if the check clears the bank.

As stated earlier, while lien laws are easy to follow, they vary from state to state. You are urged to acquaint yourself with the laws and procedures of the state in which you do or intend to do work.

SECTION X

GENERAL ADMINISTRATION

Chapter 24

BUSINESS ADMINISTRATION

EXECUTIVES

On the ladder of success, you will always meet people ready to help you no matter which way you are going—up or down.

The aim of this book is to help you on the road to complete business success. However, you cannot achieve that kind of success without the respect of your families, your associates, your employees, vendors, customers, and, above all, yourself. You earn that respect by executing your duties as a businessperson fairly.

With the exception of a few large contracting firms, you cannot manage electrical contracting remotely from some resort, as many would like to. As the owner, you are essential to the daily operation of the business and you must attend to it even if it means a few hours a day. In any case, most electrical licensing agencies require direct supervision of the qualifier, thus restricting absentee operators.

As stated in Chapter 1, electrical contracting is a tradesperson's business, and as such it needs your attention, especially in its infant years.

Personal Affairs

Keep personal affairs separate from business. An effective method is the legendary grandma's cookie jar. It applies to business and personal finances.

Grandma kept a cookie jar for the home mortgage and one for the store rent, a jar for groceries and one for clothes and so on for every other expected expense, including one for her nest egg. She even had one set up for family fun and entertainment.

When money came in she spent it 'all' in every cookie jar she had set up.

She was never short on her commitments—and grandpa loved it. She never set up a new cookie jar until there was an assured income for the new commitment.

This is not an antiquated method; rather, it is the way successful people and companies run their affairs. They set budgets within their means. Above all, they don't mix personal and business finances. When and if they do, they keep them readily accountable.

In evaluating your relationship with your business, list what you are willing or not willing to pledge to it. Make an honest assessment and limit your expectations to the extent of your pledge. For example, don't expect full salary if you only work part-time; or don't expect to double or triple your income unless you invest the resources (money and time) that it takes to generate such a return.

Business Affairs

Keep business independent from your personal affairs. As an executive, keep yourself up to date on all that affects your business. What may seem trivial today may be the way of tomorrow. The world is full of such stories—from the telephone, to the airplane, to computer chips, to software. In their infancy, people considered them trivial and worthless ideas.

If you are in business for the full ride, then you can progress toward your goal only if you make every step count and acquire the business knowledge you will need to keep up with the fast-moving world of electrical contracting. What you do or learn today forms the foundation of tomorrow. Businesses that fail to keep up with the times will fall by the wayside.

The skills that make the difference in people's lives are not the ones you may dread such as equating figures, measuring statistics, and legal concerns—for those you can hire professionals—but those that will help you make wise decisions in all other aspects of business as you keep an eye to the future.

For example, investing all your learning resources into improving your technical skills alone is a poor business investment, as it does nothing for the business side of contracting. You need to expand and balance your knowledge across both fields, for both are essential to success.

You have to invest your time wisely and keep yourself up to date with the latest innovations. You can spend idle time in your office on non-business related activities or you can invest it in your business future.

The following is a list of things most businesses need that you can do every day in one hour or less:

- Check all promotional mail yourself. True, a good

part is junk mail, but the wealth of information you get from the rest justifies the time spent.

Companies are expending a great deal of resources to keep you abreast of the latest news. Only your mailbox can yield such information. As your company's name takes hold on mailing lists, you can be certain that whatever information you need will eventually show up in your mail. Don't shy away from mailing lists and don't let others decide what is good or bad mail. Open the mail yourself.

- Set up a classified directory. Information you collect is useless unless you can find it when you need it. You could use a three-ring binder or a filing cabinet. Whichever medium you choose, set up the directory in so that it can be expanded and remains accessible to anyone in the organization. Make it part of the company's library.

- Touch base with your customers, new and old. A good business relationship with your customers is better than having a salesperson knocking on doors.

BUSINESS MANAGEMENT

Knowledge determines how we conduct ourselves and how we perceive the different functions of the electrical contracting business. The following is a collection of suggestions and hints:

Estimating

Buying sophisticated equipment without mastering the craft of estimating will not give you the type of estimates you seek—the ones that reflect your personal expertise as a mechanic—nor will it give you the edge over the competition.

Nowadays, estimators search for equipment in the same way hackers search for golf clubs that drive the ball straight and long, never realizing that the problem lies with their skills rather than with the equipment (See Chapter 8 - Estimating).

Marketing

It is no secret that repeat business is dependent on the quality of the product. In contracting, that product is service.

Forecast Your Business

You should advertise and look for work while you have work. This will enable you to choose better customers and better jobs. It is no different from borrowing money while you have money—this helps you borrow at a better rate.

Invest in Your Presentations

This can put the odds in your favor and get you more money for your work. When you go into a meeting, be mentally and physically ready to close the deal. Look to the real needs of the customer.

A good knowledge of the work and an enthusiastic presentation are refreshing to prospective customers.

This stuff is what makes loyal customers and helps you to blow away the competition.

General Contractors

Unless you are seasoned and financially stable enough to deal with the terms and conditions a general contractor imposes on you, you should eliminate the general contractor from your list of prospective customers.

You have a choice. You may take a job from a general contractor and when you finish it spend most of your time on closing the job and collecting your final payment, or you can invest your time 'now' in looking for prime work directly from owners and the like.

In prime work, down payments and prompt payments are most often the norm, for you are dealing directly with the owner (See Chapter 6 - The Starting Point; and Chapter 7 - Where to Look for Work).

Contracting the Job

Negotiations

Most standard contract forms are written for general use. Often the customer doesn't himself know why a specific clause is either part of or applicable to your agreement.

Most likely, the lawyer added it for general protection; and if you ask, chances are he will cross it out. If you don't ask, then the customer will begin to wonder why you did not (See Chapter 4 - Contract Basics; and Chapter 16, Negotiations).

Doing the Job

Mobilization

A good mobilization sets the stage for a profitable job. You can improve the job's anticipated profit by negotiating labor-hours with your lead-person before the job starts. In contracting, profits are generated by the number of productive labor-hours you can sell and your expertise in controlling their cost (See Chapter 20, Mobilizing the Job; and Chapter 21 - Controlling the Job).

Good Relationship

Establish a good relationship with other subcontractors on the job. There will be times when you need to touch base regarding payments and other job conditions that may affect everyone on the job.

Doing the Job

Redesigning, substitutions, buying, and your ability to manage your work force form the cornerstones of electrical contracting (See Section VIII, Doing The Job.)

Change Orders

Don't be in a hurry to start working on change orders. Before you begin work, be sure they are approved and executed. Fax copies are only good until you have to submit them in court (See Chapter 18 - Contract Management).

Time and Material

Whether time and material work is a unilateral directive, a change order, or a contract, a prudent contractor will secure in writing the name of the authorized representative of the customer at the job site. Once you start, have your daily worksheet verified and signed everyday by this person (See Chapter 5 - Service and Contracting Work).

Collecting Your Money

Protection

The best protection you can have, besides your legal rights and your financial strength to withstand litigation, is the foresight to choose your customers wisely and the smarts to custom-make a relationship for each new customer. The reputation of your customer should be the measuring stick for how much you should risk (See Chapter 23 - Collecting Your Money).

Paydays and Payroll Taxes

Every employee expects payment in full on payday. On that day, each employee entrusts you with the funds you have deducted from his gross wages to deposit in his behalf, along with your contributions, with the Internal Revenue Service (IRS). The IRS requires you to deposit these funds with your bank when they are due.

Using these funds for any other purpose is not only a criminal act but a sure way to put yourself out of business with a personal debt to the IRS of 100% of the money withheld plus interest and whatever penalty is applicable until the debt is repaid in full.

General Administration

Be a Legal Entity

Register your business with the appropriate Federal, State, County, City or Town agency and pay your dues. A non-legal entity has no standing in a court of law.

Insurances

Maintain all mandatory insurances—Workmen's Compensation, General Liability and the like.

Leading

If we want to lead while everyone is skirting a problem, we must attack it head-on.

While lawyers are talking about judicial doctrines and code interpreters and regulators are talking about new rules and regulations, you must stay committed to the purpose of the business—making a profit.

A good administrator implements systems that enlist the help of everyone in his organization, thus sharing the work among those who can contribute without duplication.

Any administrative system has its weak points as well its scores of critics ready to condemn it. This is true of any company. Once you adopt a system, police and maintain it with confidence. The worst thing is not to have a system at all.

You make your own decisions. If you don't, eventually someone else will make them for you.

Shadow employee

A shadow employee is someone you would love to have around and on your side in moments of need. This craving is so strong that often we allow an impostor to work his way into our confidence, only to be disappointed when we finally look to him for help. They tend to disrupt the morale of other people in the organization.

Personnel

Surround yourself with qualified and dedicated working people who are capable of working within the framework of the industry and are accountable for their actions. Often, we can't be Mr. Electrician or Mr. Businessperson full-time; therefore, we must rely on key personnel to carry out the work diligently.

In a given day, you may need to attend to many different facets of contracting, from closing a bid to negotiating a contract, to interviewing a job applicant, to meeting prospective customers. As the chief executive of the company, you must make the time to attend to these duties with your full concentration. Failure to grasp this position can cost you the very business you are trying to build.

Your Next Job

If you adhere to good business rules, then there will always be many 'next jobs' for you to work on.

Your supplier

Your supplier is pivotal to your estimating success as well as to your field production. Pay the bills promptly. If you have a problem, be a straight shooter—apprise him of the problem and work it out in an honorable way. Suppliers don't want to lose customers.

Finances

Making a profit is okay. It's the only reason we are in business.

A Survival Tip for Single Operators

The company profit is the collective profit of all the jobs. One job cannot pay you full salary unless your pay rate is equal to the labor rate you used to bid the job.

For example, if you bid a job at $16 per hour and pay yourself out of that same job at $22 per hour, unless you complete that job in about two thirds of the allocated labor-hours, you are bound to lose $6 per hour.

When this happens, you are cutting into your job profit and, most likely, into the allotted overhead, which you need to pay operating expenses such as rent, phones, auto expenses, insurance, and all the other stuff that keeps you in business.

There are two ways you can earn $22 per hour or more. Either by drawing from a pool of jobs you manage yourself and hiring others to do the work at $16 per hour or less, or by working on jobs you bid at $22 per hour or more.

If you find it difficult to hire people at the rate you bid the jobs, then you are not offering competitive rates for the type of work you are bidding.

Be aware that bidding jobs at $22 per hour or more may put you out of the mainstream as a single operator and force you either to contract a higher volume of work, or take different types of jobs to meet your salary expectations.

Failure to understand this equation is the cause of failure for many single operators and small contractors as well. You cannot bid a job at a lesser rate than it actually costs you (See Chapter 9 - How to Develop Your Own Numbers).

Overhead Allowance
To keep the business going and expanding, keep a special account for part of the overhead allowance for the replacement or addition of vehicles and equipment.

Credit exposure
If need be, ask the supplier or bank to run a credit check on a new customer. Regardless of how good the credit report is, you should never invest all your resources into one job. A large job that needs all your resources is not worth the risk. One delayed payment can send you crashing.

To keep your company financially healthy, everyday you should check, review, and pay special attention to:

- Bank balances

- Accounts receivable

- Accounts payable

- Leads and quoted jobs status

You cannot rely on others to perform this task. Learn the meanings and interrelations of these factors the same way you mastered wire sizes and their relative ampacities—by heart. Only then will you be in control of your business finances (See How to Read Financial Statements later on in this chapter).

Bank Accounts

For most contractors, the most effective method is to maintain three checking accounts (cookie jars)— Operating, Payroll, and Special Accounts. The two-monthly fees, if any, are well worth the investment.

Deposits are made into the Operating Account. Once they clear, transfer the amount earmarked for payroll into the Payroll Account and the amounts earmarked for depreciation and insurance premiums, rents and the like into the Special Account.

When running the payroll, calculate and transfer into the Special Account all applicable payroll taxes—unless you make weekly payroll tax deposits to the bank.

The Special Account is your passport to a trouble-free operation. Like grandma, we will have the money to pay those off-the-cuff bills that usually show up at the wrong time of the month. It might take a while for you to get used to this method, but once you do, it is a safe bet you won't want to do it any other way.

How to Read Financial Statements

The Balance Sheet

If you cannot compile or read a financial statement, it will be difficult for you to know where your company stands and what portion of the money is rightfully yours to keep. The balance sheet, which is the financial resume of the company, is there to assist you.

The balance sheet reveals how much money and other assets the company owns and where they are to be found; how much money people owe the company and how much the company owes other people—suppliers, banks, etc. It also shows how much the company owes you personally and what portion of the company's assets are yours.

A balance sheet serves companies as well as individuals by summarizing their financial status for lending institutions or anyone else concerned.

The main categories in a balance sheet are assets, liabilities, and equity. It is called a balance sheet because the total assets always equal the combined total of the liabilities and the owner's equity (or capital), which together represent the claims against the assets.

The following definitions and examples were condensed from "A Handbook of Small Business Finance," by Jack Zwick, which is published by the Small Business Administration and available from the Superintendent of Documents, U.S. Government Printing Office, Washington, D.C. 20402.

Assets

Anything the business owns that has money value is an asset. The assets in a small business commonly include cash, notes receivable, accounts receivable, inventories, land, buildings, machinery, equipment, and other investments and are classified as current assets, fixed assets, or other assets.

- *Current assets* are cash and assets that are expected to be converted into cash during the normal operating cycle of the business (generally, within a year). They include notes receivable, accounts receivable, marketable securities, and inventories, as well as cash. However, if inventories are not to be used up (that is, converted into accounts receivable or cash) within a year, they should be recorded as fixed assets. The same is true of notes receivable and accounts receivable that are not expected to be converted into cash within a year— they should be treated as fixed assets.

- *Fixed assets* are those acquired for long-term use in the business. They include land, buildings, plant, machinery, equipment, furniture, fixtures, and so on. These assets are typically not for resale, and they are recorded on the balance sheet at their cost to the business, less depreciation.

- A fixed asset is treated as a long-term cost, with that cost allocated as depreciation over the working life of the asset. Thus, the value of a fixed asset as shown on the balance sheet is not necessarily the same as the resale value of the asset.

- *Other assets* include patents, trade investments, goodwill, and so on. Goodwill is recorded on the balance sheet only to the extent that it has actually been purchased.

Assets are also sometimes classified as tangible or intangible. Literally, tangible means 'able to be physically touched.' Current and fixed assets are normally tangible; other assets, typically intangible.

Liabilities

Liabilities are the claims of creditors against the assets of the business—in other words, debts owed by the business. They do not include owners' claims. Among the more common liabilities are notes payable, accounts payable, accrued liabilities, and allowance for taxes.

- *Current liabilities* are those due for payment within a year. Long-term (or fixed) liabilities are debts, or parts of debts, that are not due for payment within a year. The allowance for future income taxes represents the taxes that will have to be paid on the profits of the current year, but that are not due for payment until later. Accrued liabilities are similar to the allowance for future income taxes in that the expenses are charged against profits of the current year, although payment will not be made until later. The most common example is accrued wages, which must be accounted for whenever the last day of the accounting period does not coincide with the last day of a pay period.

Equity

The assets of a business minus its liabilities equals its equity. This equity is the investment of the owner or owners plus any profits that have been left to accumulate in the business (or minus any losses).

If the business is incorporated, its books will show a capital stock account. This account represents the paid-in value of the shares issued to the owners of the business.

If the business is a proprietorship or a partnership, the capital accounts appear under the name or names of the owners. Increases in equity as a result of undistributed earnings are also recorded there, as are decreases in equity if the business shows a loss instead of a profit.

Valuation Accounts

Depreciation and other factors reduce the value of some assets. Because it is important to state balance-sheet values correctly, the balance sheet is usually set up to show that provision has been made for such reductions in value. This is done by using depreciation, or valuation accounts. Some of the more common of these accounts are:

- *Accounts receivable.* These are analyzed according to the length of time the money has been owed. An estimate is then made of what proportion of them will turn out to be uncollectible. This 'allowance for bad debts' is usually computed for a given accounting period either as a percentage of the average balance of receivables or as a percentage of the net credit sales for the period. The balance sheet shows it as a deduction from the asset 'accounts receivable.'

- *Losses in the value of inventories* may occur as a result of price changes, style changes, physical deterioration, pilferage, and so on. If such losses are likely to occur, an estimate of possible shrinkage should be made. This estimate appears on the balance sheet as a deduction from the value of the inventory.

- *Fixed assets*, other than land, decline in value. This decline in value may be due to wear and tear, technical obsolescence, or other causes. A periodic charge for depreciation should be made and shown on the balance sheet as a deduction from the value of the asset.

For the following examples we are using the financial statements of the sample company John Doe Electric.

John Doe Electric Co.

Balance Sheet (Simple Format)

12/31/20__

Assets

Current Assets:

Cash	$20,000
Accounts Receivable	40,000
Inventories	45,000
Total current assets	**$105,000**

Fixed assets:

Machinery and equipment	$20,000
Buildings	28,000
Land	12,000
Total fixed assets	60,000
Total assets	**$165,000**

Liabilities and Equity

Current liabilities:

Accounts payable	$20,000
Notes payable	30,000
Accrued liabilities	6,000
Reserve for taxes	4,000
Total current liabilities	**$60,000**

Equity:

Capital stock	$50,000
Surplus	$55,000
Total equity	**$105,000**
Total liabilities and equity	**$165,000**

Figure 54: Balance Sheet Simple Format

John Doe Electric Co.

Balance Sheet (Advanced Format)

12/31/20___

Assets

Current Assets:

Cash		$20,000
Accounts Receivable	40,000	
Less allowance for doubtful accounts	3,000	37,000
Inventories	45,000	
Less allowance for inventory loss	5,000	40,000
Total current assets		**$97,000**

Fixed assets:

Machinery	$20,000	
Less allowance for depreciation	4,000	$16,000
Buildings	28,000	
Less allowance for depreciation	6,000	$22,000
Land		12,000
Total fixed assets		50,000
Total assets		**$147,000**

Liabilities and Equity

Current liabilities:

Accounts payable	$20,000
Notes payable	30,000
Accrued liabilities	6,000
Reserve for taxes	4,000
Total current liabilities	**$60,000**

Equity:

Capital stock	$50,000
Surplus	$37,000
Total equity	**$87,000**
Total liabilities and equity	**$147,000**

Figure 55: Balance Sheet Advanced Format

Figure 54 shows a simple balance sheet. It represents the financial position of the John Doe Electric on December 31, 20___.

Total assets of $165,000 are offset by liabilities and equity totaling $165,000. The balance sheet balances. The assets are grouped as current assets and fixed assets (John Doe Electric has no 'other assets'). Current liabilities are identified as such, although there are no long-term liabilities.

When the valuation accounts are included in the balance sheet, the statement becomes more accurate and therefore more useful. Figure 55 shows how they affect the asset figures that appear in Figure 54.

Note the following changes:

- Accounts receivable have been reduced by $3,000 to an estimated $37,000 collectible.

- Inventory values have been reduced by $5,000 to $40,000.

- Total current assets, therefore, show a reduction of $8,000 from $105,000 to $97,000.

- Machinery is now valued at $16,000, or $4,000 less than the original $20,000.

- The value of the buildings has been reduced by $6,000 to $22,000.

- Total fixed assets have thus declined by $10,000.

- Total assets have declined by $18,000.

- Surplus is now $37,000 and total equity $87,000, each one $18,000 less than in Figure 54.

- Total liabilities and equity now balance total assets

at $147,000.

The balance sheet can be expanded still further to make it even more useful. For more advanced study, send for the handbook at the Washington D.C. address shown above.

The Profit-and-Loss Statement

A profit-and-loss statement of John Doe Electric for the Year Ended December 31, 20__ whose balance sheet appears in Figure 54 and Figure 55 is simplified as follows:

Sales	$120,000
Cost of contracts sold	70,000
Gross margin (gross profit)	$50,000
Selling Expenses:	
Salaries	15,000
Commissions	5,000
Advertising	5,000
Total Selling Expenses	25,000
Selling margin	25,000
Administrative expenses	10,000
Net profit	$15,000

Figure 56: Profit-and-Loss Statement

Sales

The item 'Sales' includes all sales of contracts or services. The sales figures shown in Figure 56 above represent net sales. This is computed by subtracting sales discounts and sales returns and allowances from gross sales.

Cost of Contracts Sold

The 'cost of contracts sold,' the total price paid for the contracts sold during the accounting period, includes productive labor, material, and direct job expense costs.

Selling Expenses

These are expenses incurred directly or indirectly in making sales. They include the salaries of the sales force, commissions, advertising expenses, and so on.

Portions of rent, heat, light, power, supplies, and other expenses that contribute to the company's sales activities may also be included under selling expenses.

In small businesses, however, such mixed expenses are usually charged to general expenses.

General and Administrative Expenses

General salaries and wages (non-productive labor), supplies, and other operating costs necessary to the overall administration of the business are included in this group of expenses.

Non-operating Income

Some small businesses receive additional income from interest, dividends, miscellaneous sales, rents, gains on sale of capital assets, and so on. In such cases, the 'net profit' shown in Figure 56 is really a net operating profit. The non-operating income would be added to it and any interest paid subtracted. The result would then be the net profit before State and Federal income taxes. The profit-and-loss statement, like the balance sheet, can be expanded to include more details.

Interpreting the Profit-and-Loss Statement

In the profit-and-loss statement shown in Figure 56, note that the *gross margin* (sometimes called gross profit) is computed first, and then the net profit.

The gross margin equals sales less cost of sales. It does not take into account the overhead expenses (other than direct job expenses) of being in business—the selling expenses, office expenses, and so on.

John Doe Electric reports a gross margin of $50,000 on net sales of $120,000. The gross-margin percentage, then, is about 42%. This indicates that the contracts sold cost the company about $58 per $100 of sales.

The net profit of the business is the final profit after all costs and expenses for the accounting period have been deducted. John Doe Electric made a net profit of $15,000, or about 12.5% of sales.

Use with caution

The balance sheet tries to present a 'true and fair picture' of the financial position of a business at the *close* of the accounting period.

The profit-and-loss statement tries to present a 'true and fair' picture of the results of operations during the accounting period.

These reports, constructed according to accepted principles of accounting, are among the most important tools for a businessperson. However, they are drawn up under conditions of uncertainty, and many of the transactions involved are necessarily incomplete at the end of the accounting period.

These balance sheets do not reflect resale of liquidating values; they reflect the cost, or cost less depreciation, of the assets held by the business as a going concern.

The figures depend to some extent on the judgment of your accountant, who decides which accounting techniques are best suited to your business.

The above should be kept in mind when analyzing financial statements.

Ratio Analysis of Financial Statements

The two types of financial statements, the balance sheet and the profit-and-loss statement, are necessary and useful. However, they are only a start in helping you understand your position, where you are going, and how you are going to get there.

To get your monies worth, study the various relations between some of the figures.

A number of indicators have been worked out for this purpose. In many ways, these indicators, or comparative measures (usually expressed as ratios), are more useful for analyzing your business operations than are the dollar amounts. They provide clues for spotting trends in the direction of better or poorer performance. They also make it possible for you to compare your company's performance with the average performance of similar businesses.

Some important points must be kept in mind, however.

- *—Businesses are not exactly comparable.* There are different ways of computing and recording some of the items on financial statements. As a result, the figures for your business may not correspond exactly to those for the businesses with which you want to compare it.

- *—Ratios are computed for specific dates.* Unless the financial statements on which they are based are prepared often, seasonal characteristics of your business may be obscured.

- *—Financial statements* show what has happened in the past. An important purpose in using ratios is to obtain clues to the future so that you can prepare for the problems and opportunities that lie ahead. Since the ratios are based on past performance, you must use them in the light of your best knowledge and judgment about the future.

- *—The ratios* are not ends in themselves, but tools that can help answer some of your financial questions. But they can do this only if you interpret them with care.

Measure of Liquidity

Liquidity may be thought of as the ability to pay our bills. It is the first objective of financial management. Measures of liquidity are intended to help us answer questions such as this:

"Do we have enough cash, plus assets that can be readily turned into cash, so that we are sure of being able to pay the debts that will fall due this accounting period?"

The current ratio

The current ratio is one of the best-known measures of financial strength.

The main question it answers is this: "Does the business have enough current assets to meet its current debts—with a margin of safety for possible losses such as inventory shrinkage or uncollectible accounts?"

The current ratio is computed from the balance sheet by dividing current assets by current liabilities.

For John Doe Electric, it is computed as follows:

$$\frac{\text{Current assets}}{\text{Current Liabilities}} = \frac{\$97,000}{\$60,000} = 1.61 \text{ (or 1.61 to 1)}$$

Is this a good current ratio? Should the owner of John Doe Electric be reasonably satisfied with his firm's performance on this point?

These questions cannot be answered with an unqualified yes or no. A popular rule of thumb for a favorable current ratio is 2 to 1, but whether a specific ratio is satisfactory depends on the nature of the business and the characteristics of its current assets and liabilities.

If you decide that your current ratio is too low, you may be able to raise it by:

- Paying some debts
- Increasing your current assets from loans or other borrowings with a maturity of more than a year
- Converting non-current assets into current assets
- Increasing your current assets from new equity contributions
- Plowing back profits

Working Capital

Working capital is the difference between current assets and current liabilities.

John Doe Electric's (Figure 54) working capital is $37,000 ($97,000 less $60,000)

Its working capital turnover equals sales over working capital, which is 3.24 ($120,000 / $37,000).

Bankers look at net working capital over periods of time to determine a company's ability to weather financial crises. Often, loans are tied to minimum working-capital requirements.

The acid-test ratio

This ratio, sometimes called the 'quick ratio,' is one of the best measures of liquidity. It is computed as follows:

$$\frac{\text{Cash + Government securities + Receivable}}{\text{Current liabilities}}$$

For John Doe Electric, which has no Government securities, this becomes $57,000 divided by $60,000, giving John Doe Electric an acid-test ratio of 0.95 (or 0.95 to 1).

The acid-test ratio is a much more exacting measure than the current ratio. By not including inventories, it concentrates on the truly liquid assets, whose values are fairly certain. It helps to answer the question: "If all sales revenues should disappear, could my business meet its current obligations with the readily convertible, 'quick' funds on hand?"

Net quick funds equals quick assets less current liabilities.

Quick assets equal cash plus receivables plus securities.

An acid-test ratio of about 1 to 1 is considered satisfactory, subject to the following conditions:

- The pattern of accounts receivable collections should not lag far behind the schedule for paying current liabilities. In making this comparison, think in terms of paying creditors early enough to take advantage of discounts.

- There should not be much danger of anything happening to slow up the collection of accounts receivable.

Unless you feel comfortable about these two qualifications, keep the acid-test ratio somewhat higher than 1 to 1.

A general principle concerning the current and acid-test ratios is that the higher the ratios are, the better. This may be true from your creditors' point of view, because they stress prudence and safety, but it is in your interest as the owner of the business to be strong and trim rather than fat. Idle cash balances and receivables and inventories out of proportion to our selling needs should be reduced. The key to successful financial management is to conserve the resources of your business and to make these resources work hard for you.

Measure of Profitability

Is our business earning as much profit as it should, considering the amount of money invested in it? This is the second major objective (after liquidity) of financial management, and a number of ratios have been devised to help measure a company's success in achieving it. A few of them are explained here.

Assets' earning power. The ratio of operating profit (earnings before interest and taxes) to total assets is the best guide for appraising the overall earning power of your company's assets. This ratio takes no account of what proportion of the assets represents creditors' equity and what proportion represents your own equity, or of varying tax rates. For John Doe Electric, it is computed as follows:

$$\frac{\text{Operating profit}}{\text{Total assets}} = \frac{\$15,000}{\$147,000} = 0.10, \text{ or 10 percent}$$

Return on the owner's equity. This measure shows the return you receive on your own investment in the business. In computing the ratio, the average equity is customarily used—the average of the 12 individual months, if it is available, or the average of the figures from the beginning and ending balance sheets. For John Doe Electric, the beginning and ending equity figures are (assumed) $87,000 and $97,000, giving an average of $92,000. The return on the equity is then:

$$\frac{\text{Net profit}}{\text{Equity}} = \frac{\$15,000}{\$92,000} = 0.16, \text{ or 16 percent}$$

A similar ratio uses tangible net worth instead of equity. Tangible net worth is the equity less any intangible assets such as patents and goodwill. If there are no intangible assets, there will be no difference between the two values.

Net profit on sales

This ratio measures the difference between what your company takes in and what it spends in the process of doing business. The ratio depends mainly on two factors—operating costs and pricing policies. If your net profit on sales goes down, for instance, it might be because you have lowered prices in the hope of increasing total sales volume. Or it might be that costs have been creeping up while prices remained the same. Net profit on sales is computed as follows:

$$\frac{\text{Net profit}}{\text{Net sales}} = \frac{\$15,000}{\$120,000} = 0.125, \text{ or } 12.5 \text{ percent}$$

This means that for every dollar of sales, the company has made a profit of 12.5 cents.

Investment turnover

Investment turnover is the ratio of annual net sales to total investment. It measures what volume of sales you are getting for each dollar invested in assets. John Doe Electric will compute its investment turnover as follows:

$$\frac{\text{Net sales}}{\text{Total assets}} = \frac{\$120,000}{\$147,000} = 0.82$$

Return on Investment (ROI)

The rate of return on investment (profit divided by investment) is probably the most useful measure of profitability for the small business owner. Practice varies as to what specific items from the financial statements are to be used for "profit" and which for "investment." For example, "profit" might be considered to mean net operating profit, net profit before taxes, or net profit after taxes. "Investment" could mean total assets employed or equity alone. It is important to decide which of these values to use in computing return on investment and then to be consistent. In this discussion, net profit after taxes and total assets will be used. For John Doe Electric, then, the return on investment, assuming a net profit after taxes of $12,000, is computed as follows:

$$\frac{\text{Net profit}}{\text{Total assets}} = \frac{\$12,000}{\$147,000} = 0.08, \text{ or 8 percent}$$

Common-Size Financial Statements

Sometimes, all values on the financial statements are reduced to percentages. Balance-sheet items are usually expressed as percentages of the total assets figures, while profit-and-loss statement items are expressed as percentages of net sales. A statement in this form is often called a "common-size" balance sheet or profit-and-loss statement.

This type of analysis has little or no value, however, unless the percentages are compared with figures for other businesses in the same line of activity or with past records of your own company.

Using the Ratio

Ratios will not provide you with any automatic solutions to your financial problems. They are only tools—though important ones—for measuring the performance of your business. It is the use to which you put them that will determine their real value.

Compare your ratios with the averages of businesses similar to yours. Also, compare your own ratios for several successive years, watching especially for any unfavorable trends that may be emerging.

If warning signs appear, look for the causes and for possible remedies. Studying one ratio in relation to others may help here, but you will probably also need to look into more detailed records of your business in the areas concerned.

Sources of Industry Ratio Data

The following are among the best-known sources of industry ratio data:

Key Business Ratios. Published annually by Dun and Bradstreet, Inc., 99 Church Street, New York, NY 10007.

Covers 125 lines of business, including construction industries.

Statement Studies. Published annually by Robert Morris Associates, National Association of Bank Loan Officers of Credit Men, Philadelphia National Bank Building, Philadelphia, PA 19197.

Based on data collected from member banks of the association.

Covers approximately 300 lines of business.

Analysis for Small Business (SBMS No.20) U.S. Small Business Administration. This publication may be purchased from the Superintendent of Documents, U.S. Printing Office, Washington, D.C. 20402.

Chapter 25

Forms

HOW TO GET THEM

Everyone dislikes filling out forms. In business, however, you cannot do without them.

If used properly, forms become the best logical connectors in a complex control system that makes all parts of a business work smoothly and in the right sequence.

The forms shown in this book can also be used as templates for your computer programs or printed stationery. They can be downloaded online at www.theestimatingroom.com.

Chapter 26

OFFICE

OFFICE OPERATION

The office is where we conduct business and, consequently, where we keep records. How to keep them in order is the subject of this chapter.

The most effective way to expedite tasks in an office is to have the related paperwork readily available. This includes:

- Customers' and vendors' addresses including zip codes, faxes, beepers, mobile and telephone numbers

- List of employees, including social security numbers

- The company's federal and state identification numbers

- Insurance policy numbers and expiration dates

- Vehicle titles, registrations, plates and serial

numbers

- Equipment maintenance contracts with serial numbers and expiration dates

- Any other expiration dates, serial numbers or account numbers related to the business

Amazingly, most of this information crosses our desks at one time or another, but it's always hard to find when we need it.

How we maintain the flow of paperwork directly affects our rate of success.

Nowadays, government and municipal agencies, insurance companies, customers, and vendors inundate us with requests to update our files. If we fail to comply promptly, chances are that they will fine us, cancel our insurance, or delay our payment.

Procrastination often stems from disorganization, a disease that afflicts many well-intentioned contractors. However, aside from penalties, cancellations and delays are frustrating and time consuming to say the least. The misplacement of a document such as a completed change order can cost you its face value and more.

The following system is tailor made for electrical contracting:

Set up General Files

The following topics deal with specific filing methods: Chapter 10 - Estimating the Job - Step #3 The Estimating Folder; and Chapter 17- Protecting the Job - Documentation. Review them if necessary.

Filing Cabinets

For a new business, two four-drawer and one two-drawer 'legal size' filing cabinets are the basic requirements. Label one four-drawer 'Jobs' and the other 'General Administration.' The two-drawer, which belongs next to you, should be labeled 'Business Administration.' Each cabinet should be set up from the top drawer down as follows:

Jobs File Cabinet

Before using this cabinet, decide whether you want to keep jobs by their name, in which case you will need alphabetical dividers, or by number, in which case you will need an index-sheet in the first folder.

Drawer #1 – Estimates

Completed estimates belong in this drawer. Active estimates and quotes belong in the Business Administration cabinet next to you.

Drawer #2 – Active Jobs

This drawer holds active jobs only. A job remains active until all moneys due including retainers are collected. Use job folders as laid out in Chapter 17.

Drawer #3 – Shop Drawings

Because certain jobs have voluminous shop drawings, file these drawings in a separate file and drawer such as this. To be consistent, employ this method for all jobs.

To generate a paper trail, leave a copy of the shop drawings' transmittal in the 'Active Job' folder in the Shop Drawings section.

Annotate the transmittal copy to show where you filed the actual shop drawings and all pertinent data reflecting submissions and approvals dates.

Drawer #4 – Completed Jobs

File all completed jobs in this drawer. Completed means all monies collected and final certificates of approval and releases executed. Consult the statute of limitations in your state to find out how long you have to hold on to these records.

General Administration File Cabinet

Drawer #1 – Payroll

File all matters concerning employees and payroll in this drawer. Label each folder as follows:

Next Week's Payroll

This folder is your 'Things to Do' list for payroll closing day.

File everything to do with computing payroll checks, including payroll reports, forgotten hours or overtime from the week before, raises or expenses due and the like.

Before running the payroll, go through this folder and leave behind all that is not applicable to this week and save it for next week.

Never replace the 'Next Week's Payroll' folder; it just collects information for the upcoming payroll.

Weekly Labor Reports

This folder holds blank payroll report forms. File the actual reports in the Next Week's Payroll folder.

Active Employees

Terminated Employees

W-4 Forms

W-2 Forms

Payroll Tax Report

This folder holds copies of the quarterly payroll tax reports and supporting documentation and copies of checks or deposits made for each quarter reported.

Insurance Payroll Reports
Where applicable, keep copies of all payroll insurance reports here.

Other
You may expand this drawer to handle any other records pertaining to payroll or employees.

Drawer #2 – Accounts Payable

Unpaid Bills
This folder holds incoming invoices pending approval and distribution annotation.

Approved Bills
This folder holds bills approved for payment until they are paid in full. Neither the Unpaid Bills folder nor the Approved Bills folder is replaced.

Behind the first two folders, Unpaid and Approved Bills, set up 26 alphabetical dividers. Dedicate a folder for each vendor containing information regarding the business relationship such as discount allowed, guarantee, agreements, and the like. Also in this folder, file all paid invoices for that specific vendor.

Drawer #3 – Accounts Receivable

Keep accounts receivable documentation in the job file.

However, you should keep pertinent information not associated with any specific job but relevant to the customer in a file remote from the job file.

In Chapter 17, this folder was identified as the Intelligence File. This is a good place to keep such information along with statements and open invoices.

Aged Receivables
This folder should be the first in line in this drawer. It should contain a list of moneys due with the customers' names, invoice numbers and dates, indicating how old the invoices are.

Running Invoices
Most companies keep running invoice numbers in a folder or clipboard. This method tallies sales for any specific period and allows quick location of customer invoices by reference number. You can replace this folder at the end of each period (say, a month or a quarter) by filing it away in a storage cabinet.

Alphabetical Folders
These should follow the above two folders with alphabetical dividers. Keep one folder for each customer.

Drawer #4 – Tools and Equipment

This drawer is productive. It records the whereabouts of hard-to-find equipment.

You can also keep files for equipment you own with relevant serial numbers, maintenance contracts, and bills of sale. To accommodate this system, split the drawer into two sections.

In the first section, file literature of interest for equipment. File each folder according to the type of equipment; for example, electric drills, wire-pulling machines, pipe benders, high potential testers, and so on. You can expand this list with each piece of mail you receive on new equipment. To discourage procrastination, keep a number of empty folders in this drawer ready to accept the next literature.

In the second section, set up a folder for each piece of equipment you own with its respective title, operating manual and guarantee.

Business Administration

In this two-drawer cabinet, you can keep information necessary to conduct daily business along with the sensitive files that are off limits to others.

Drawer #1 – Daily Business

Use the first few folders for blank forms such as proposal/contracts, change orders, work orders, releases of liens and other forms. The next folders in this drawer should be set up as follows:

Quotes

Copies of bids or quotes should be filed in this folder for follow up and until they are signed or voided or lost to competition.

Active

Use this folder for service work and small jobs for which a formal job folder isn't necessary, i.e. work that you supervise and dispatch personally. When this kind of work is completed, shift each work order to the Completed Work folder below. This method gives you quick access to active and completed work.

Completed Work

A 'Completed' folder is set up for each month or quarter, depending on the volume of work for the period. If you choose quarterly, then the folder should read, 'Completed Work 1st Quarter 20__" or "2nd Quarter 20__" and so on. When the period ends, file the folder in a secondary cabinet and start a new folder for the new period.

Alphabetical Folders

This section of the drawer allows you to keep individual folders for (1) jobs that are either too large for the active folder or need your special attention or (2) any other job you wish to keep an eye on.

Drawer #2 – Company

Keep the company records of your own business in this drawer. Unless this drawer is secured, keep only copies here and file the originals in a safer place, preferably remote from the office.

Divide this drawer into several sections, each designated for a different level, i.e. Federal, State, etc. Then subdivide each classification into folders as follows:

Federal Taxes
- Approved Documents – In this folder, keep your Federal Identification Number and other approved documents such as the Subchapter S Application, IRS form #2553 'Election by a Small Business Corporation.'

- Corporate Income Tax – File annual tax reports and the latest IRS bulletins here. Also file other information relevant to the filing of the company's income tax return.

- Quarterly Withholding Taxes – Keep copies of quarterly tax reports 941 and 940 and the latest IRS bulletins and tax tables here.

State
- Approved Documents – If the company is a corporation, keep copies of the Certificate of Incorporation and the Articles of Incorporation in this folder. If the company is not a corporation, then use this folder to keep copies of any state

certificates you are required to obtain.

- State Corporate Income Tax

- State Franchise Tax

- State Intangible Tax

- State Sales Tax

- State Unemployment Tax

- Etc.

County

- Certificates of Competency – Your electrical licenses. Relocate this folder to the section in which it belongs. For example, if you are licensed by the state, then place it in the state section; if you are licensed by the city, then place it in the city section.

- County Occupational License

- County Taxes

- Etc.

City

- City Occupational License

- City Taxes

- Etc.

Financial

In this section, set up folders for your bank and other financial institutions with which you deal. In each folder, keep copies of the institution's standard agreement and any special terms extended to you. Each folder should also be used for general correspondence.

- Checking Account

- Savings or CD Account

- Mortgages or Loans

- Visa, American Express, Master Card, etc.

- Mobil, Exxon, etc.

Human Resources

File the agreements you make with people for their services in this section in their own folders. Individual labor incentive programs with your lead-persons are also filed here.

- Lead-persons:

- John Smith, Foreman

- Tom Smith, Foreman

- Charles Doe, Super

- Etc.

- Professional:

- Accountant

- Lawyer

- Etc.

Insurance

- Workers' Comp

- General Liability

- Auto

- Office and Warehouse Contents

- Fire and Theft

- Etc.

Auto and Equipment

Keep a folder in this section for each auto, truck, and piece of equipment you own with its title and registration. Also keep repair bills and scheduled maintenance cycles in these folders.

General

This section is divided with 26 alphabetical dividers for filing items that do not fall into any of the above categories but should still be kept in this drawer.

Conclusion

Files necessary to support the system are archived for future reference. Ask your accountant how long you should keep each file.

A final note on setting up a filing system that works for the duration of the business and that will expand itself with ease as you grow: Don't skimp by trying to save a few pennies here and there or trying to save the time that it takes to write a few labels. If you fail to maintain a good filing system, eventually it will crumble... and your business with it.

Chapter 27

WAREHOUSING

COSTS AND BENEFITS

Warehousing of tools and material is the mainstay of electrical contracting. Some contractors use warehousing to store equipment and large quantities of standard material acquired at greater discount, giving them an edge on the next bid.

Other contractors use warehousing to store leftover material from jobs, giving them the comfort of having parts at hand to carry out their next service call.

Either way, the cost of warehousing is something that you must balance against its benefits. This task is complex because neither cost nor benefits are tangible.

Cost of Warehousing

The cost of warehousing is measured based on the number of square feet of usable space.

For example, if the rent for a 1000 sq. ft. space is $1000, then the cost is $1 per sq. ft. However, if we invest an additional 500 sq. ft. of shelving or mezzanine, then our cost per square foot of usable space drops to about $0.66—a one-third saving.

In laying out warehousing space, you must consider:

- The cost of operation including rent, utilities, and maintenance personnel

- The costs associated with creating usable space

- The return on your investment

- The ease of operation

Of the four elements, 'ease of operation' is the most important here. The other costs can be figured out easily; however, your investment in warehousing can be considered cost-effective only if:

- It increases field production

- The stored materials maintain at least their original value

- The equipment depreciates at the same rate as the economics of your business and the IRS allows you to depreciate them.

For example, if the material is stored in garbage can-like containers so that you have to dig your way through one-half of the container just to find a few fittings, then you should not waste valuable space and time just for the sake of storing this material.

In fact, if you eliminate this kind of storage, you can reduce the size of the warehouse to store equipment and tools only. This move will save more than it cost to buy those few fittings from a supplier as you need them.

However, if you keep a warehouse with a shelving system where you can store and find what you need readily, then the benefits will outweigh the cost of additional warehousing.

A system that holds ten different-sized fittings for Flex, EMT, RGC, and PVC, including a section for items such as Devices, Grounding, Wire Termination Fittings and the like, can be assembled relatively inexpensively in a 300 sq. ft. area (for layout see below).

However, it could become more expensive if you fail to maintain it.

The principal function of a storage system for service work is to keep you from having to run to a supplier, buy every fitting ever made in every size, and store it. That would be a poor investment, for every day that the fitting is not used its cost increases in direct proportion to the cost of warehousing.

Whether you use a certain fitting or not, rent is still payable on the space it occupies. This takes you into that gray area of tangible and intangible warehousing costs and benefits that only your business can dictate and only you can decide its worth.

The most cost-effective storage system is the one that stores leftover material from jobs in the least amount of space and so that they can still be found readily when needed.

Don't throw away material, for it is part of your last job's profit regardless of whether it came from demolition work or from the supplier.

If you manage leftover material through a well laid out warehousing system, besides being available on demand, you can turn it into cash through your next job.

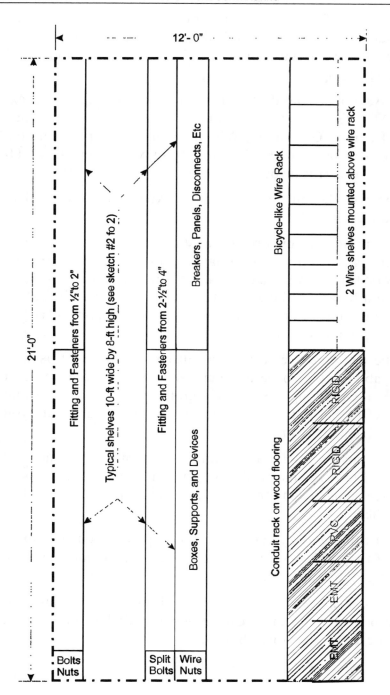

12'- 0"

21'-0"

Fitting and Fasteners from ½"to 2"

Typical shelves 10-ft wide by 8-ft high (see sketch #2 to 2)

Fitting and Fasteners from 2-½"to 4"

Breakers, Panels, Disconnects, Etc

Boxes, Supports, and Devices

Bicycle-like Wire Rack

2 Wire shelves mounted above wire rack

Conduit rack on wood flooring

RIGID

RIGID

PVC

EMT

EMT

Bolts
Nuts

Split
Bolts

Wire
Nuts

Sketch #1 of 2

Small Warehouse Floor Plan

A TYPICAL SHELF LAYOUT APPX. 10 ft. X 8 ft.

Typical 5-1/2" W x 11"D x 4-3/4" H Bin Cartons

Regardless of the bin carton content's size, for fitting identification, always lie-wrap on the face of the carton an actual 1/2" fitting.

Sketch #2 of 2

SECTION XI

QUICK START

Chapter 28

QUICK START - CHECKLISTS

OVERVIEW

For a consistent and comprehensive review of administrative tasks related to selling, producing, and closing a job, this chapter offers a series of checklists. The intent is to help you develop a set of business policies that will be adaptable to all facets of contracting on the fly by anyone on your staff.

Once you have considered a certain checklist, make it a part of your standard procedures—the bylaws of your company.

The checklist becomes a handy tool and a good reminder for those on the go. To avert nasty surprises, hand them out to your staff before they are forced to apply their best guess to a problem.

RECORDING THE INVITATION TO BID

Based on the premise that preserving your resources is a continuous task, check the following questions establishing whether to accept or reject an invitation to bid.

Invitation to Bid

- ☐ Check GC's bidders list
- ☐ Other prospective subs
- ☐ Competition Labor force

- ☐ Project viability
- ☐ Estimating workload
- ☐ _____

Reply to the Invitation to Bid

- ☐ Confirm you are bidding the job
- ☐ Request complete set of drawings
- ☐ Request specs and addenda
- ☐ Prevailing wages schedule

- ☐ Other special schedules
- ☐ _____
- ☐ _____
- ☐ _____

Post the Job on the Bidding Schedule Board

- ☐ Due date and time
- ☐ Apply for bond, if required
- ☐ _____

- ☐ Invite vendors
- ☐ _____
- ☐ _____

File the Invitation to Bid

- ☐ Construction bulletin, if any
- ☐ The GC transmittal
- ☐ _____

- ☐ Your written reply
- ☐ _____
- ☐ _____

Check for Completeness

- ☐ Drawing #, date, revisions
- ☐ Labor Prevailing Wage Sheet

- ☐ Construction Schedule
- ☐ Normal

☐ Specifications   ☐ Fast track

☐ Alternates schedule   ☐ _____

☐ Addenda   ☐ _____

Filing Documents

☐ Estimate folder   ☐ Intelligence folder

☐ Estimate 3-ring binder ☐ _____

ESTIMATING THE JOB

Estimating Checklist – Job Settings

As you explore the plans and specifications, check the following items then verify them with a jobsite visit.

Job Accessibility

☐ Low overpass   ☐ Tolls

☐ Small or narrow bridge ☐ _____

☐ Narrow tunnel   ☐ _____

☐ Tonnage limits   ☐ _____

Elevator Type and Usage

☐ Service elevator   ☐ _____

☐ Passenger elevator   ☐ _____

Facilities and Other

☐ Toilets   ☐ Parking

☐ _____ ☐ _____

Permanent Utilities

☐ Electric power   ☐ Sewage

☐ Gas   ☐ _____

☐ Water ☐ _____

Temporary Utilities
☐ Electric power ☐ _____

☐ Gas ☐ _____

☐ Water ☐ _____

Security
☐ Neighborhood ☐ _____

☐ Storage ☐ _____

Labor force
☐ Public transportation nearby ☐ No public transportation

☐ Labor availability ☐ _____

☐ _____ ☐ _____

Exterior Electrical Work – General Checklist

For exterior electrical work, check the following items then verify them with a jobsite visit.

Abandoned Obstacles and Obstructions
☐ Parking lot and under road pavement ☐ Concrete anchors

☐ Railroad tracks ☐ Monument foundations

☐ Fuel tanks ☐ Trees and hedges

☐ Light pole pedestals – concrete ☐ _____

☐ Sewer lines ☐ _____

Ground Condition
☐ Water table ☐ _____

☐ Easy digging   ☐ _____

☐ Hard digging   ☐ _____

Walls Exterior

☐ Concrete   ☐ _____

☐ Stucco   ☐ _____

☐ Blocks   ☐ _____

Other _____

☐ _____   ☐ _____

☐ _____   ☐ _____

☐ _____   ☐ _____

Interior Electrical Work – Estimating Checklist

For interior electrical work, check the following items then verify them with a jobsite visit.

Interior Work Checklist

☐ Existing service   ☐ Voltage

☐ Amperage   ☐ Grounding system

☐ Meter amperage   ☐ _____

Systems

☐ Fire alarm   ☐ _____

☐ Sound   ☐ _____

☐ Security   ☐ _____

☐ Data   ☐ _____

☐ Phone   ☐ _____

☐ TV / Cable   ☐ _____

☐ Access control   ☐ _____

☐ Intrusion detection   ☐ _____

☐ Master clock   ☐ _____

☐ Nurse call   ☐ _____

Lighting Fixtures

☐ Included   ☐ Excluded

Exception:

Tile cutting, fireproofing, and structural support for lighting fixtures in suspended ceiling shall be:

☐ Included   ☐ Provided by others

☐ _____   ☐ _____

Temporary Light and Power Utility Company Charges

☐ Included   ☐ Excluded

Power Source Remote from Jobsite

☐ Included   ☐ Excluded

☐ _____   ☐ _____

Maintenance during Regular Working Hours

☐ Included   ☐ Excluded

Maintenance during Off-Hours – Premium Time

☐ Included   ☐ Excluded

☐ Provided by others   ☐ _____

Burned Out Lamps Replacement

☐ Included   ☐ Excluded

☐ Provided by others   ☐ _____

Wiring for Trailers and Other Temporary Construction Facilities

☐ Included   ☐ Excluded

☐   Provided by others   ☐ _____

Appliance Cords and Caps

☐   Included   ☐ Excluded

☐   Provided by others   ☐ _____

Emergency Generator Exhaust Piping, Muffler, Thimble, Fuel Lines

☐   Included   ☐ Excluded

☐   Provided by others   ☐ _____

Remote Enunciator Panel

☐   Included   ☐ Excluded

☐   Provided by others   ☐ _____

Battery and Battery Charger

☐   Included   ☐ Excluded

☐   Provided by others   ☐ _____

Day Tank Furnish and Install

☐   Included   ☐ Excluded

☐   Provided by others   ☐ _____

Propane or Gas Fueling and Start Up Account

☐   Included   ☐ Excluded

☐   Set up by others   ☐ _____

Air Conditioning Disconnect Switches and Fuses

☐   Included   ☐ Excluded

☐   F & I by others   ☐ _____

Motor Starters

☐ Included   ☐ Excluded

☐ F & I by others   ☐ _____

Variable Frequency Drive – Wiring Only

☐ Included   ☐ Excluded

☐ Provided by others   ☐ _____

Motorized Dampers – Wiring Only

☐ Included   ☐ Excluded

☐ Provided by others   ☐ _____

Temperature Control System – Empty Conduit Only

☐ Included   ☐ Excluded

☐ F & I by others   ☐ _____

Fire Alarm System

☐ Included   ☐ Excluded

☐ F & I by others   ☐ Empty conduit only

☐ _____   ☐ _____

Smoke Evacuation System

☐ Included   ☐ Excluded

☐ F & I by others   ☐ Empty conduit only

☐ _____   ☐ _____

Magnetic Door Holder

☐ Included   ☐ Excluded

☐ F & I by others   ☐ _____

Toilets Auto-flush System

☐ Included   ☐ Excluded

☐   F & I by others   ☐   Empty conduit only

☐   _____   ☐   _____

Remove Existing Violations

☐   Included   ☐   Excluded

☐   Provided by others   ☐   _____

☐   _____   ☐   _____

Building Structure

Ceiling

☐   Height and space   ☐   Acoustic

☐   Concrete   ☐   Gypsum

☐   Metal   ☐   _____

Walls Interior

☐   Concrete   ☐   Stucco

☐   Drywall   ☐   _____

☐   Blocks   ☐   _____

Floor

☐   Level for rolling scaffolds   ☐   _____

☐   Crowded with furniture   ☐   _____

☐   Crowded with equipment   ☐   _____

Doorway

☐   Wide enough for equipment   ☐   _____

☐   _____   ☐   _____

Safe Storage

☐   _____   ☐   _____

☐ _____   ☐ _____

Violations

☐ _____   ☐ _____

☐ _____   ☐ _____

Other _____

☐ _____   ☐ _____

☐ _____   ☐ _____

☐ _____   ☐ _____

Requesting Quotes from Your Vendor

For a complete bill of material, provide your vendor with:

Quantity Takeoff/Buy-out Sheet Footnote Clauses

☐ These quantities are offered as a courtesy to the vendor. The vendor shall be responsible for the final count. Our intent is to purchase a complete package in accordance with the plans and specifications for this project.

☐ Specs for each item for which you are requesting a quote including spare parts, test, certifications, O&M manuals, and warranties.

☐ One line diagrams   ☐ Flow charts

☐ Sketches   ☐ _____

☐ _____   ☐ _____

☐ Bid due date   ☐ Quote needed by date

☐ _____   ☐ _____

Bidding Information

To prevent a last minute rush at bid time, verify its requirements and scope of works as early as possible. Most often, your vendors will provide you with bill of materials long before they quote prices. Check and do:

General Conditions

- ☐ Bid bond
- ☐ Certified check
- ☐ Letter of credit
- ☐ Performance bond
- ☐ _____

- ☐ Payment bond
- ☐ _____
- ☐ _____
- ☐ _____
- ☐ _____

Special Conditions

- ☐ Set aside for minority compliance
- ☐ Prevailing wages project
- ☐ Liquidated damages

- ☐ _____
- ☐ _____
- ☐ _____

Bid Pricing Schedules

- ☐ Lump sum
- ☐ Alternates
- ☐ Unit prices
- ☐ Pay line

- ☐ Allowances
- ☐ _____
- ☐ _____
- ☐ _____

Addenda

- ☐ _____
- ☐ _____

- ☐ _____
- ☐ _____

Documents Review

Specifications

- ☐ Instruction to bidders
- ☐ Special conditions
- ☐ Special provisions

- ☐ _____
- ☐ _____
- ☐ _____

Drawings

- ☐ Architectural

- ☐ _____

☐ Structural   ☐ _____

Special Items

☐ Survey and layout   ☐ Utilities charges

☐ Trenching / backfilling   ☐ Hoisting material

☐ Concrete: precast, pour in   ☐ Storage
   place, coreboring

☐ Patching and painting   ☐ Site security

☐ Site restoration   ☐ Garbage removal

☐ Temporary light and power   ☐ _____

☐ Maintenance of temporary   ☐
   light and power   _____

☐ _____   ☐ _____

BIDDING AND SELLING THE JOB

Proposal/Contract

For a detailed explanation and a copy of the Proposal/Contract form, see Chapters 8 and 18.

This section contains checklists for the various parts of the Proposal/Contract. Consider those items that are applicable to your presentation. Avoid redundant statements. Present your Proposal/Contract in a clear and concise form. When it is done properly, it will favor you—the writer.

Words to Avoid

Words to Avoid are a collection of words and sentences you should stay away from, especially in writing 'Scope of Work' and 'List of Exceptions.' In a dispute, they tend to bite you unexpectedly.

☐ **All** – Represents the entire or total number, amount, or quantity. It means the whole thing. It has no boundary. It's not clear, for it means different things to different people. It can include items of work you don't intend to furnish, install, or maintain. *All* has cost many well-intentioned contractors dearly.

☐ **Any** – Means one, some, every, or all without specification, whichever, etc. It is not specific enough for proposal writing. You should use *any* only for promotion and to instill confidence. For example, "Permit fees, if *any*, shall be paid by others. In this case, *any* diminishes the possible outcome and relieves you of the expense, if *any*. On the other hand, if you write, 'we shall remove *any* violation' or 'install *any* work shown on ...,' we all know how much *any* could cost.

☐ **Complete** – For getting you into trouble, *complete* is not much different from *all* and *any*. While it's a good selling word, it can cost you plenty in a dispute.

☐ **Work** – Used in electrical '*work*,' it means all work related to that specific trade. For example, 'Install all electrical *work* as per plans ...' In this context, it could well include *any* electrical apparatus shown on *any* plans (starters, motor drives, electric hand dryers and the like not specifically designated elsewhere). In such a context, you should substitute *work* with *electrical wiring*.

☐ _____

☐ _____

Legal Notice - Suggested Clauses

☐ The information in this proposal is privileged and confidential for the sole use of the individual or entity to whom it is addressed. Any dissemination, distribution, or copying is prohibited by law.

☐ _____

Method of Payment Clauses

☐ We propose to furnish labor and materials as specified herein for the sum of $_____ payable as follows:

Lump sum

☐ The customer shall pay for the work in full:

☐ Before the work commences

☐ Upon the physical completion of the work (stipulate what constitutes physical completion).

☐ Upon passing final inspection (stipulate by whom).

☐ _____

Monthly

☐ Monthly requisitions payable by the 10th of each month

☐ Monthly requisitions as per bidding documents

☐ Monthly requisitions as per contract breakdown submitted by <your company name> before commencing work. Requisition shall be submitted to the customer on the 25th of each month and shall be paid no later than the 10th of the following month

☐ _____
_____
_____

Weekly

☐ Weekly requisitions payable every Thursday before noon.

☐ _____

Payment Plan

Down Payment

☐ _____% or $_____Down payment upon acceptance of proposal.

☐ _____% or $ _____Down payment upon starting work.

☐ _____

Interim Payment

☐ ____% or $_____Upon roughing of _____

☐ ____% or $_____Upon trimming of

☐ _____ _____

Final Payment

☐ ____% or $_____Upon physical completion

☐ ____% or $_____Upon final inspection by <stipulate whom>.

☐ _____

Retainer, if any

☐ Suggested clause:

'Full retainer, as part of the owner's contract document, shall be allowed until <your company name> has earned 50% of the contract amount, after which it shall be reduced to one-half.'

☐ _____
_____

Valid Until Cancelled

☐ Suggested clause:

'If this proposal is not accepted within ____ calendar days, <your company name> has the right to withdraw it without notice.'

☐ _____
_____

Scope of Work

☐ Suggested clause:

The work is based on plans and specifications prepared by <architect or whomever prepared the drawings> identified as section <title of section, e.g. Section 16 Electrical> of the specifications, drawings numbers, and date: <list drawings numbers and their respective dates price is based on> including addenda number <list of addenda by number> with the following exceptions:

Proposal/Contract – Typical List of Exceptions

Performance and Payment Bond

☐   Fees for performance and payment bonds, if required, are not included.

☐   _____

Drawings

☐   No other work, aside from the work shown on the drawings
    listed above, is included in this proposal.

☐   _____

Fees

☐   Are not included. The customer shall pay them directly to the
    issuing agency.

☐   Are included. The customer shall pay them directly to the
    issuing agency and deduct the cost from our contract amount.

☐   Are included.

☐   _____

Utilities Charges

☐   Utility charges, if any, shall be paid by others

☐   _____

Survey and Benchmarks

☐   Included   ☐   _____

☐   Provided by others   ☐   _____

Asphalt, Concrete Cutting

☐   Included   ☐   _____

☐   Excluded   ☐   _____

Trenching

- ☐ Trenching is not included.
- ☐ Trenching and backfilling of standard soil is included.
- ☐ Trenching of rock, under-pavement, road layers, coral, tree-roots, stumps and the like is not included.
- ☐ _____

Dewatering

- ☐ Included   ☐ _____
- ☐ Excluded   ☐ _____

Compaction

- ☐ Included   ☐ _____
- ☐ Excluded   ☐ _____

Site Restoration

- ☐ Included   ☐ _____
- ☐ Excluded   ☐ _____

Cutting and Patching

- ☐ <Your company name> shall do its own cutting. Patching, painting, fireproofing and similar restoration work shall be done by others.
- ☐ Cutting and patching is included.   ☐ _____

Demolition

- ☐ Prior to any demolition, <your company name> shall be allowed to rework and use existing conditions so as to accommodate the new work.
- ☐ _____

Trash and Debris Removal from Site

- ☐ Included   ☐ _____

☐ Excluded   ☐ _____

CUSTOMER ACCEPTANCE

One of the most overlooked parts of the Proposal/Contract is the customer's acceptance clause. Because most of us expect to sign the general contractor or the owner's subcontract agreement, we lose many opportunities when the customer chooses to sign our contract and we haven't taken the time to think it through. Invest a few extra minutes, follow these guidelines and, more often than not, it will be time well spent.

Acceptance Clause

☐ The price, specifications, and conditions set out herein are satisfactory and accepted. You are authorized to proceed with the work. Payment shall be made as outlined above. Unpaid balances are subject to 1.5% per month interest rate until paid in full.

☐ _____

The Customer/Agent Statement

☐ I <signatory name> am authorized to sign and accept this contract because I am the customer, or I am his authorized agent.

☐ The customer's signature

Signed by _____ Title _____ Date_____

Timing Your Bid

Submitting Your Proposal/Contract

To Several GCs - Public bid

☐ Broadcast your scope of work as soon as possible to those general contractors on your bidding list. The scope of work should also include alternates, allowances, and similar options. This action will position your company well for selling the job to the winner.

If necessary, amend your scope of work so as to keep your prospective customers appraised and ready for you to insert your final price into their bid tabulation at bid closing time. If you don't follow up this process, you will often be shut out of the bidding process.

If you have done your homework as described above, you can afford to quote your price at the very last minute so it is not broadcast to your competition in time for price cutting.

Contracting the Job

Negotiation

For complete discussion, see Chapter 20.

The opportunity to negotiate freely the terms and conditions of a contract presents itself once, and that time is before you sign it. Negotiating the job goes beyond the legal ramifications of a contract. It involves translating the party's offer and acceptance into a fair and equitable agreement—leveling the playing field, if you will.

The following checklist should put you in a negotiating frame of mind without losing sight of what you are after. Whatever you get, make sure you write it down, preferably on the contract itself:

Method of Payment

☐ Down payment ☐ Bimonthly or weekly

☐ Final payment upon physical completion

☐ Retainer, if any, reduced one-half once 50% of contract is earned

☐ No retainer ☐ _____

☐ _____ ☐ _____

Substitutions

☐ Special equipment ☐ _____

Limit the Change Order and Back Charge Amount

Each change order cannot exceed 10% of the contract amount without adjusting the overhead and profit percentages accordingly (upward). Unless you want to build another half a building at the same markup, the contract must stipulate this.

Insert this suggested clause in your contract: 'Change orders in excess of 10% of the base contract amount shall be treated as Supplemental Contracts, and shall be quoted and governed independently from the terms and conditions set herein.'

☐ 'No back charges will be accepted by <your company name>, without a 10 days notice from the date the event occurs.'

☐ _____

Completion Date

☐ Make sure there is a definite completion date in the contract.

Premium Time

☐ Contract work shall be performed during regular time.

☐ _____

Surplus Material – First Refusal

☐ In most alteration jobs, you cannot claim ownership of surplus material and equipment unless it is stated in your contract. So you won't inherit junk and the associated cost of removal from the jobsite, ask for 'first refusal.'

Scope of Work

☐ Survey and benchmarks

☐ Concrete cutting and core-boring

☐ Excavation

☐ Trenching

☐ Backfilling

☐ Compaction

☐ _____

☐ _____

☐ _____

☐ Garbage removal

☐ Fireproofing

☐ Hoisting and warehousing

☐ _____

☐ _____

Letter of Intent

The purpose of the letter of intent is to inform you that, based on your proposal and the owner's contract documents, if any, you have been awarded the job. Its objective is to get things moving—releasing shop drawing, filing for permit applications and insurance certificates, and, sometimes, starting the work while the general contractor prepares the subcontract agreement for you to sign. The letter is a good instrument until the unscrupulous general contractor comes into play. For in-depth discussion on this subject, see Chapter 19.

Nevertheless, in accepting such a letter you should review the following:

Does the Letter of Intent include:

☐ Reference to your proposal	☐ Directive to release material
☐ The contract amount	☐ Directive to pull permits
☐ Alternates and allowances	☐ Directive to mobilize the job
☐ Copy of Notice of Commencement	☐ Deadline for the execution of a subcontract agreement
☐ The GC's signature	☐ Is the Letter of Intent dated?
☐ _____	☐ _____
☐ _____	☐ _____

THE SUBCONTRACT AGREEMENT

If the subcontract agreement the General Contractor expects you to sign has not been part of the bidding documents, nor were you made aware of its existence until after the job was bid and won, and nor was it ever part of your Proposal/Contract, beware of such an agreement. These are the worst aftershocks a subcontractor has to deal with if he wants the job. For an in-depth discussion, see Chapter 19.

The checklist that follows dissects the subcontract agreement in six parts: Offer, Performance, Compensation, Consequence, Remedy, and Acceptance. Each part is divided into clauses and each clause into paragraphs, sentences, and even words that can make a difference in leveling the playing field—our focal point. So, when you receive your subcontract agreement, consider it all carefully before signing on the dotted line.

Offer

The offer is your Proposal/Contract inclusive of the scope of work and its list of exceptions in response to the general contractor's solicitation or invitation to bid. So, dig through the subcontract agreement you are about to sign and compare notes with your original intent. Use the following checklist as your worksheet:

Does the Offer Include...?

☐ Base price	☐ Drawings list
☐ Alternate price	☐ Specifications
☐ Allowance	☐ Addenda and revisions
☐ Payment schedule	☐ Customer acceptance
☐ Scope of work	☐ _____
☐ List of exceptions	☐ _____

Performance

This is where your skills as a mechanic and a businessperson are put to the test. Pay attention to each of the following items, for this is where many well-intentioned subcontractors slip up.

☐ Scope of work	☐ Work condition

☐ Owner's furnished material (Who will receive, unload, store, uncrate, and check it against damages?)

- ☐ Commencement date
- ☐ Progress schedule
- ☐ Performance schedule
- ☐ Completion date
- ☐ Substantial completion
- ☐ Final completion
- ☐ Labor force
- ☐ Possession of work prior to completion

- ☐ _____
- ☐ _____
- ☐ _____
- ☐ _____

Compensation

Being paid for all you do is the essence of any business and, for that matter, of anyone's financial life. No truer statement can apply to subcontracting, for so much can be lost due to hidden and unexpected costs. The subcontractor cannot afford to overlook any amount earned and its timely payment. Likewise, the subcontractor cannot afford to extend credit behind his projected cash outlay without compensation. Check and review:

- ☐ Pay when paid
- ☐ Extra work
- ☐ Schedule of values
- ☐ Delays
- ☐ Requisition
- ☐ Final payment
- ☐ Retainer
- ☐ _____
- ☐ Material on site
- ☐ _____

Consequence

Failure to deliver on a promise carries consequences. For our purposes, a consequence is a double-edged sword. Either party of the contract can be assessed as being subject to a penalty for failure to perform or even coming up short on a commitment. A fair contract is one where penalties for default are in balance with the damage and are equally applicable to all parties. Here are some favorable and unfavorable consequences for you to consider:

Right to Stop Work

☐ Each requisition submitted by the 25th of the month is due by the 10th of the following month. If any requisition, or part thereof, remains unpaid 30 days after its due date then *<your company name>* has the right to stop work.

Note: To induce acceptance of this clause, you may negotiate the 30-day grace period accordingly, perhaps starting with a 10-day period and working your way up. Whichever grace period you agree to, at least it will give you an ultimate cutoff date for stopping work without consequence.

Liquidated Damages

☐ No liquidated damages shall be assessed to *<your company name>* without its participation in the decision-making process of revising progress schedules and deadlines that affect the completion date of the project.

Note: Short of this, the process is like being sent to jail without a trial.

☐ Back Charges   ☐ Termination

☐ _____   ☐ _____

Remedy

The best remedy is only to take jobs you can execute well. This will establish a good working relationship with the general contractor, which is often the best cure to prevent disputes before they arise.

Despite good intentions, disputes are sometimes inevitable. So, right from the start you should verify and maintain accurate documentation. Should the occasion arise, you will be prepared to mount a defense that will get you paid for all that is due you. There are two places where you can settle a dispute—in a Court of Law or through Arbitration.

Court of Law

□ Court decision can be appealed

□ You can call as many witnesses as you need

□ Most judges lack construction background

□ _____

Arbitration

□ Arbitration is final

□ Witnesses are limited

□ Most arbitrators have construction background

□ _____

Legal Notices

□ If you want to preserve your rights, follow the contract procedures to the letter.

□ Obtain the legal addresses for serving notices under the terms of your agreement.

□ Record all critical schedules of events in your calendar with at least 15 days advance notice.

□ _____
_____
_____

Acceptance

If a deal is to last, it has to be good for all parties concerned. If you know you have negotiated an agreement grossly lopsided your way, don't sign it—it will backfire on you sooner than you think. However, if you have negotiated a smart agreement, protect it well. It would be infuriating to lose a deal due to an irregularity. Review the following checklist, and if need be backtrack over your steps—in the end this will give you peace of mind.

Customer Signature

☐ Original

☐ Notarized (if required)

☐ Title and date

☐ Agreement dated

☐ _____

☐ _____

Record Keeping – Prior to Sending the Agreement Back

☐ Clearly mark all changes on the agreement.

Note: Handwritten changes, even on the margin of the agreement, are as good as typewritten, if not better.

☐ Initial every page and every change you've made.

☐ Retain a complete photocopy.

☐ Stamp date your photocopy and note the method of delivery.

☐ Allow ten working days for the original to return.

☐ _____

☐ _____

Conclusion and Follow-up

Once you have settled on the basics of the agreement, the general contractor will send you two unsigned copies of the subcontract agreement for you to execute. The general contractor will not sign your copy until after you have signed it. Go through the agreement thoroughly and verify that it contains what you have agreed. To assist you, use the 'Negotiation' and 'Subcontract Agreement' checklists presented above. Once you are satisfied, sign it and send both copies back to the general contractor for his signature. When you get your copy back, don't just file it away; to confirm the validity of the agreement, check that:

Signatures

☐ Both signatures—yours and that of the general contractor—are on the same contract and both are originals—not photocopies.

☐ Both parties have initialed all revisions.

☐ Was the agreement altered after you signed it?

Note: Tedious as it may seem, it is worth comparing each paragraph to your photocopy set. If you are too busy, get someone else to do it, but get it done.

☐ Retain a photocopy for office use and file the original in a safe location, preferably away from the office.

☐ _____

PROTECTING THE JOB

Planning and Progress Schedule (PPS)

PPS is a self-imposed punch list, if you will. It starts with the laying out of the job and concludes with the completion of the owner's final punch list.

PPS provides a snapshot for any given time in the past (actual activities) and in the future (planned activities) of the job. When diligently maintained, PPS is a powerful tool for tracking down and being paid for productivity losses, change orders, and other related costs that otherwise may go undetected.

For an in-depth discussion on how to develop and implement PPS and the usage of its related forms, see Chapter 21.

THE DIARY

Daily Job Diary Sheet

Along with the PPS, the diary, when kept accurately, facilitates payment for undue delays and productivity losses. For an in-depth discussion and forms, see Chapter 21.

The daily report sheet for a diary should be consistent in form and should include the following:

Typical Diary - Sheet

☐ Day of week   ☐ Date

☐ Weather   ☐ Temperature :High _° low _°

☐ Rained from _am to __pm   ☐ Other weather conditions

Labor Force

☐ Project manager:_____   ☐ Foreman:_____

☐ Journeymen:__(how many)   ☐ _____

☐ Mechanics:_____   ☐ Apprentices:_____

☐ Helpers:_____   ☐ Others:_____

☐ Workforce Total:_____   ☐ _____

Worked on

☐ Contract Work   ☐ Change Orders

☐ _____   ☐ _____

Changes to Scope of Work

☐ Change description _____

☐ Change occurred due to _____

Materials

(If necessary, attach bill of materials or shipping ticket)

□ Ordered   from   □ Received from _____

□ Back   ordered □ Returned to _____

□ Received   □ Returned to shop _____

□ Sent   for   repair □ _____

Rentals: Equipment and Tools

□ Type:_____   □ Model
                                 _____

□ Received from:_____ at____:____ ( ) am ( ) pm

□ Returned to: _____ by _____

□ Picked up by: _____at ____: ___ ( ) am ( ) pm

□ Back charge vendor for downtime from _____am to __ pm

Visitors

□ Name:_____   □ Owner

□ Architect   □ Engineer

□ Other_____   □ _____

Inspection

□ Type   □ By_____

□ Passed   □ Failed

□ Rescheduled for _____   □ _____

□ Inspector's Name _____   □ Phone # _____

Other Events

□ _____

□ _____

□ _____

□ _____   □ _____

□ _____   □ _____

□ _____   □ _____

Intelligence File

Most newcomers frown at the thought of setting up an intelligence file, especially on business associates. However, the fact is that many people wish they had done so long before they got hurt.

Many of these items may seem hard to get, but as you sharpen your skills, you'll become more vigilant and begin to notice that most of this information flows right through your office at one time or another. For example, permit applications, notices of commencement, occupational licenses and the like are crucial sources of information that you can easily access during the construction of the job.

This special issue folder contains confidential information about your customer and, if necessary, you should keep it off limits to others. For an in-depth discussion, see Chapter 21.

Content

☐ Postal stamped envelopes where a discrepancy exists or is suspected between the date received and the date claimed in the contents of the envelope.

☐ Fax transmittals where a discrepancy exists or is suspected between the actual date and time received, the sender's electronic header, and the body of the fax itself.

☐ Your customer's transmittal soliciting (inviting) you to bid the job. Some will list the particulars of the documents they send, such as drawings, specs, addenda, schedule of prevailing wages, etc.

☐ Photocopy of your customer's check.

☐ Photocopies of checks from other parties on behalf of your customer.

☐ Customer personal data, home address, phone, etc.

☐ Credit reports, if any

☐ Your customer's job superintendent's personal data: home address, phone number, or at least the super's vehicle license plate number and model, Social Security # and any other license # you can get.

☐ Customer's Occupational and Proficiency License #

☐ Other subcontractors' names and phone #, foreman's name, etc.

☐ _____

Filing Notices

With regard to Mechanic's Liens law, each locality has its own set of rules. For detailed information, see Chapter 23 - Mechanic's Lien.

BUYING THE JOB

The Vendor's Quote

Another part of your profit-making equation is the vendor who is expediting the quote from the manufacturer to your estimating table. However, when the line of communication between him and the manufacturer gets blurred, so does the bill of material. Special components needed to complete your scope of work such as spare parts, startup services, shipping charges and the like that should be clearly listed in the bill of material are not. You can find them only in the small print section, usually at the end of the quotation form—the section in light blue-gray that you had no time to read.

In verifying a vendor's bill of material, you should follow this checklist:

Vendor's Quote – Bill of Material

Quantities

- ☐ Vendor quantities
- ☐ Lump sum
- ☐ As per plans and specs

- ☐ Our quantities
- ☐ Unit prices
- ☐ _____

Materials and Equipment

- ☐ Per plans and specification
- ☐ Equal to

- ☐ Substitute
- ☐ _____

Shipping Method

- ☐ FOB jobsite
- ☐ Freight not allowed

- ☐ Freight allowed
- ☐ _____

Delivery

- ☐ Sidewalk drop
- ☐ Rigged in place

- ☐ _____
- ☐ _____

Deposits

- ☐ Returnable crates/reels
- ☐ _____

- ☐ Other returnable packaging
- ☐ _____

Exceptions to the Bill of Material

- ☐ Spare parts
- ☐ Manuals and certifications
- ☐ _____

- ☐ Personnel training
- ☐ Allowance manufacturer tests
- ☐ _____

Purchase Order

Equipment

- ☐ Factory Assembled
- ☐ _____

- ☐ Field Assembled
- ☐ _____

Lighting Fixtures
☐ Factory Assembled ☐ Field Assembled

☐ _____ ☐ _____

Lamps
☐ Factory Assembled ☐ Field Assembled

Emergency Ballasts
☐ Factory Assembled ☐ Field Assembled

Whips
☐ Factory Assembled ☐ Field Assembled

☐ Factory Assembled ☐ Field Assembled

Other Parts
☐ Roughing trims ☐ Catastrophic Clips

☐ _____ ☐ _____

Light Poles
☐ Anchor Bolts and Templates ☐ Fuses and fuse holders

☐ _____ ☐ _____

Spare Parts
☐ Lamps ☐ Fuses

☐ _____ ☐ _____

Switching Gear
☐ AIC rating ☐ Shunt trip breakers

☐ TVSS ☐ Disconnects/Starters

☐ _____ ☐ _____

☐ _____ ☐ _____

The Purchase Order Number

☐   Your purchase order number must appear on all correspondence, invoices, shipping tickets, bills of lading, packages and crates, enclosures, and shipping devices.

☐   _____

The Order Clauses

☐   Please furnish the bill of material listed here as per our buyout sheet(s) dated ___/__/__ and attached hereto for the lump sum of $_____

☐   Please furnish the bill of material listed here as specified herein and in the job's contract documents for the lump sum of $_____

☐   Please furnish a complete bill of material with quantities as per plans and specifications for the lump sum of $_____

Payable as Follows Clauses

☐   Net 30 days   ☐   2% 10 days

☐   Paid when we get paid   ☐   _____

Notice

☐   No delivery will be accepted without a 24-hour advance notice.

Vendor's Confirmation Clauses

☐   The price, specifications, and conditions set herein are accepted.

☐   Within ___ days from the issuance of this purchase order, the vendor shall submit a bill of material write-up for the purchaser approval.

☐   Within ___ days from the issuance of this purchase order, the vendor shall submit to the purchaser no less than ____ sets of shop drawings.

☐ The vendor shall not release material for manufacturing until the owner has approved the shop drawings.

Items shipped under this purchase order shall be readily identifiable from the exterior package with their designated type. (i.e. Type A, B, etc.)

☐ Spare parts and documentation shall be clearly identified as per item #___ above, and shipped directly to the purchaser's office unless otherwise noted.

☐ The vendor shall give the purchaser a 24-hour advance notice prior to any delivery.

☐ Facsimile (Fax) correspondence shall be accepted as an official means of communication.

☐ Within ___ days of the issuance of this purchase order, the vendor shall confirm this purchase order by signing it where indicated and returning it to the purchaser. If the vendor fails to do so, then the purchaser has the option to cancel this purchase order anytime thereafter.

Vendor's Signature

☐ I <printed signatory name> am authorized to sign this purchase order for I am the vendor, or am acting for the vendor.

Vendor's Signature _____ title _____date __

☐ _____

DOING THE JOB

The Process

A job well done contributes the largest share of profit to your company. Here is where your expertise as a mechanic and as a productive labor manager will shine brightest. Every labor dollar spent that fails to generate revenue is a dollar wasted. Indulge yourself by not insisting on being paid for every labor hour spent and you will soon go out of business. For an in-depth discussion, see Chapter 24.

Change Orders

While change orders are written to revise the contract amount up or down, some do not affect the contract amount. The latter serves an important role in documenting changes to the scope of work without the aftermath of back charges or, most importantly, being accused of modifying the work without authorization.

Change orders are generated for a variety of reasons, most commonly:

Change Order – Most Common Causes

- ☐ Errors in plans and specifications
- ☐ Site conditions or obstacles
- ☐ Change to the scope of work for owner's convenience
- ☐ Your scope of work interfering with that of others
- ☐ Specified product availability
- ☐ _____
- ☐ _____

Basic Requisites for Collectable Change Orders

- ☐ Change order number
- ☐ Date

☐ Addressed your change order to your customer's designated person and address as called for in your contract

☐ Job name   ☐ Job address

☐ Owner   ☐ Owner's contract number

☐ Date of submission   ☐ _____

☐ _____   ☐ _____

Change Order Clauses

☐ We agree to make changes as specified below for the lump sum price of $_____

☐ Scope of work – describe it in a logical and easy to understand format showing the location first, for example:

Building A (if there is more than one)

Second floor, Room 220

Relocate:

2 A. C. units

5 Exhaust fans

Furnish and install

100ft of ductwork

Room 275

Replace, etc.

Applicable Exceptions

☐ Cut, patch, and restore   ☐ _____

☐ _____   ☐ _____

Work to Be Done During

☐ Regular working hours   ☐ Premium time

☐ _____   ☐ _____

Supplementary Information

For more details, please find attached:

☐ Cost breakdown	☐ Catalogue sheets
☐ Shop drawings	☐ _____

Signature

☐ Your company name   ☐ Your signature, title, and date

Customer Acceptance

☐ The price and specifications of this change order are satisfactory and hereby accepted. All work shall be performed under the same terms and conditions of the original contract agreement, unless otherwise stipulated herein.

Customer Signature

☐ I <printed signatory's name> am authorized to sign this change order for I am the customer, or acting for the customer.

Signature _____ Title _____ Date _____

Work Order

Upon the acceptance of your change order, it is prudent to issue a work order for the field. This procedure eliminates unnecessary broadcasting of price and other confidential information; it will also tell the field whether to start on a given change order. When signed by the customer, the work order is a valid record keeping instrument for documenting T & M (time and material) costs.

Besides using the work order as a daily verification sheet for your change order work, you may use it as an independent form for work you are doing for other customers or for subcontractors on the same project.

Work Order Basics

☐ Work order number	☐ Date
☐ Customer name, address, contact person	
☐ Job name and address	☐ Owner's name

☐ _____ ☐ _____

☐ Order date ☐ Order taken
_____ by_____

Terms

☐ Charge to contract ☐ Day work

Work Based On

☐ Change order No._____ ☐ T & M work

☐ Punch list by ☐ A/E directive

☐ Correction ☐ _____

Assigned To

☐ Name ☐ Start date

☐ Completion date ☐

Performance Record

☐ Dispatched: ___:___ a.m. ☐ Arrived at jobsite ____: ____

☐ Out ___: ___ In ___:___ ☐ Out ___:___

☐ Date ☐ Day of the week

☐ Workman or crew number ☐ Number of hours worked

☐ _____ ☐ _____

Billing

☐ Number of hours charged ☐ Hourly rate

☐ Labor total $_____

☐ Total material and direct
job expenses $_____

☐ Work order total $_____

Scope of Work

☐ Clear description of work

Attach plans and specs if necessary

Attach only documentation that helps clarify the scope of work

Customer Acceptance Clauses

☐ T & M

I hereby acknowledge the satisfactory completion of the work described herein and have verified that the number of hours spent on this work along with the materials listed are true and correct.

☐ Change Order

I hereby acknowledge the satisfactory completion of the work described herein. The work has been completed in accordance with the terms and conditions of <your company name> Change Order number _____ dated _____

☐ Correction Work

I hereby acknowledge the satisfactory correction of the work described herein.

☐ Work Order

I agree to pay all of <your company name> costs related to the collection of any sum due under this Work Order, including legal fees and other expenses.

Customer signature

☐ I <printed signatory name> am authorized to sign this Work Order, for I am the customer or am acting for the customer.

Signature _____ title _____ date _____

Inspections

Nothing can be more devastating to a progress schedule and to your working relationship with a general contractor than a series of inspection failures. Poor planning is most often the culprit here.

The following checklist should simplify the task.

Electrical – Pre-inspection Checklist

Before you call for an inspection, verify that the following items of work conform to the plans and specifications and industry standards:

Temporary Service

☐ Ground rod ☐ GFCI receptacles

☐ Riser bonding ☐ _____

Note:

Get temporary signed off. It if fails, get a written explanation.

Rough Residential Inspection

☐ Cable installed flat at least 1-1/4"

☐ Receptacles spacing ☐ Bonding for metal boxes

☐ Wire size ☐ Bonding for metal boxes

☐ Service bonding/grounding ☐ Multi-gang boxes – cable strapping

Note:

Get rough inspection signed off. If failed, get a written report.

Residential Final Inspection

☐ Identify circuits at panel ☐ Lighting outlet cover plates

☐ Required GFCI receptacle ☐ Required disconnect switches

☐ Check nameplates' rating against wire size and over-current devices

Note:

Get final inspection signed off. If failed, get a written report.

Pre-inspection Work

- ☐ Permit and re-inspection fees paid
- ☐ Permit and inspection signature card displayed at the jobsite
- ☐ A set of approved plans bearing the building department's stamp of approval
- ☐ The work area is accessible for inspection
- ☐ OSHA approved ladder or scaffold
- ☐ Work ready for inspection
- ☐ Work complies with equipment's manufacturer label
- ☐ Material used is approved for that use
- ☐ _____

At Inspection

- ☐ Get the inspector's name, telephone, and extension or cell number
- ☐ If passed, get the permit card signed and dated
- ☐ If inspection fails, get a written report
- ☐ _____
  _____

Closing the Job

Every job has a beginning and an end. For a successful conclusion—collecting what is due you as quickly as possible—you must adhere to some predetermined conditions. By the way, this phase of the job does not have to be a last minute chore, as most subcontractors make it out to be.

An efficient way of compiling closeout documents is to set up a folder or three-ring binder just for that purpose right from the start. When the job is done, this phase of the job will be almost complete as well. You won't have to spend countless hours retracing your steps.

Remember, you may get out of installing some work in the job, but if you want your final payment, it is unlikely that you will get out of delivering every document listed in your contract requirement. The following is a partial closeout document list.

Close-out Documents

□ As-built drawings   □ Field test reports

□ Final inspections   □ Certifications

□ Mnftr. tests reports   □ Training of owner's personnel

□ O & M (Operating and Maintenance manuals and logbooks)

□ Spare parts   □ _____

Warranties

□ Warrantee from you   □ Warrantee letter from vendors

□ Maintenance warrantee   □ _____

Field

□ Directories   □ Tags

□ Markers   □ Engraved plates

□ Signs   □ Safety devices

□ Keys

Footnote:

Closing the job well is stamping your seal of quality to your work.

Index

NOTES

NOTES

NOTES

NOTES

NOTES

NOTES

DATE DUE

SEP 2 0 2012		
SEP 1 3 2012		

Demco No. 62-0549